COLD WAR SAGA

By Kempton Jenkins

Foreword by Marvin Kalb

NIMBLE BOOKS LLC

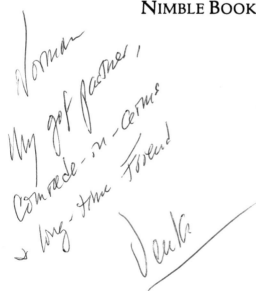

Norman
My golf partner,
Comrade-in-arms
& long-time friend

Ken

NIMBLE BOOKS LLC

Nimble Books LLC
1521 Martha Avenue
Ann Arbor, MI, USA 48103
http://www.NimbleBooks.com
wfz@nimblebooks.com
+1.734-330-2593

Printed in the United States of America
ISBN-13: 978-1-60888-009-6

∞ The paper used in this publication meets the minimum requirements of the American National Standard for Information Sciences—Permanence of Paper for Printed Library Materials, ANSI Z39.48-1992. The paper is acid-free and lignin-free.

DEDICATION

To my late beloved wife "C", and my three boys, Peter, Michael, and Timothy, who shared this challenge and historic opportunity with unflinching love, devotion, and good humor.

And to my beloved wife Lucy, who five years after my losing "C," agreed to pick up the baton and shepherd me through my final years in the Foreign Service of the United States with the same love and devotion.

Contents

v

FOREWORD BY MARVIN KALB

If this book was not a "saga," as its title suggests, then it would be an odyssey, a journey through the Cold War by a professional American diplomat who skillfully plied his craft in such important places as East and West Germany; the old Soviet Union, heart of an imperialist empire; Thailand, where the contest for the soul of Asia was played out by the United States and Communist China; Venezuela, a doorway to Latin-America's chronic struggle between Castro's brand of communist rule and Washington's style of democracy; and, of course, the United States, which, shortly after World War II, took upon itself the awesome task of containing Stalin's expanding sphere of power and influence.

Two Americans, President Harry Truman and an ex-traordinary diplomat/writer named George Kennan, identified the problem, and then created the policy of global "containment." It fell to a succession of later Presidents: Dwight D. Eisenhower, John F. Kennedy, Lyndon B. Johnson, Richard M. Nixon, Gerald Ford, Jimmy Carter, Ronald Reagan, and George H. W. Bush to implement the policy and bring it to victory. That is our diplomat's generous view, and for those of us who have known him over many years, as I have, it is not a surprising view.

Our diplomat and author is Kempton Jenkins. The reader is indeed fortunate to have such an astute guide through this historic period of American diplomacy. Jenkins synthesizes his personal and professional life and in the process produces a clear narrative of one diplomat's role in—and view of—the Cold War. Thick texts of diplomatic history have been written (and they, too, are valuable), but there are times when one can catch a better glimpse of the arc of history through the prism of a single pair of eyes. Jenkins has good eyes. His recollection of his journey through the Cold War is eloquent, at times touching, and always informative.

The Jenkins story is therefore the story of a diplomat at work and a family at both work and play. When a diplomat goes abroad to represent his country's interests, to live in a foreign city, to raise his family in an environment decidedly different from, let us say, Washington, D.C., he is normally accompanied by a wife, a child or two or three and, in this case, an Airedale dog named Tigger—an experience that carries with it all of the pleasures and problems associated with uprooting a family, finding an appropriate school or tennis court and then plunging into the study of the host country's language, history, and politics. No Foreign Service family walks through the experience without the delights of discovery, but also with bumps and bruises from unexpected encounters.

In Jenkins' case, during a rewarding assignment in Vene-zuela, the affairs of state had to take second place to the jarring revelation that wife Cecile, "C," as she was called, an intelligent, utterly charming person, had come down with cancer. "C" and the family had to return to Washington for special treatment. Her death, when it came, devastated everyone. In time Jenkins returned to his beloved craft and five years later met and married a widow named Lucy, who, like "C," took to the special rigors of diplomacy with an easy grace as if she had been at it for decades. Jenkins was lucky twice.

It happens that the career of diplomat Jenkins spans much of the Cold War. Know him, and you know it. From the administration of President Harry Truman to President Reagan, Jenkins had a series of fascinating assignments. He dealt with the rebuilding of West Germany; a crisis with the Soviet Union, especially concerning the issues of Berlin and nuclear weapons; the way Communist China cast a menacing shadow over Thailand and the rest of Southeast Asia; and the way Fidel Castro's Cuba sent a chill through those parts of Latin America that did not want any of the reputed "blessings" of Communism. Jenkins tells many interesting and important stories, and he populates them with fascinating individuals.

One of the most significant figures of the Cold War with whom Jenkins worked was Ambassador Llewellyn Thompson, a quintessential career diplomat, who was steeped in the Soviet experience under Stalin. In his preface account of Thompson's showdown with Gromyko, Jenkins reveals Thompson's cool discipline as he rebutted Gromyko's threat that New York could be incinerated if the U.S. did not abandon its Berlin position. Earlier in 1954, Thompson had led the negotiations that produced the historic withdrawal of Soviet forces from Austria. And, subsequently during the nuclear confrontation with the Soviets over Cuba, "Tommy," as he was affectionately known to us in the Moscow press corps, was the prudent voice that persuaded President Kennedy to leave an escape hatch for Soviet Chairman of the Council of Ministers Nikolai Khrushchev—the "quarantine" decision that led to Khrushchev's withdrawal of nuclear missiles from Cuba. Jenkins' account of his two years in

Moscow portrays this brilliant diplomat and the critical impact he had on the Cold War.

Henry Kissinger, Secretary of State during the tail end of the Nixon administration and all of the shortened President Ford administration, was German-born, a Harvard scholar, and conservative theorist. One day, when Jenkins was Assistant Secretary of State for Congressional Relations, he got a call from an aide to the feared Wayne Hays, Democratic Chairman of the House Appropriations Subcommittee, which oversaw the State Department's budget, among many other things. If Kissinger would stop by for a birthday party for Hays, the Chairman "would be thrilled." Kissinger and Jenkins both realized that Congressional support for the Vietnam War was eroding swiftly. Kissinger agreed to attend. When the Secretary entered a Capitol Hill chamber crowded with more than 200 legislators, there was suddenly "heavy applause." In his thick accent, with dramatic pauses, Kissinger said, "I know it is unusual for a Republican cabinet officer to be here, but I wanted to wish the Chairman 'Happy Birthday.'" More applause. "He is one of the great parliamentary diplomats in our history." Kissinger could stretch the truth to fit his needs at the drop of a hat. Jenkins writes: "The next morning, at 9:30 am, Hays called me and said, 'Jenkins. I don't know how you managed that, but you tell the Secretary that anything he needs up here, I will deliver." And Hays did deliver, on more than one occasion. Jenkins understood that domestic politics often trumped diplomatic needs. He learned that no policy could succeed, that no war, including the one in Vietnam, could be won without domestic support.

Anatoly Dobrynin, Soviet Ambassador to the United States, was accredited to President Kennedy first and ended his career with President Reagan twenty-five years later. He represented the USSR's interests from Khrushchev to General Secretary of the Communist Party of the Soviet Union, Mikhail Gorbachev. He was "second to none," writes Jenkins, in the "access game." He was as fluent in English as he was in manipulating the American political system. He loved getting invited to the Kentucky Derby, and he pretended to be pals with American industrialists. Though he was on a first-name basis with Kissinger, and Kissinger with him, "most of us," Jenkins says, "were distrustful of Dobrynin." Jenkins points to the way Dobrynin ran roughshod over other East European ambassadors, as though he, representing the Soviet Union, had the right to dictate the Kremlin's party line to them.

Anecdotes bring diplomacy to life. One example is worth noting. In the early 1970s, as Kissinger—first with President Nixon and then with President Ford—attempted to negotiate a nuclear arms reduction treaty with the Soviet Union, he ran into a buzz saw of opposition from Senator Henry "Scoop" Jackson, a Democrat from Washington who wanted to be president. Through guile and determination, Jackson managed to introduce the Jackson-Vanik Amendment, which tied Jewish emigration from the Soviet Union to American trade with the Soviet Union. The amendment not only froze trade opportunities between the two countries, it also blocked any progress on strategic arms negotiations. By working on Capitol Hill, Jenkins learned a vital lesson—

America is a land of many minorities, each with an equal opportunity to lobby Congress and influence foreign policy.

Toward the end of this rich swing through the Cold War, Jenkins addresses two questions central to understanding this period of history. The Cold War ended when the Soviet Union collapsed, in large part because of its internal rot, and because its communism ideology had failed. And President Reagan, as many partisans have alleged, did not "win the Cold War" by his vigorous opposition to communism, or by his demand that Gorbachev "tear down this wall." President Reagan played his part, but, Jenkins insists, so did every other president from President Truman to President Bush. "All in all," as Jenkins puts it at the very end, "a remarkable national commitment to the forty-year policy of containment. It worked!"

Though Jenkins can be generous in his judgments of American policy and policymakers through this period, he is also one of those diplomats who recognized that Vietnam was a disaster. If one day the State Department needs a good argument for a bigger budget, every member of Congress should be given a free copy of *Cold War Saga*.

Marvin Kalb, once Chief Diplomatic Correspondent for CBS and NBC and host of "Meet the Press," is the Edward R. Murrow Professor Emeritus at Harvard and founding Director of the Shorenstein Center on the Press, Politics and Foreign Policy at the Kennedy School of Government. He has known Jenkins since the early 1960s, when they were both based in Moscow, Jenkins for the State Department, Kalb for CBS.

PREFACE: A MOSCOW CONFRONTATION WITH GROMYKO, 1961

It was approximately 7:30 p.m. on January 13, 1961, when I found myself walking briskly on a bitterly cold night from Spaso House, the storied United States ambassadorial residence in Moscow, to the U.S. Embassy on "the ring" about a mile away. The perpetual light dusting of snow covered up some of the tackiness of Moscow's fading architecture, and the snow crunched under my feet as I walked. I was warmed, however, by adrenaline: I'd just come from the most dramatic negotiating confrontation I had ever experienced in my career in the Foreign Service (or would ever experience again).

The session, held at the Soviet Ministry of Foreign Affairs, was the third of four "discussions" between Ambassador Llewellyn "Tommy" Thompson and Soviet Foreign Minister Andrei Gromyko to discuss access to Berlin. Gromyko was joined by Deputy Foreign Minister Vladimir Semyonov, who had been ambassador to Germany, and I accompanied Tommy as the Second Secretary and German Specialist at the U.S. Embassy. In retrospect, these sessions may have been as close to the eruption of World War III as we came in the Cold War.

The session began with an uninterrupted forty-minute diatribe by Gromyko, who pounded his chair arm as he denounced the obduracy of the United States and its Allies in clinging to the "archaic claims" of four-power sovereignty over the former German capital. The high point in Gromyko's attack came when he reiterated Khrushchev's ultimatum to the West that it needed to accept East German sovereignty over West Berlin, or find itself forcefully expelled. Gromyko made a clear threat of nuclear war if the United States persisted in rejecting Moscow's reasonable proposals. The United States would have only itself to blame for any catastrophe that might follow—one which could include such an unthinkable act as the incineration of New York City.

Ambassador Thompson, who will be recognized in history as one of the most skilled professional practitioners of diplomacy the United States has ever produced, sat calmly listening to Gromyko's vitriol, chain-smoking the entire time, while I noted down Gromyko's words (although fluent in English, Gromyko spoke in Russian, which was then translated by the ubiquitous Soviet Foreign Ministry English language expert, Victor Sukhodrev). For me, taking notes in this historic situation, the double presentation was of course critical. I was able to sketch out Gromyko's denunciations in Russian and then refine his remarks from the English translation Sukhodrev provided.

At the end of this incredible performance, Gromyko looked at Ambassador Thompson, who continued to drag on his ever-present cigarette. After what seemed like fifteen minutes, but was probably only thirty seconds, Thompson snuffed out the cigarette, gazed at Gromyko impassively, and said nothing. Finally Gromyko blurted, "Well, Mr. Ambassador?!" to which Thompson very deliberately and very softly responded, "Mr. Foreign Minister, I deeply regret that the policy of your government has required you to put on such a performance. You know as well as I that if there is to be a nuclear exchange between our two great nations, the incineration will be in the Soviet Union, which will disappear from the face of the earth. I will report your remarks to my government with deep disappointment." With that, Tommy and I rose and departed, leaving Gromyko ashen-faced and embarrassed in front of his colleagues, Sukhodrev and Deputy Minister Semyonov.

Without exchanging a word in the presumably wired atmosphere of the Foreign Ministry, Tommy and I strode out into the Embassy car and returned to Spaso House. Once there, in what was to become standard procedure for our Berlin sessions, Tommy had me go to the Embassy where I dictated a virtually verbatim account of the meeting in the form of an "Eyes Only" flash telegram to the President and the Secretary of State, while he, by hand, wrote down his impressions of the session. Within the hour I returned to Spaso House with my draft and sat in Tommy's study while he read and refined my notes. He allowed me the privilege of reviewing his impressions (and even making some suggestions). When we had two agreed texts, Tommy handed them to me and I went downstairs to take the car back to the Embassy. On this occasion the driver had mysteriously disappeared. When I called the Embassy no car was available. With that, I folded the drafts, pressed them into my pocket, and set off on foot for our Embassy from which these two historic messages would be cabled by the fastest means back to Washington.

As I walked through the snow my heart still beat with the excitement of the confrontation with Gromyko. I mulled over the admiration I felt for the cold-blooded, totally compelling response that my Ambassador had given to the obviously flustered Gromyko. Although I was somewhat nervous making my way through the back streets of Moscow in possession of such an important document, but after brief reflection, I realized I had probably never been safer in my life; it was of utmost importance to the Soviet government that the account of this meeting be sent back to Washington, and I'm sure that as I walked, a typical KGB cocoon of flanking observers surrounded me, out of sight.

While this incident was hardly typical of my thirty-year career in the U.S. Foreign Service (1950-1980), it does indeed clearly depict the Cold War, a situation that drove U.S. policies from the end of World War II until the collapse of the Soviet Union in 1991.

ACKNOWLEDGEMENTS

This project was first stimulated by my involvement with the Oral History program of the Association for Diplomatic Studies and Training (ADST). The Oral History program has recorded more than 1,500 interviews with senior diplomats covering the entire post-war era; an outstanding resource for historians, journalists, and students. One can access the program at:

http://memory.loc.gov/ammem/collections/diplomacy/ .

As I have reflected on my thirty-year involvement in the Cold War, I am deeply impressed by the dedication, brilliance, and courage of my Foreign Service colleagues with whom I was privileged to work. Above all, I am proud to have been a Foreign Service officer of the United States.

Inspiration throughout my career came especially from the unsung heroes Ambassadors Llewellyn Thompson and Maurice Bernbaum, as well as the more obvious heroes of that critical era in our history, General George C. Marshall; Secretaries of State Dean Acheson and Henry Kissinger; Averill Harriman; George Kennan; and the historic Presidential leadership of Presidents Harry Truman and Jerry Ford.

My friends in journalism who shared these experiences not only encouraged me to pursue this project; they were key contributors to the efforts of the United States in concluding the Cold War successfully.

A special note of gratitude to the legendary doyenne of the White House press corps, Helen Thomas, who from the first reading of my introduction, pressed me to write this account.

This product was greatly enhanced by the editorial reviews and recommendations of Professor Don Rowney of Bowling Green State University (my alma mater), and the distinguished Civil War historian (and Moscow correspondent of the *Baltimore Sun*), Ernest Ferguson.

And thanks to Diane Nine, my diligent agent who found a home for the product, and Hannah Rosenberg, who struggled through my handwritten drafts to turn them into a manuscript.

Ann Clark Espuelas, copyeditor extraordinary, labored long and hard to purge the numerous amateurish errors from my manuscript. I am sure her enthusiasm was enhanced by the fact that she is my daughter-in-law's sister!

Peter Hannaford, longtime friend and editor supreme, who polished my manuscript as only he could.

ASSOCIATION FOR DIPLOMATIC STUDIES AND TRAINING (ADST) AND DIPLOMATIC AND CONSULAR OFFICERS, RETIRED, INC. (DACOR)

Since 1776, extraordinary men and women have represented the United States abroad under all sorts of circumstances. What they did and how and why they did it remain little known to their compatriots. In 1995 the Association for Diplomatic Studies and Training (ADST) and Diplomatic and Consular Officers, Retired, Inc. (DACOR) created the Diplomats and Diplomacy book series to increase public knowledge and appreciation of the role of American diplomats in world history. The series seeks to demystify diplomacy through the stories of those who have conducted U.S. foreign relations, as they lived, influenced, and reported them. Kempton Jenkins's Cold War Saga, 41st in the series, fulfills these aims with panache.

NIMBLE BOOKS LLC

ADST-DACOR Diplomats And Diplomacy Series

Herman J. Cohen, *Intervening in Africa: Superpower Peacemaking in a Troubled Continent*

Wilson Dizard Jr, *Inventing Public Diplomacy: The Story of the United States Information Agency*

Brandon Grove, *Behind Embassy Walls: The Life and Times of an American Diplomat*

Parker T. Hart, *Saudi Arabia and the United States: Birth of a Security Partnership*

Cameron R. Hume, *Mission to Algiers: Diplomacy by Engagement*

Dennis Kux, *The United States and Pakistan, 1947–2000: Disenchanted Allies*

Jane C. Loeffler, *The Architecture of Diplomacy: Building America's Embassies*

William B. Milam, *Bangladesh and Pakistan: Flirting with Failure in Muslim South Asia*

Robert H. Miller, *Vietnam and Beyond: A Diplomat's Cold War Education*

David D. Newsom, *Witness to a Changing World*

Nicholas Platt, China Boys: How U.S. Relations with the PRC Began and Grew

NIMBLE BOOKS LLC

Chapter I. Postwar Washington: A New World Capital

February 12, 1950, was a blustery cold day in Washington, D.C. I found myself standing in front of the antebellum mansion on Lee Highway in Arlington, Virginia, where my wife and I had rented a small apartment converted from latter-day slave-quarters, waiting anxiously for the mail. Earlier that morning, two of my close friends, Bill Porter and Herb Hutchinson, had called and alerted me that they had received official word about their results in the Foreign Service Exam—one passed and one failed. Having concentrated all my energies over the previous two years on passing the exam, which would open the door to a career as a U.S. diplomat, this particular mailman became an object of intense focus for me. He did come. I did pass!

My new wife Cecile ("C") and I had arrived in Washington in August 1948, fresh from graduation from Bowling Green University and our wedding in Evanston, Illinois . I had been accepted to pursue a Master's degree at George Washington University in International Law and she'd been hired as an executive secretary to the dean of students at George Washington University.

Barely three years after the Japanese surrender, Washington was awakening to the fact that it was the real capital of the world, with all of the challenges that entailed. The city (and its suburbs) had, over the short course of eight years since the beginning of the war, grown from a sleepy, segregated southern town to a jam-packed, wartime capital. At the end of the war, enthusiastic, dedicated young veterans piled into a town already bursting at the seams with thousands of young women who had answered the call during the war to fill the needs of a war-time government. Housing was in very short supply; comfortable old homes and Georgetown's row houses had quickly been converted into one-floor apartments and "rooming houses." Streetcars provided critical transportation, air-conditioning was unheard of, and rigid segregation prevailed—blacks were unseen in Washington's few department stores (Garfinkel's and Woodward & Lothrop) except as janitors. There were few restaurants. The Occidental and the Old Ebbitt Grill, which still survive, were the most notable.

In the following tumultuous two years (1948-50), Washington was transformed into not only a national capital but the "capital of the free world" as well. Our heroic war-time ally, the Soviet Union, also was transformed into an aggressive, imperialist power, brutally taking over Poland, overturning a Czech government, and absorbing Bulgaria, Romania, and Hungary. And in Germany, dominated in the East by Soviet troops and in the West by the Allied troops, Berlin was controlled through an uneasy four-power mechanism, although much of the city lay within the Soviet occupied zone.

By 1948 Stalin had moved to force the three Western powers out of Berlin, but he was checked by a historic counter-initiative: the Berlin airlift. This was the first of several instances where the West had to clearly demonstrate that it would not shy from the use of force to maintain this particular outpost of democracy. Berlin emerged as the centerpiece of the subsequent fifty-year struggle to block Soviet expansion, and the program of "containment" which would become enshrined as the Western response to Moscow's global aspirations.

Within the U.S., the political process was also at a dramatic point. In November 1948 "C" and I retired around midnight after listening to radio accounts of Thomas E. Dewey's victory over President Truman; but, lo and behold, when the alarm went off at 7:00 a.m. the next morning, President Truman had pulled off an historic upset. We, and practically all of our veteran friends, were thrilled. "C" and I generally perceived President Truman as an heroic, embattled president who had had the vision and courage to convert the United States from elated victory in World War II to an unflinching policy of containment of Soviet imperialism. Immediately at the end of the war, the United States and its allies had undertaken a radical demobilization, with U.S. forces dropping to fewer than six hundred thousand army troops from our wartime peak of twelve million troops. Thus, President Truman and the U.S. armed services faced a daunting challenge in terms of what Stalin called the "correlation of forces," a challenge most directly reflected in the neuralgic confrontation of those forces in Berlin.

Blair House

This was the climate in which I worked to complete my Master's degree in International Law at George Washington University and prepare for the Foreign Service exam. There were four of us pursuing this GWU program, and we enjoyed a unique arrangement between the university and the Carnegie International Law Library, housed in part of what is now the official U.S. guest house, Blair House, right across Pennsylvania Avenue from the White House. We were allowed to use the Carnegie Endowment board room for our research in the world's best specialized international law library. The board room had a bay window overlooking Pennsylvania Avenue. To our delight, each day President Truman would walk with different lunch guests across Pennsylvania Avenue from the White House to dine in the original Blair House, passing directly under our bay window. The White House living quarters at that time were closed as the now-famous "Truman balcony" was built.

Our excitement was magnified by the fact that the President was invariably accompanied by such historic figures as General George Marshall, Defense Secretary James Forrestal, State of Secretary Dean Acheson, and Paul Nitze. Often the President, usually in a Panama straw hat, would look up at us in the overhanging window and tip his hat! It is hard to believe in today's world that he and his team were accompanied by a single uniformed Secret Service officer, then were met at Blair House by just two more stationed at the front steps.

Like most of my fellow students, I had to supplement my spartan G.I. Bill allowance with odd jobs. Two of my fellow Foreign Service aspirants and I went to work part-time as parking lot attendants. When the city-operated lot where we worked, owned by the prominent Washington brewer, Christian Heurich, failed, we persuaded Mr. Heurich to let us operate the lot on our own and cover his taxes. Thus was born Colonial Parking (the George Washington University mascot was a "Colonial"), which today is a major parking business in Washington and elsewhere with hundreds of locations. We made $8,000 the first year, operating on a shoestring. On the first day of the month, my wife would join us to collect the monthly payments from our customers. Many of those customers were officials in the State Department, which we dreamed of joining. (I still enjoy free parking, which is worth considerably more than our original investment, but far short of what we could have realized had we incorporated and held on to a small share of the business).

That eagerly anticipated letter from the State Department on February 12, 1950, dramatically changed my life. From that day forward I began to believe that I would enter the Foreign Service, hoping that I could pass the oral exam. As it is today, the exam system was extremely competitive, and good fortune was essential to success. Today some 25,000 candidates take the annual exam, and only a few hundred actually make it through, a fact of which I am very proud. The Foreign Service, after the initiation of public competitive exams shortly after World War II, has been an openly elitist organization—the Marine Corps of the civilian bureaucracy. Societal changes in the United States have properly led to a much more diversified "corps" today in terms of gender and race, but the merit-based competitive selection process remains.

My oral exam in May was a source of on-again, off-again worry. I would receive accounts from my friends of the fearsome interrogation they experienced and from others who bragged that it was "not that tough." My own anxiety heightened when a close friend (Richard E. Johnson) who was a Harvard graduate, a naval officer during the war, and an intern on the State Department's China desk informed us that he had been deferred.

When my day arrived, it was very hot and my exam was in the non-air-conditioned office building known as the Walker-Johnson annex. As fate would have it, I was the last of the four candidates; as I waited I tried to focus on the *New York Times* and perspired heavily. Finally, I was called before the board of four senior Foreign Service Officers, chaired by the infamously gruff Ambassador Joseph Green. The questioning opened pleasantly with queries about my wife (they noted that she had been an English major), my undistinguished navy career, and my parking lot business! Then Mr. Green started living up to his reputation with staccato questions about the Civil War, U.S. government policies between the wars, and more. I choked. I couldn't even remember four generals on each side of the Civil War, nor could I identify the authors of ten well-known books, such as *Moby Dick*. I tried desperately to be pleasant, even amusing ("You've got me again!"), but by the end, I was convinced that I had flunked the oral. I was told to "go have some lunch and be back by 2:00 p.m." My wife was crestfallen for me, and we went off to Billy Martin's Tavern in Georgetown for a martini lunch to drown our sorrows.

At 2:00, I arrived back at Walker-Johnson to face the music. Joe Green, to my amazement, congratulated me and explained that they were impressed by my good spirit and understood my nervousness. He added, "if your wife had not been an English major, we would have sent you back to take a crash course in literature," a fact that "C" never let me forget.

Within a month, with my new status as an "FSO (Foreign Service Officer) eligible," I was employed by the State Department and plunged into a fascinating career. First assignments are usually quite pedestrian and boring, yet, I was placed in the Office of Public Affairs as an assistant to the radio/TV (yes, TV was just emerging) officer, former CBS (Columbia Broadcasting System) correspondent Bill Wood.

In the eight months that I remained in Washington, two dramatic international events exploded that dominated Washington and especially the State Department: North Korea invaded South Korea, and Senator Joseph McCarthy made a speech in Wheeling, West Virginia, in which he charged that he had a list of thirty-five known Communists and homosexuals who worked at the State Department. The Office of Public Affairs was smack in the middle of the department's effort to deal with these historic crises. We scheduled Secretary Acheson and other top officials, such as Niles Bond, director of Korean Affairs, for radio appearances and helped develop "press guidance." We also produced a new television program called "Diplomatic Pouch" to present foreign policy issues to the public. The first program was on Korea and featured Niles Bond. Bill Wood's experience led quickly to his being in the center of things, and I was allowed to tag along, taking notes and preparing follow-up directives.

The dramatic announcement of the Korean invasion put Washington back onto a war footing overnight. By chance, the night of the announcement "C" and I and a close FSO-eligible friend of mine, Paul Smith, and his wife had gone to the Chesapeake shore for a house party and some swimming. Once there, we quickly decided—not, of course knowing anything about Korea—that it wasn't worth it (jellyfish and warm beer) so we faked a phone call and told our hosts that we had been called back to the State Department. You can imagine our shock when, driving back to Washington, we learned on the radio that North Korean troops had invaded South Korea. Even though it was a somber moment, we had to chuckle that our hosts must have assumed that we were truly important.

President Truman's decision to commit the United States to defend South Korea united the country for the first two years of the war as our small occupying force faced near-defeat in front of the massive North Korean Forces, supported by the newly communist People's Republic of China. It was only after two years of brutal warfare that public support for the war faded.

Dark Days of McCarthyism

Meanwhile, the cancer of McCarthyism spread until the country became bitterly divided. What had been an ebullient self-confident national mood, following our great victories against Japan and Germany, turned sour. President Truman, who had the vision and political savvy to rally the U.S. Congress and public to face up to Soviet aggression in Iran, Greece, and Turkey, was increasingly denounced not only by Senator McCarthy but, to their everlasting disgrace, by otherwise respectable Republican leaders such as Robert Taft. The most distressing example of the intellectual cowardice of our leadership occurred when, after McCarthy had attacked General George Marshall as an enabler of communism, General Dwight D. Eisenhower nonetheless proceeded to Madison, Wisconsin, and gave a speech supporting McCarthy's reelection in Wisconsin. Given the fact that General Marshall discovered, mentored, and promoted General Eisenhower, it was especiall disappointing.

The national paranoia about the dangers of communism in the United States was reflected throughout society. Conservative congressional leaders seized on the communist victory in China and Moscow's absorption of Eastern Europe to whip up a national mood of fear. "Somebody lost China," and the ideology of communism was a serious danger within our own schools, they insisted.

Later, when I returned from having been posted to Germany for home leave in 1954, I repeatedly encountered hostility and suspicion because I "worked for the State Department." Boyhood friends, country club members, and the general public. especially in Lake Forest, Illinois (my wife's hometown), were all suspicious of me.

This disappointing chapter in U.S. history was finally ended when the McCarthy hearings backfired on him, thanks in part to CBS correspondent Edward R. Murrow and one very courageous senator, Republican Margaret Chase Smith of Maine, who stood up in the Senate and led a successful effort to censure McCarthy's behavior. Other than Smith and CBS, few emerged from the episode with any honor. Even President Truman and Secretary Acheson squirmed and sought ways to "compromise" on what was clearly a fundamental issue of principle.

One episode during my State Department assignment captured the seamy nature of the McCarthy phenomenon particularly vividly. Through the FBI, the State Department learned that McCarthy's chief operator—a widely reviled young man named Roy Cohn—had been compromised because of his blatant homosexual activity. Homosexuality had become one of McCarthy's principal charges against the State Department because in those days it was assumed that the security reliability of any homosexual was vulnerable to "communist blackmail." With considerable preparation, the deputy undersecretary of state, Carlisle Humelsine, trooped up to McCarthy's office expecting the senator to back off his unfounded charges against the department when confronted with the reports about Cohn. To much dismay, rather than backing off, McCarthy presented Humelsine with irrefutable evidence that the highly respected former Undersecretary of State, Sumner Welles, had been arrested at Thomas Circle for molesting young boys. The effort was dropped.

As a sidebar of interest, future attorney general Robert Kennedy was one of Cohn's assistants in these historic hearings. It is ironic that as a presidential candidate, Kennedy was seen as an ultraliberal opponent of the Vietnam War, given his staff job with McCarthy, and his earlier aggressive leadership in President Kennedy's cabinet for building up our engagement in the Vietnam War.

In retrospect, the knee-jerk reactionary effort of McCarthy to exploit Soviet advances to establish a national sense of fear seriously undercut the determined efforts of President Truman's administration to confront and engage our new adversaries. Thanks to McCarthy and the irresolute response of our administration, national attention was too often focused on the threat of communism in our schools, a paranoid reaction to a political philosophy that never worked, instead of on the critical need to build our military capacity, and to create international coalitions to face down Soviet expansion.

Such reactionary tactics are hauntingly familiar today, in a world poisoned by fear-mongering about the "War on Terror" and President George W. Bush's administration's failure to mobilize national sacrifice and build international alliances to confront the real terrorist threat while strengthening our economy and education system. Fear is not a sound basis for national policy, nor does it reflect the historic reality that the United States today remains the sole world power.

Thus, after two and a half years in Washington "C" and I had seen the ebullient mood of victory in World War II dissolve before the stark, aggressive Soviet moves to repress patriotic forces and take control of Poland, Czechoslovakia, and Hungary and initiate the attack by North Korea. And we watched an heroic performance by President Truman to show down and evict Soviet forces in the northern one-third of Iran, to launch a full-scale effort to support the Greek and Turkish governments as they faced Soviet support for communist Greek insurgents attempting to seize control in Greece, and to commit U.S. forces to block the takeover of South Korea.

Proud as we felt about the U.S. response to these imperialist moves by Moscow, we were depressed and concerned by the eruption of the poisonous McCarthy phenomenon that divided our country and shattered our national self-confidence.

These were the dominant realities as we sailed for Europe on our first overseas assignment—to Germany.

Chapter II. Across Devastated Europe, Face to Face with the Cost of Hitler's War, 1951-1952

March 12, 1951, was a rainy day as "C" and I boarded the SS *DeGrasse* at New York's French Line dock. We were among a group of eighteen new Foreign Service officers and wives en route to our first posting to replace military administrators with civilian authority in defeated Germany. Our excitement was palpable, and life aboard ship was out of a prewar movie: a great French breakfast, consommé on the deck at 11:00, lunch at 12:30, and an outstanding dinner followed by VSOP cognac.

The voyage, a first for all of us, passed through rough seas, and the *DeGrasse*, built before the war, had limited stabilizer capacity. It creaked and rolled, and several of our group reacted predictably, turning green and sick. Nonetheless, the ping-pong tournament went on; the lucky and healthy sailors among us gorged on magnificent food; every night we danced to the ship's small orchestra; and we watched the latest movies. After four days everyone had found their sea legs and the weather improved.

The trip was also a final bonding experience. We had all been studying German together and benefiting from lectures by academic experts on German history for those three months prior to sailing. On board, our families grew together. I was impressed by the diversity of our group in terms of wartime combat experiences and academic achievement. Admittedly, we all spent a lot of time gauging each other: he will certainly become an ambassador, or, how did *he* get in? But above all, we were excited and enthusiastic about our band of brothers—and the future.

We sailed into the harbor at Le Havre, France, on the morning of March 20 to a shock. After shipboard French luxury, we were overwhelmed by the ruins and ashes of war: sunken rusty ships, bombed out warehouses, flattened apartment buildings, and mountains of rubble. Dockyards are never characterized by aesthetic beauty, but Le Havre in March 1951 was a vivid reminder of the unprecedented destruction and chaos that Europe had endured. There was little construction activity; Marshall Plan funds, which had primed basic industry production by 1951, had yet to make a noticeable difference in the reconstruction of the devastated cities and towns. Crippled veterans were everywhere. George Kennan, in his memoirs, characterized Europe then as gripped in "a pall of fear and seemingly resigned to fall into Stalin's hands."

The only splashes of color were the political posters and painted slogans on the walls, largely red, calling for a Communist rule. In the immediate postwar years, the French Communist Party (FCP) was France's largest, and there was genuine fear that a Communist takeover could well happen. The FCP had a heroic image, having been a major element in the anti-German resistance. The Soviet Union's lead role in the victory over Germany also enhanced the influence of the

FCP, which held genuine appeal for the apathetic, deprived French population. By 1947 the Communists had enrolled 907,000 members, as the public grew anxious about a descent into anarchy. The public, too, was sincerely respectful of the "invincible" Red Army, which, although it had paid a terrible price, had utterly destroyed the bulk of Hitler's army. Communists dominated and often controlled the powerful trade union movement. They demonstrated their power with snap strikes that easily stalled all activity and revealed the impotence of the French governments, which went through endless changes. In the early postwar elections, the FCP won 25 to 40 percent of the vote.

A similar political pattern had been established in Italy when the Communist Party of Italy (CPI) controlled the labor unions and the communal movement in agriculture. Italy had the largest Communist party outside of the Soviet Bloc. In the 1953 elections, more than six million voters chose the Communist Party—more than 23 percent of the vote. It is difficult to imagine in today's prosperous Italy the devastating influence of the CPI; unions were largely CPI-controlled and massive strikes were frequent. And yet when viewed against the backdrop of destruction and postwar political chaos in Italy, it is not surprising that the clear-cut discipline of the Communist movement, so like the order of Mussolini's Italy, would seem more comfortable to many than the disorder and social corruption of postwar Italy. More than half of Italy, largely the residential north, had been devastated in the post-1943 German occupation and subsequent slow, grinding infantry war that finally liberated the South.

Thus, as we drove across France and Luxembourg and then into Germany to our first assignment in Munich, we were deeply impressed by the incredible destruction and human cost of the war. Everywhere, it seemed, my eyes met the painful sight of amputees hobbling on crutches, pathetic efforts to provide some kind of mobility to war veterans. Wheelchairs were more like wheelbarrows than chairs, and begging was widespread. The ruins of the Maginot and Siegfried lines were haunting, but these impressions were overwhelmed by the human suffering and total loss of human dignity, which were the true costs of Hitler's brutality.

Stalin's expansionist intentions were clear to all of us: to seize power in Western Europe by working through the trade union movements in France and Italy, while nailing down absolute authority over the Eastern European countries now occupied by the victorious Red Army. Allied hopes in 1944 to 1945 that Stalin would in fact become a peaceable partner as well as a wartime ally were thus quickly disabused. Perhaps the most revealing event in establishing the new power configuration was the demand from Moscow that the Czech government reverse its initial decision to participate in the Marshall Plan, thereby dooming the Czech economy and prefacing the Moscow-directed coup in Prague that placed Czechoslovakia firmly under Communist control and Moscow's direction. In short, by 1950, Europe was firmly divided by the Iron Curtain, and the western side of the division in Europe was under heavy pressure to join the new Soviet Empire.

While Western leaders focused on the hardening divide between Soviet-occupied Eastern Europe and the West, Stalin offensively moved ahead to mobilize supporters in Western Europe and lay the groundwork for Soviet influence in the Third World. In 1947, he established the COMINFORM, successor to the prewar COMINTERN, to coordinate—read "run"—international Communist party activity, and to solidify Moscow's absolute control of satellite parties and international "cultural" and trade activities.

Thus, although the Iron Curtain had clanged down, Stalin was still able to brush through it into Western Europe where he sought to create the conditions for further Soviet expansion. American policymakers grew increasingly alarmed. The Berlin Blockade in 1947, Mao's victory in China, and the 1951 aggression in Korea drove the final nails into sincere hopes among Western leaders that a peaceful post-World War era was possible. The Cold War was on, and U.S. policies and programs turned quickly.

Legacy of Yalta

Some conservative voices in the United States continue to insist that Moscow's control over Eastern Europe was a product of the wartime Yalta Conference. Yalta has grown into a myth in American politics. The consensus among conservatives is that an enfeebled Franklin Roosevelt was out-negotiated by Stalin and gave away the independence of Central and East European nations to Stalin. This simplistic evaluation ignores basic realities: Soviet troops fought for (at a disastrous cost in human life) the liberation of these countries from German occupation and were firmly in control of these territories as the war ended. U.S. troops might have been able to rush in and occupy Czechoslovakia and capture Berlin ahead of Soviet forces, but General Dwight Eisenhower and his Allied partners decided without hesitation that they did not want to accept the casualties that such a move would cost and that the Soviets deserved the right to capture Berlin and Czechoslovakia, given their overwhelming contribution to Allied victory. Second, to attribute the Yalta division of territory to President Roosevelt ignores Winston Churchill's role as the principal promoter of this "division," which in fact only confirmed the earlier decision in Tehran, where Churchill again was the dominant figure on the Western side. This decision, as the late author David Halberstam wrote in *Vanity Fair*, was not a "sell-out", it was a fait accompli.

Munich, too, in early 1951 was largely destroyed, especially in the city's center. The contrast to the largely unaffected, beautiful pastoral landscape of Bavaria was stark. However, here more than in Northern Germany, large pockets of relatively undamaged buildings and homes projected the tradition of the distinctly attractive architecture so typical of

Bavaria; restaurants, often in the surviving basements of their former sites, were serving typically excellent Bavarian food and beer, opera was active, and restoration of the city center was underway.

Refugee Resettlement

The eight career Foreign Service officers in our contingent were immediately drafted into emergency duty to process the thousands of displaced persons (DPs) seeking to win entry into the United States under the Displaced Persons Act of 1948. Congress had passed the act as an emergency program to allow the resettlement of some 150,000 refugees from Eastern Europe and the Soviet Union who had been residents in the teeming refugee camps in Germany since 1945. The refugees, who had either been impressed into involuntary labor brigades by the Nazi authorities or had fled the combat zones as Red Army troops "liberated" Eastern Europe, were a heavy burden on Allied occupation forces and the slowly reviving European economies. I was disappointed not to participate in the more political process of nation-building that our group had been recruited to implement, but in retrospect, we gained invaluable exposure to the realities and costs of the historic uprooting of millions caught between the brutalities of Hitler's invasion and the Soviet overrunning of Eastern Europe.

As the war ended, some six million refugees from the Soviet Union and Eastern Europe overwhelmed Allied authorities in Germany. Originally the UN (through the United Nations Relief and Rehabilitation Administration, UNRRA, with more than $10 billion in U.S. aid) established more than 300 camps in Germany and Austria and initiated a massive resettlement program for these pathetic survivors in Western countries. By 1951, under a new congressionally authorized and funded program, we were engaged in cleaning up the remaining 200,000 cases, largely for resettlement in the U. S. This law terminated on December 31, 1951; thus our team was thrown into the breach to complete the resettlement by year's end.

Each of us was assigned a local translator, who in my case was a Czech refugee, fluent in Russian, Ukrainian, and German. Each day we interviewed in depth some twenty candidates. While the process itself was depressing and often boring, as we worked our way into it, we became more and more impressed by the personal tragedies these people had experienced. For each case we had a background file that included the case history prepared by the American charity group "sponsoring" the DP in question; a local police record (usually Nazi-era material); and U.S. Army intelligence material about the units in which the DP had worked as a laborer, camp guard, or German-allied military unit.

The most straightforward cases (and those were the ma-jority of which we received) were the thousands of forced-labor battalion members who had been rolled up as German forces advanced into the Soviet Union. Entire Ukrainian, Polish, and Russian families were pressed into these labor battalions under the forced-labor plan designed by Albert Speer, Nazi minister of construction, to replace the millions of German workers drafted into the Wehrmacht for the invasion of the Soviet Union. These cases were simple and easy to approve.

However, embedded among these hundreds of thousands were thousands of eager former collaborators who willingly joined Nazi programs and now were presenting themselves as "victims" of the Nazi regime. Our ability to weed out these elements from the masses of legitimate refugees was compromised by the essential quick switch in U.S. policy, from defeating Hitler to containing Stalin, and the inevitable policy shift to view the "refugees" from the Baltic States, Hungary, and Ukraine, for example, as fleeing Soviet domination. In more concrete terms, each refugee was sponsored by American organizations, such as: the National Catholic Welfare Organization; the Lutheran World Foundation; the United Jewish Assistance Group; and ethnic groups such as Ukrainian-American and Hungarian-American organizations. These non-governmental sponsors did tremendous work providing assistance to the refugees in the camps, setting up sponsors in the United States to assist in resettlement, and helping to locate and reunite families.

The complicating factor in this process was that the sponsoring agencies were essentially disinterested in what the refugees in question had done under German direction. As long as the applicant was Ukrainian, the Ukrainian-American community wanted him and his family admitted to the United States. The Hungarian-American agency was particularly aggressive in pressing us to ignore the wartime records of Hungarian applicants.

In fact, several hundred Hungarian "refugees" had been active members of the infamous Prinz Eugen SS Division, one of the most brutal Nazi units during the war. The Germans had created this SS Division to harness their enthusiastic Hungarian supporters. It was one of several such divisions formed as the Nazi government exploited the minority of supporters who emerged in the German occupation. Some of these actually became first-line forces on the Eastern Front (the Romanian and Baltic divisions), while others were employed as guards at concentration camps. The Baltic SS Division had understandably found eager anti-Soviet recruits as Germany moved into the Soviet Union. As in the case of the Prinz Eugen Division, however, these volunteer Baltic troops were often used as willing concentration camp guards and were especially brutal. The same was true in the case of the tens of thousands of Ukrainians, several of whom had been the backbone of the Nazi-sponsored independent Ukrainian government that retreated with German forces back into Germany itself. The Ukrainian-American agency made every effort to win approval for all Ukrainian refugees, largely ignoring collaborative activity in recognition of the new Cold-War reality.

In our efforts to sort out these historic and complex population movements, sensitive above all to the human tragedies we learned of each day, we often found it difficult to do as the law required and at the same time, what was right. In one particularly painful day for me, I interviewed a young Ukrainian Jew who had survived Babi Yar (the Nazi extermination center for Ukrainian Jews) and who had been convicted by a Nazi court in 1945 of stealing firewood, a crime "involving moral turpitude" under our immigration law, and therefore rendering him ineligible for a U.S. visa. I destroyed the "criminal record" and issued the visa. The same day I was faced with a case, strongly supported by the Lutheran World Federation, of a Latvian refugee who had been a colonel in the Baltic SS Division and clearly active in the German concentration camp activities. In his case, I "lost" the entire file, thereby blocking his application.

I was too young to fully assimilate the historic dimensions of the tragedy I saw, yet I sat in judgment of these people whose lives I could change with a quick stamp of approval. Yes, visa work was boring and clerical, but I just couldn't lose the feeling that I was magic to them. It was humbling. This personal hands-on experience also introduced us to the bitterness between these peoples, and to the political influence of ethnic minorities in the U. S. The latter experience was invaluable in my thirty-year career, as I often found myself dealing with diaspora politics in Washington. As a twenty-four-year-old diplomat, I was humbled by the pain and tragedy represented by these thousands of refugees. The combined refugee resettlement programs were truly God's work, but remorse rather than fulfillment was its effect on me.

Meanwhile, Munich had become an incredibly vibrant center of struggle between the multitudes of émigré survivors. Anti-Nazi survivors denounced German collaborators; Jews suffered continuing discrimination from other ethnic groups who reflected the centuries of anti-Semitism in Russia, Poland, and Eastern Europe, and the hundreds of thousands of minority groups Stalin had uprooted and resettled (or killed) as German troops rolled over Western provinces of the Soviet Union were viewed as uncivilized barbarians by their more Western counterparts. One of the most striking examples of this latter phenomenon was the Kalmyks (remnants of the Mongol invasion of ancient Czarist Russia). Some two thousand Kalmyks were housed in our DP camp, Funkkaserne. By all odds, they were the best organized and most self-supporting in their immaculate cabins. They were quickly accepted for resettlement and U.S. visas.

The Radios

The historic experiences of all these peoples and their overwhelming anti-Soviet hostility made them very attractive for U.S. and Allied recruitment for the rapidly evolving anti-Soviet programs, in particular the intelligence and propaganda efforts. The Central Intelligence Agency had established headquarters in Munich for Radio Liberty, which was directed into the Soviet Union, while Radio Free Europe was aimed into what was becoming the Warsaw Pact. To this day, "the Radios" (now overseen and funded by the

Board for International Broadcasting) are staffed by refugees (and their children) from our displaced persons camps. This activity was bitterly attacked by Moscow, which complained about "nests of Fascist vipers" dedicated to overthrowing the Soviet government. In the 1950s, assassinations were not infrequent as Soviet agents tried to blunt the effectiveness of "the Radios." Munich also served as a recruiting source for Western intelligence services, which regularly ran agents into the Soviet area. In the 1990s it was learned that Soviet infiltration of Western intelligence sources quickly aborted many of these efforts. The dramatic British cases of Donald MacLean, Guy Burgess, and Kim Philby (and the much later Soviet recruitment of senior CIA program leader Aldrich Ames and top FBI Soviet experts) have explained the frequent failures of Western efforts to infiltrate our agents behind the Iron Curtain. At the same time, U.S. and especially British recruitment of KGB and other Warsaw Pact agents in Washington and London succeeded in aborting or "turning" Soviet efforts in the West. In short, Munich in 1951 was a key center for the rapidly growing intelligence war between East and West, an ugly manifestation of the global Cold War.

Some revisionist historians, usually born after World War II, have insisted that "each side" was guilty of missing opportunities to avoid the Cold War. They contend that the West, by offering to rebuild the West European economies, locked Moscow into a defensive position. They ignore the Western assistance programs that were offered to East

European countries, who declined under heavy pressure from Moscow. And the Soviets themselves benefited from massive economic and military equipment assistance during the war and in the first few years after Germany's collapse. By 1951, the Soviet-imposed Iron Curtain had dropped with a vengeance across Europe.

Idyllic as the Bavarian countryside was, the ever-present reality of the Iron Curtain could not be avoided. My SS *DeGrasse* colleague Jim Carrigan and his wife Jane were posted to Hof in Northern Bavaria, where Jim served as the civilian replacement for the former U.S. military governor. U.S. troops patrolled the border of the adjacent Soviet zone and Jim served as the channel for U.S. assistance, selecting Hof officials and students for trips to the United States, working to bring officers of the German Bundesgrenschuetz (border police who became the core of the soon-to-emerge German army) to the U.S. and symbolically reassuring the local population that the U.S. government was present and committed. For the residents of Hof and its surrounding population, Soviet presence was a continual source of anxiety. As the border between U.S. and Soviet zones ran, villages were often split in half. "C" and I visited a town, Moedelreuth, which provided a vivid example. The day we were there, a wedding was held in the western half. The bride's relatives in the eastern half stood, forlornly, on the far side of the fence, guarded by the detested VOPOs (East German police under Soviet Control), unable to join the bridal party as vows were exchanged. It was surreal to witness the bride and groom in full wedding dress and tails being married in front of the isolated relatives under a typical huge red banner calling for the victory of Communism on the wall of the Moedelreuth's only factory, located across the Iron Curtain.

This was in 1951. Stalin was at the height of his paranoia, purging Jews and other "foreign elements." The gulags were bursting at their seams, and Stalin was rebuilding the Red Army until it reached more than five million men. Hof sat astride the so-called Fulda Gap (which had been the historic invasion path), where U.S. and allied forces numbered fewer than a million. In short, the Iron Curtain was a very real presence to us, and even more so to the Bavarians, who clung to the U.S. presence as a security blanket.

We also experienced the historic East-West confrontation when we visited Vienna. Soviet troops still occupied Eastern Austria, and Vienna itself was divided into sectors. Already, in 1951, the Western sector was showing signs of revival, while the Soviet sector was dormant and depressed. Soviet forces withdrew from Austria in 1955, and the influence of their occupation quickly dissipated.

We saw an even more dramatic manifestation of the Iron Curtain in our 1951 visit to Berlin. The Soviet sector looked as though the war had ended the week before, while activity in the free Western sector was already vigorous. We were free to move about in all sectors of Berlin under the occupation settlement, but the massive Soviet troop presence in the Soviet sector was daunting.

The vigorous intelligence battle we witnessed in Munich was considerably more intense in Berlin, where U.S.-Allied elements were face-to-face with their Soviet adversaries. By 1951, the division of Europe was solidified and the grinding of the two tectonic plates—Western and Soviet—was well under way, and one destined not to end until the last act of the Cold War: the collapse of the Soviet Union.

Earlier, in 1947, as he worked to mobilize congressional support for the Marshall Plan, Dean Acheson stated that "the U.S. and Soviet Union now stood like Rome and Carthage, divided by an unbridgeable chasm." He added that "the Soviets were aggressively squeezing three of the world's most delicate nodal points; Iran, Turkey, and Greece."

The end of the Displaced Persons Act on December 31, 1951, freed my Foreign Service colleagues and me to rejoin the American effort to build a new Germany. The military government was formally converted into civilian control under John J. McCloy, the first High Commissioner. Unfortunately for me the personnel system transferred me to the U.S. Consulate General in Munich to become a "passport officer."

"C" and I loved living in beautiful Bavaria. We had an attractive, small house on the edge of a forest, with ample time to prowl around historic Munich, its museums, and its fine restaurants. I became an active member of the local tennis club, where we made numerous friends among the Bavarian members. We became particularly close to Paul and Imogene "Mutti" Kinkledey and their son Hermann, my seventeen-year-old tennis partner. They provided us with an intimate insight into the experience of German civilians as the war ended.

Like most of those engaged in Germany in 1951, we were perplexed and troubled by the haunting images of German bestiality in attempting to obliterate Europe's Jewish population. I visited the infamous Dachau concentration camp, not far from Munich, to better assess the behavior of many of the "displaced persons" seeking enrollment in the U.S. subsidized resettlement program. The vivid memory of that visit will never leave me.

Paul Kinkledey was very forthcoming about his experience during the war, unlike many Germans, who tried to blot out their memories and lived in a state of denial. He described the creeping, pervasive Nazi campaign to replace German despair during the Weimar period between the wars with rabid nationalism. He first noticed that only German and Austrian operas were being performed at Munich's opera houses, book reviews of non-German authors disappeared from the press, and such authors' books themselves became no longer available. School texts were cleansed, and finally book-burnings began. Paul was working as an economist at the Bavarian state bank, and noticed that Jewish films were also banned. He, however, like most businessmen, was distracted by the devastating effect of

massive inflation and greeted positively many of the economic reforms and the end of inflation. By mid-1935, he said,
the full force of the Nazi programs gradually became clear,
and so did the increasingly tight political control of the
Gestapo. He had spoken out against the firing of Jewish
colleagues, and was quickly warned that "one more outburst
like that and you will be dealing with the Gestapo and its
local Bavaria police allies." Paul described how fear was at
the base of his and practically all of his friends' actions. "We
knew by the late 1930s, our Jewish colleagues were being
sent off to internment camps and feared the worst. Dachau
and its horrors were not fully appreciated until I was con-
scripted and sent off to the Russian Front, by which point
survival had become the central thought in my mind."

Paul and Mutti Kinkledey were emblematic of the dozens
of Germans "C" and I met in my two assignments in postwar
Germany: decent; bewildered by the historic costs of the two
World Wars; torn by guilt that they had been impotent in
resisting the destruction of civilized Germany; and eager to
reach out and start life anew as part of the West, facing the
Soviet behemoth occupying the eastern half of Germany.

The Kinkledeys had had a savior in the United States in
the 1945-50 period when Germans faced practical starvation.
Professor Glenn Seaborg, president of Cal Tech and one of
the atomic bomb development team, had lived with their
family in the early 1930s while attending the University of
Munich. Beginning in 1945, his care packages were critical for

the Kinkledeys as they coped with the destitution in their lives.

In sum, my experience from 1950 to 1952 in Munich was much more important than I realized at the time. My colleagues and I were deeply immersed in attempting to understand how a "civilized Western Christian country" could descend into a vicious evil society, and then bring down upon the world the most brutal war in the history of mankind. I am not sure that question has ever been answered satisfactorily, but certainly many Germans remain even more perplexed, troubled, and guilty about it.

By the end of that first assignment, I had seen and experienced the rise and peak of Allied efforts to deal with this issue through the messy but effective de-Nazification program. I accepted that "guilt and accountability" were a complicated challenge and that degrees of guilt were the reality. The Nuremburg trials were the capstone of Allied efforts to resolve this issue. Though imperfect in the eyes of many, the trials did serve their purpose and allowed a page to be turned.

This closure was accelerated by the rise of the Cold War confrontation with a different but equally brutal adversary: Stalin's Soviet Union.

Thus, as I concluded my assignment in Munich in 1952, we experienced a historic watershed in U.S. policy: shifting from cleaning up the remnants of Nazi aggression to a new, unprecedented confrontation with Soviet imperialism.

CHAPTER III. NORTH TO THE GERMAN LOWLANDS

The *berumpte Deutsche tiefebene* (German lowlands), Lower Saxony, had a complex history; the British Royal Family was drawn from its major city, Hannover. Hannover and its neighbor Hamburg were strongholds of German Communism between the two wars, and it was the principal area to which displaced Germans fled from the Prussian territories occupied by the Soviet forces and then ceded to Poland as the war ended. With the German surrender in 1945, Lower Saxony, Hamburg, and the northern peninsula Schleswig-Holstein fell under British occupation. In 1952 the U.S. high commissioner for Germany, John J. McCloy, negotiated an agreement with his British counterpart to expand our "reeducation program" from the U.S. occupation zone into the British zone, as well.

It was this opening I seized upon when the Displaced Person (DP) visa program was completed in Munich in the spring of 1952. While "C" and I truly loved the life we led in Bavaria, the proffered position as a consular officer in our Consulate General in Munich to assist U.S. tourists held no appeal, and it was far from the "nation-building" that I had originally been sent to Germany to carry out. Designed to convert the defeated German nation into a democratic European partner, the replacement of our military government by civilian teams was visionary, high-minded, and remarkably well received by the overwhelming majority of

33

the German people in the U.S. zone. When McCloy and his high-powered civilian team replaced U.S. military governors, he committed to a sweeping fundamental program to create a democratic media system, reform the historically narrow nationalistic school system, promote economic development, and strengthen the German labor movement.

The McCloy program paralleled the recasting of Japan under General McArthur. In both cases, the farsighted programs were eventually successful; democratically solid allies of the U.S.—and the West in general—the examples of Germany and Japan dramatically established the wisdom of "nation-building," if that action was provided with sufficient funds and dedicated top leadership. McCloy was supported in Frankfurt by outstanding U.S. economists, publishers, journalists, and academic experts— and the results showed.

(I belabor this issue, particularly, because as this is written in 2009 we are mired deep into Iraq and only after five years of an extremely expensive mismanaged occupation are we reprioritizing our efforts around "nation-building.")

It was this policy-pivot by High Commissioner McCloy that opened the opportunity for me to avoid a humdrum consular post in Munich. With Consul General Sam Woods' begrudging approval, I traveled to McCloy's headquarters in Frankfurt and met with his deputy for "information," Elmer Lower. Typical of the quality of McCloy's team, Lower eventually returned to New York and became the CEO of Mutual Broadcasting. Lower, with obvious concern about my youthfulness (I was twenty-five), agreed to gamble that my enthusiasm and command of German might be enough.

Thus, "C" and I, and our new Airedale, Tigger, drove into Hannover to join a four-man U.S. vanguard to set up a full-bore "public affairs" program. Headed by an outstanding middle-aged academic, Francis Lindeman, our team included a seasoned bilingual veteran of the lend-lease program in the USSR who had a Master's in Russian Studies from Columbia, Wallace Littell, and a wonderfully wise school principal from Louisville, Kentucky, Liz Wilson. We all spoke German, and had no doubts about the importance of the opportunity we faced.

We were warmly received by the British official community. While maintaining two tank divisions in Lower Saxony (designed to face a Soviet invasion force in the lowland corridor), the British footprint was much gentler than its U.S. counterpart in the U.S. zone, where housing developments, schools, athletic facilities, and the ubiquitous PX and community facilities were developed to allow the U.S. troops to feel "at home."

Lower Saxony had been much more heavily damaged by bombing during the war than Bavaria. Our bare-bones new offices opened quickly and we set about to promote appreciation of the U.S., its democratic methods, and planned economic development.

We were viewed first with curiosity and then increasingly as friendly sources of revitalization, and finally, together with the British army tank units, as a security blanket, with almost 500,000 Soviet troops fewer than 100 miles away. The surprising absence of hostility from the people of our recently defeated enemy was explicable to some degree by the absolute nature of that defeat. Millions of German men from ages sixteen to sixty had been killed, mostly on the Eastern Front. Hannover and its industry were in ashes, food was in short supply, and fuel was hard to get. Malaise was the predominant mood. Those who had been enthusiastic about Hitler's nationalism and military conquests (and most observers agree that covered much of the population) were thoroughly cowed or dead by the time we arrived in 1952. Their efforts were now directed at "getting by" and cleaning up. It was therefore no surprise that we were seen as contributors to their efforts to rebuild their lives.

Amerika Haus

We established a cultural center *Amerika Haus* (AH) in the center of town in a property donated by the city and refurbished by us. Liz Wilson directed the AH, which quickly became immensely popular. It held some 3,000 books, mostly in English, and was the center for weekly programs about the U.S. and also about Europe's and Germany's problems. The most lively program in which I participated was a debate among a U.S. visiting economist, a French professor, and a German economist about the "Saar

Frage"—what to do about coal production and how to govern the French occupied province, Saarland. Often debate and audience participation were a revolutionary experience for most Germans, who had never known that kind of interaction. Students were very enthusiastic, and as the AH became increasingly the cultural center in which to be seen, the older generation became more involved.

It was a bit of an embarrassment when our popular AH was visited by a two-man Congressional staff delegation led by the infamous McCarthy staffer Roy Cohn, who ransacked through the library of American literature and school books, weeding out those with "left-leaning tendencies!" McCarthy was riding high at home and the paranoia that he generated produced absolute incredulity among Hannoverians. Here we were, 100 miles from the Red Army, and those two ridiculous staffers were ordering us to remove Mark Twain from the shelves! However, that was a passing incident and Cohn and his associate, hotel heir David Shine, were ridiculed in the local press as *Schone* and *Kein* ("already nothing").

Meanwhile Francis Lindeman developed close ties with the editors and writers of the two principle newspapers— one socialist and one conservative—and launched a program to send them and several of their young journalists to the U.S. for extended visits and exchange programs with U.S. newspapers. We also provided funding to modernize their presses.

Pic Littell designed and put in place a very successful cultural exchange program, selecting and sending more than 150 academics and student leaders to the U.S. He also set up a very well received "alumni group" program for the exchangees when they returned from the U.S. In addition, he recruited more than a dozen U.S. historians to spend a semester in Hannover's academic institutes.

My own principal focus was to create a network of film committees in each county (*kreise*) to include teachers, student leaders, church officials and business leaders; the draw was my ability to provide each committee with one or two 16-mm Victor film projectors, train projectionists, and establish a steady stream of 16-mm films. National Geographic features, educational school films, political feature films, our presidential campaign between Eisenhower and Adlai Stevenson were very popular, as well as more general films about sports, among others. In the ruins of war, a film projector was a thing of wonderment. Many younger Germans who had known only war were as thrilled as their elders were at exposure to the Western world. I say "Western world" because no German in Lower Saxony could forget for a moment the looming Soviet presence, so closeby.

The first step in this process was to agree on the targets for our efforts: teachers and student groups; church leaders; trade union officials; and the media, such as it was. There were two predominant youth groups. The more conservative Christian Democratic Union (CDU) and the Socialist Falken (the youth division of the SPD). With the election of

38

Eisenhower and growing influence of Conservative Republican congressional leaders, the U.S. administration was clearly signaling that our efforts and support should concentrate on the CDU groups. Our contigent was able, however, to preserve a fairly balanced approach to include both parties. We were able to persuade these two state level youth offices—and parallel state offices of the church, ministry of education, and trade unions—to set up training programs for us in each county. Then we roamed the towns of Lower Saxony, providing hands-on projector training and scheduling lectures and visits by our traveling "bookmobiles."

As the years of Soviet occupation of East Germany subsequently wore on, the West Germans and we became somewhat more resigned and less fearful. But, in 1952 Stalin was still alive; his brutal purges of Jews, military veterans, and helpless innocent Soviet survivors were filling the Gulags. For those who lived along the Iron Curtain, the effect was palpable and oppressive. East Germany at that time had a population of some 17 million. Soviet occupation troops numbered 450,000-500,000—a density of one Soviet occupier for each thirty-five Germans stranded in the Soviet zone. Constant maneuvers and frightening "incidents" along the border and at the checkpoints kept their awareness fresh.

For the German residents of Lower Saxony the psychological effect of twelve years of Hitler, dominated by the suicidal war, the subsequent forced acknowledgement of concentration camp horrors, and new Soviet terror produced desperation, resignation, and congenital fear. Our program was seized upon by the German population to whom *Amerika* was a dream, and we provided some access to that dream. Heady stuff for our young, fluent, and enthusiastic team.

As the presidential election between Eisenhower and Aldai Stevenson unfolded, we took advantage of the intense interest among Germans to launch a simulated campaign tour throughout Lower Saxony. I played "Ike" and Littell played Stevenson. We had an excellent 16-mm film of the two conventions (dubbed into German) that we played at gatherings across Lower Saxony and then we debated each other. The audience ate it up. In the Q & A periods, invariably there was a strong focus on whether the next U.S. administrator could be counted on to "stand firm" in front of the massive Soviet forces so close by.

Some of our most challenging debates took place at the military bases (*kasernes*) where the German border police were training. With the help of the British military leadership in Lower Saxony, we called on the director of the academy for the newly evolving German army where the officer recruits were being trained—a small West Point-type campus. He readily agreed to including us in the academy's program; Littell, Lindeman, and I lectured once a month on such things as the presidential election and U.S. foreign policy. We also were allowed to repeat these programs at the individual bases for the so-called "Border Guards." These *Bundesgrenschutz* troops were eighteen- to twenty-two-year-

olds who had missed the war, officered, however, by seasoned veterans of the *Wehrmacht* who had mostly served on
the Russian front in the War. The dynamic between the
young enlisted men who were strongly committed to the
West, and the U.S. particularly, and the officer corps was
dramatic. The latter were usually cynical about the reliability of U.S. and British forces and constantly pressed us as to
why we had not been allies against the Soviets all along. The
lack of contrition and sense of guilt for having launched the
brutal invasion of Poland and the USSR disappointed us.
But, as we strove to answer their questions and accusations,
we were heartened by the virtually unanimous support from
the younger men. Speaking out to disagree with officers and
"seniors" in general had never been acceptable in the rigid
German society, especially under the Nazis. We built on
these "debate" events to establish regular film programs and
provide speakers (including British and American officers) at
the *kasernes*. We quickly had a very active program with
these officers and men who were to become the core of the
new West German army.

Historically, Hannover had been the site of one of Europe's most vibrant trade fairs; the *Hannoversche Messe* was a
major annual event over several centuries. Hannover lay
astride the principal trade routes from Eastern Europe to
Hamburg, a powerful site for merchants from Moscow, the
Middle East, and Central Europe. The war, of course,
interrupted this role for Hannover. The second year of our
time in Hannover, local business leaders, supported by the

British concession, decided to revive this historic event. As the U.S. representatives in Hannover, we were asked to encourage U.S. participation, which we did. The effort was an amazing success—many Western European and British corporations built exhibit halls, and we persuaded several American companies to participate, especially agricultural implement producers such as John Deere and Caterpillar.

The political impact of aggressively showcasing U.S. industrial might was dramatic—a lesson I never forgot, and which was an invaluable experience in future posts.

Littell also set up a very effective program throughout Lower Saxony whereby we held three-day "retreats" for German teachers – in which there were usually about twenty participants—to talk about education challenges, and obviously the political reality of the Cold War. Often these were in camps, very close to the Soviet zone border in the Hartz mountains. We provided the food, films, wine, and beer. Without exception these meetings quickly developed into deep conversations about their fear of the Soviets, and a pouring out of their sense of guilt about the Nazi period. Sitting up late at night around a fire, the compelling soul-searching the participants revealed was truly unforgettable. Departures at the close of these sessions were inevitably emotional. The emotion was heightened by the omnipresent Soviet guard towers whose floodlights were clearly visible at night.

Tennis: Diplomatic Tool

In addition to my professional capacity, one of the most effective tools I found to break into the initially stiff formal North German reserve was tennis. As in Munich, I immediately joined the Hannover Tennis Club and quickly found eager partners—eager because tennis balls, of which I had an endless supply, were scarce and cars and gas to travel to other clubs for matches were hard to come by. Hannover had been home to Germany's finest players, and three of their top international players who had survived the War were leaders of the Club's team: the Baron von Cramm, Henner Henkle, and Hans Denker. It was a privilege to be on their team and it opened great and unusual opportunities for us to travel around the state together. Once again, anxiety about the ever-present Soviet behemoth to the East and psychological scars from the Nazi era permeated our conversations.

With the election of Eisenhower, a change of guard had occurred with former Harvard president James B. Conant replacing McCloy. After two years in Hannover, the new High Commissioner decided to consolidate our Hannover activities with those in neighboring Hamburg and Schlewig-Holstein, and "C" and I were off to Hamburg, heavily damaged by fire-bombing but even then a beautiful city. Conant, who had visited our mission in Hannover, was equally committed to our efforts there.

We made regular visits to the tense checkpoint at Helmstedt where all allied traffic had to park on the highway

43

to Berlin, across the Soviet zone, about 100 miles away. At the checkpoint, British, U.S., and French military units processed all vehicles and Western passengers prior to crossing some fifty yards to the Soviet troop-manned checkpoint. Needless to say, the Soviet process was unfriendly, lengthy, and included sniffer dogs and under-car and trunk inspections, all carried out by machine-gun bearing young Red Army soldiers. Soviet tanks were parked ominously and the soldiers tried manfully to appear threatening. The drive to Berlin, which we did twice, was fascinating but depressing. Already in 1952 the contrast between the West German villages struggling to rebuild and the depressed Soviet zone with no signs of rebuilding efforts was dramatic. We were instructed to stick strictly to the Autobahn, neither to stop nor engage in any conversation with the occupied East Germans. Soviet troops and installations were visible all along the route.

The U.S. also put a strong program priority on the counties that bordered the Soviet zone. We were eagerly welcomed by the inhabitants whose fear of the nearby Soviets was obvious. It was also the area in which a high proportion of German refugees from Prussia and Danzig had been settled as refugees (*Flüchtlinge*) and it was, not surprisingly, in these counties among the *Flüchtlinge* where the nationalistic neo-Nazi party had most of its support— unified by the appetite for a "right to return." Never larger than ten percent in any local elections, these political groups were a tough target for us—especially the older generation.

The political rallies and so-called *"Heimat* (homeland) days"
rang weirdly like Nazi rallies with uniforms and parades.
Even here, however, we could see that the younger generation was "looking West" and not enthusiastic about these
embittered elders who insisted they must focus on recaptur-
ing their lost homeland.

Hamburg

Hamburg was, and remains, one of Europe's most beautiful cities. Even though it was probably the most heavily
bombed city in Germany, the initial clean-up and subsequent
rebuilding produced a robust port-city centered around the
beautiful lakes in the middle of the city. With a strong
Communist party in place between the wars and very
powerful labor unions, it still reflected the heritage of its
Hanseatic League autonomy and close ties with its West
European trading partners. The most English of German
cities, it was also the most commercial. Soviet post-war
brutality in the next-door Soviet zone quickly produced a
universal hostility toward the Soviet Union and a very
strong pro-American population.

Dr. Conant's decision to consolidate the Lower Saxony-
Hamburg-Schleswig-Holstein programs into one expanded
my territory and allowed me to work over the Northern
province of Schleswig-Holstein (SH)—the bottom half of
Jutland, which included Denmark. Long the headquarters of
the German navy, SH was a conservative bastion and
somewhat more begrudging in allowing us to establish our

programs. However, we had a uniquely impressive team in Hamburg, including the late "Spike" Dubs, who was murdered in Afghanistan by the Communist government there; Bruce Laingen, who went on to become the "chief hostage" in Iran when Khomeni took over; and Frank Meehan, who went on to serve as ambassador to Poland, Czechoslovakia, and East Germany. Dubs, Meehan, and I were all subsequently in Moscow together.

Hamburg was also, of course, transfixed by events in the Soviet zone, only fifty miles away. Incidents along the border and in the Baltic Sea were constant. Hamburg, as the primary sea port and commercial center, had always served the people and commerce of Eastern Germany. Now it was walled off from its natural market and hinterlands and looked to the West. The historic trading route to Berlin and eastward was blocked by the Iron Curtain.

While we were in Hamburg, Stalin died. While hard to quantify, the reaction was profound. Hope, of course, immediately flared that perhaps the divide between the East and West could soften. However, very quickly it became clear that the ascension of Georgiy Malenkov to head the Communist Party clearly would change little. And the rapid development of the infamous KGB chief Levretiy Beria's position provided little encouragement.

Among our programs in Hamburg, perhaps the predominant media center in post-war Germany, we found our efforts to encourage and support a free press was perhaps the most important of our activities. *Der Spiegel,* considered to be Germany's *Time,* had moved from Hannover to Hamburg, and the quickly respected new daily *Die Zeit* was located in Hamburg. We provided financial support, trips to the U.S., and a steady flow of material to these two major outlets. We also helped initiate television with a major station, NWDR, serving Hamburg, Hannover, and nearby Bremen.

The entire project of encouraging the development of a free, vigorous media, with a very light hand on the reins, in my judgment was one of the most significant post-war accomplishments. Under McCloy's direction, a full range of media projects including *Die Neue Zeitung,* a daily newspaper, was produced and sold throughout West Germany. A high-quality publication run by a group of German-Americans and openly identified as a U.S. product, it was fully accepted and set the standard for the new post-war German press. Several other political and cultural magazines such as *Der Monat* were widely produced—often with funding provided by the CIA, which had more flexible funding potential than the State Department.

Congressional Delegations

My first experience with that unique phenomenon of a congressional visit or CODEL (Congressional Delegation), as it is labeled, occurred in Hamburg. The chairman of the Appropriations Committee, a democrat responsible for the State Department's budget, paid a visit. Our Consul General, Clare Timberlake, decided it would fall to me to escort

47

the congressman and plan his visit. The chairman was interested and outspoken, meeting with the mayor, a powerful figure in German politics, touring the harbor and the infamous Reperbahn, the red-light district. Everything proceeded smoothly until the final formal luncheon, hosted by the mayor at the historic Rathaus (City Hall). Perhaps it was the stress of travel, but the chairman had three glasses of schnapps and proceeded to fall asleep in the middle of the mayor's speech. No serious damage done, but a definite awakening experience for this young diplomat!

Notwithstanding this finale, the CODEL was the first of many over my Foreign Service experience and brought home to me how important such events can be in terms of building Congressional understanding and support for our foreign policy, the State Department's budget, and an appreciation on the part of the FSOs who handle CODELs, as well as of the critical and unique role and culture of the Congress. Subsequent CODEL experiences further kindled my fascination with the role of Congress in foreign policy, which culminated in my final, five-year State Department assignment in 1973 as Principal Deputy Assistant Secretary of State for Congressional Relations.

Thus, by the summer of 1954 when we left Germany, we were very encouraged by the progress made by the United States in transforming West Germany and its new young population into an increasingly valuable ally as it continued to face the massive Soviet force in East Germany. This remarkable transition of the Western half of former Nazi

Germany into a viable democratic society was especially a tribute to the visionary General Marshall, who shaped the American decision to eschew the policies of revenge against the entire German people, policies that had led directly to the post-World War I collapse of the democratic Weimar Republic, and to the ascension of Adolf Hitler. And, it was also a tribute to the largely unsung leadership of John J. McCloy who, as Truman's High Commissioner for Germany, turned Marshall's vision into a reality, and sold it to our British and French allies—a project effectively continued by McCloy's successor, former Harvard president James B. Conant.

CHAPTER IV. BANGKOK: COLD WAR DOMINO

In the summer of 1954, the United States had become deeply engaged in the Cold War on two fronts, the Soviet Union and China. The collapse of Chiang Kai-shek's nationalist government, and the Communist takeover in China in 1949, dramatically altered the strategic landscape. Stalin had moved quickly to cement Moscow's influence with Mao's regime, a daunting task for Stalin because of his decades-long support for Chiang's forces (Chiang and his top military officers had trained in Moscow.) Clearly valuing the Nationalist Chinese as an ally against the Japanese, the Soviets were surprised and caught off-guard when Chiang collapsed and Mao's Communists took over China. Soviet efforts to reverse course quickly produced massive assistance and major military collaboration between Stalin and Mao.

To Western observers, almost universally, it was presumed that the Soviet-Chinese and Communist alliance was solid, and the Iron Curtain now included not only the European confrontation, but stretched across Asia to the Chinese borders. The new Eisenhower administration was transfixed by the collapse of Western influence in Asia; not only had China "fallen" (as though we ever had serious influence over that historic change), but a year later (and only three years before "C" and I arrived in Bangkok) North Korean troops attacked across the 38th Parallel and pushed our outnumbered UN troops to the Southern tip of Korea before our occupation forces could recover. And then a year later, challenged by MacArthur's offensive push to the Yalu River, thousands of Chinese troops attacked across the Yalu River and routed our forces again before we stabilized the Korean front at the original 38th Parallel border. In 1954, on my arrival in Bangkok, the UN (and U.S.) were still "at war" with China, although a cease-fire held.

On top of the "loss of China" and the Korean War, French colonial forces were soundly defeated by Ho Chi Minh and his North Vietnamese Communist forces at the historic battle of Dien Bien Phu. A fragile stand-off was established between Communist North Vietnam and South Vietnam. Momentum was clearly with the forces of Ho Chi Minh, who were seen in Vietnam as patriotic: they expelled the French colonialists from North Vietnam and were dedicated to "freeing" the rest of Indochina. The French, with massive military equipment assistance from the U.S., established a new government in Saigon, headed by a figurehead emperor, Bao Dai, and a government led by a French-educated Catholic, Ngo Dinh Diem, as president. Although clearly lacking popular support, Diem did establish a functioning government and in the two years while I was serving in Bangkok, 1954-1956, U.S. assistance and direct involvement with Diem ballooned. Warned by our French allies that Saigon was doomed, the Eisenhower administration, particularly Secretary of State John Foster Dulles, rejected French advice and redoubled our support in an effort to reinforce the anti-Communist regime in South Vietnam.

On a third front, in Malaya to the south of Thailand, the British colonial administration was under intense pressure from the "Chinese terrorists" along the heavily forested Thai-Malay border. To appreciate this threat it is important to recognize that historically, throughout Southeast Asia, the commercial classes were dominated by Chinese merchants who had been established for centuries and still maintained a strong relationship with their families in China itself. The populations in virtually all Southeast Asian capitals were heavily Chinese. Singapore's population was some 80% Chinese; Malaya's had close to 40% Chinese population; Bangkok had a majority Chinese population that dominated business; the business center of Saigon-Cholon in Vietnam was a real Chinese city; and Chinese merchant families dominated in Indonesia's cities, as well, even, in Manila.

Thus, it was in fact realistic for the U.S. government to view Thailand as a fragile domino. It seemed perhaps unrealistic to hope that Thailand could serve as a "bulwark of democracy," as Dulles pronounced our goal, surrounded by a massive, hostile Communist China, recently "liberated" North Vietnam, and Chinese terrorist forces operating on Thailand's southern border.

For "C" and me, it was a real awakening to realize that the Cold War was not limited to our confrontation with the Soviet Union in Europe, but was, in fact, a global confrontation.

Bangkok: A Different World

family and I—expanded now to include our young son, Peter, who was born in Germany—arrived in Bangkok in June of 1954 and experienced a climatic and cultural shock. The tropical heat, general "untidiness," and relaxed attitude toward sanitation was a dramatic contrast with manicured, organized Germany. Having "applied" for a post in Eastern Europe, I found myself a fish out of water in Bangkok, and especially felt my inadequacy in the Thai language. The Embassy did include two excellent Thai language career officers, as well as a Chinese language officer, but I was not one of them. However, pursuant to the Foreign Service code, you go where you are assigned and, one hoped, needed. I soon found that the skills I developed in operating with the Soviet presence in Germany were, in fact, relevant in this fragile Western outpost in Asia.

Still, it *was* an adjustment! My wife, young son, and Tigger the Airedale moved into an inadequate rooming house until the embassy-provided house became available. Snakes were a fact of life, and as you can imagine, we were especially worried about our protective and rambunctious Airedale and our toddler, Peter. Setting up our house was a genuine adventure. Our compound and three-bedroom house was surrounded by a three-inch drainage ditch covered by 1x4 planks, essential in the rainy season. Our noble dog quickly discovered that there was "life" under those planks and felt it his responsibility to protect his family; "life" was a family of cobras. He flipped the boards over and drove our cobras away by barking at them! Thereafter, our house was known as "the House of the Big Dog." In contrast to occupied Germany, this was the real Foreign Service!

My embassy assignment was to the economic section; it is part of the Foreign Service policy to rotate new officers to acquire experience in all functions. My first business event was to be introduced to the Chamber of Commerce at a luncheon. The Chamber was one of the institutions in which Chinese merchants were omnipotent. In Thailand, where approximately 20 percent of the population was Chinese (more than 50 percent in Bangkok) as mentioned above, Chinese merchants were a tremendously influential component of the population. The Chinese families, with their roots in mainland China, worked together throughout East Asia, and they still dominate business throughout the region.

There was a great sensitivity about the Chinese among the Thai, and in many ways a great antipathy. Thus, a Chinese businessman would marry a Thai, set up a corporation, invite the Minister of Defense or the Minister of Police, the Minister of the Air Force, or whomever, to be chairman of their board. They would create this board with several Thai on it, and only one Chinese, namely the man who ran the company. The Thai were paid off with handsome directors' fees, but did not get into the business of the company. This was a façade the Chinese used to get around anti-Chinese sentiment.

In Bangkok at this time, the Chinese were divided between those loyal to China and the Communist regime, and those who looked to Taiwan, where the Kuomintang (KMT, the Chiang Kai-shek regime) was based. Although many families played both sides of the fence, within Bangkok there was tremendous competition among these two factions. The Communist Chinese pretty well controlled the Chinese Chamber of Commerce. They didn't have an embassy, but used the Chamber of Commerce as their instrument of activity, while the Taiwanese had a proper embassy. On balance, the Communist Chinese dominated the scene.

The U.S. embassy has historically had a Chinese language officer on the embassy political staff. In my time it was John Farrior, who had been stationed in China before Mao's takeover and was held hostage there for a time. His parents had been missionaries in China. He was succeeded by Art Rosen, another Chinese language officer, who was Jewish, and used to laughingly say about Chinese business superiority, that he knew the really potent people in the world are "Chinese Jews."

This explains why we, in the Embassy, considered the Chamber as an important "target." On the occasion of my first encounter with the Chamber, I was introduced not only to the business community, but also to Thai pepper sauces. The food was—and Thai food remains—superb, but pepper sauce, made of the juice from ground pepper skins, is to be approached with *great* caution. I'm afraid that my enthusiasm overcame my reserve, and I actually knocked back two beers in my desperation to quench the eruption in my throat, to the great amusement of my hosts.

Another eye-opener for me was when I inquired how this restaurant, in a humble seven-story building, could produce such spectacular meals, it was explained to me gently that Hoi Thien Lao was a highly successful business because the top five stories comprised Bangkok's finest whorehouse!

Legendary Figures

A second particularly interesting business experience for me involved the legendary Jim Thompson. A longtime resident of Bangkok, Jim had been an officer of the Office of Strategic Services, the predecessor to CIA, established underground in up-country Thailand during the Japanese occupation of Thailand in World War II. Jim had been captivated by the beautiful silks woven by the peasants with whom he lived, and after the war he determined to develop a U.S. market for these unique fabrics. The trick was to establish a system to standardize the strong beautiful dyes, which had always been produced by individual silk weavers. With Thai royal family support, he succeeded in this and launched the Thai Bok silk business, which became a major success for Thailand and for Jim Thompson.

In 1953 when Jim was in New York negotiating supply agreements, his partner, a "businessman" from Laos, absconded with his dye formula and set up a competing store in Bangkok. Jim, on advice from his lawyer, a royal family member and graduate of Yale, sued his former partner in what became a prominent case in Bangkok. I was assigned to assist this American citizen as an embassy representative. In fact, I did very little but attend the trial and provide moral support. Jim won his case and the illicit competition was shut down. In the process we became close personal friends and benefited from frequent invitations to Jim's beautiful home, which was in reality a residential museum full of beautiful Thai antiques. When Jim "disappeared" several years later, his home became an official royal museum.

Jim Thompson's disappearance, several years after we had left Bangkok, has become a legend in itself and an unsolved mystery. He had traveled to a hilltop resort in Malaya (the Cameron Highlands) established by the British to escape the heat. It was a typically British empire scene: dress for dinner and all that entailed. After dinner one night, Jim announced he was going to take a walk—and he never came back. In spite of intense local British and Malay investigation, no trace of him has ever been found. Three theories exist: he fell into a tiger trap (an eight-foot pit with poisoned bamboo spears implanted in the bottom) and local authorities were so embarrassed they covered it up; he was captured by Communists who knew of his World War II intelligence officer (OSS) and subsequent CIA role; he was romantically trapped in a triangle and done in by a embittered lover. My own theory tends toward the first scenario, but Jim's OSS history was certainly an important and well-known fact.

Thompson, in fact, was one of a dozen or so members of a very brave band of U.S. officers who were infiltrated into Thailand when the Japanese occupied the country during World War II. After the war, when Thailand became surrounded by Communist regimes in China, Vietnam, and the terrorists on the Malay border, the few survivors of the OSS wartime team were held in great respect in Bangkok, among Thai officials, the royal family, and within the U.S. embassy. The small but effective U.S. business community in Bangkok had several colorful personalities. Johnny Wester, who represented the company Caterpillar in Bangkok when we were there, was another example of the unique bravery of these OSS men. Wester was a thin, almost wasted man, who related some of his experiences to me. He had lived in a secret basement in a Bangkok house throughout the occupation, shielded by his Thai assistant and family. "I never saw outside daylight in more than two years!"

Upon our arrival in July 1954, the U.S. ambassador in Bangkok was the fabled William "Wild Bill" Donovan. President Eisenhower, Secretary of State Dulles, and his brother Alan Dulles at CIA, agreeing that Thailand should become a "bulwark of democracy," persuaded Donovan to suspend his lucrative law practice in New York to lead this daunting effort in Southeast Asia. Donovan had founded the OSS during the war and played a key role in converting the OSS into CIA after the war.

Donovan looked upon all Southeast Asia as his bailiwick and brought about a tremendous buildup in CIA activities in Thailand, Burma, and Malaya, designed essentially to contain Chinese influence. Many heroic, dedicated CIA officers were involved in them. There were dramatic successes in restructuring the Thai police and the army. Donovan's activities, however, soon caused problems with "the neighbors." Typical of his high-handed approach to the area, he launched a major effort to support the Burmese rebel tribes such as the Karen, who were backed by KMT troops who had been defeated by the Communists in China. The KMT troops had slipped across the Burmese border and set up pockets of insurgency in Burma, immune from attack by the Red Chinese. The only problem with this tactic was that the Burmese government took a very dim view of having these foreign forces there. The rebels promptly began organizing opium traffic to finance their existence and purchase arms.

Our ambassador in Rangoon, Joseph Satterthwaite, was subsequently called in by the Burmese government to protest U.S. support for foreign intervention in Burma. Satterthwaite denied that the U.S. was involved in any way. The foreign minister promptly showed him a display of American equipment, PX rations, uniforms, and Collins radios, proving the U.S. presence. The ambassador was outraged when he found that, in fact, Donovan had been running a major operation in his country, Burma, out of Bangkok, and he had not even informed him.

Donovan left some six months after my arrival. My Embassy colleagues learned, with some concern, that Jack Peurifoy was to be his replacement. Peurifoy had previously held a very high profile in the press for having masterminded the overthrow of the government in Guatemala while acting as U.S. ambassador there. President Jacobo Arbenz had been a democratically elected leftist. U.S. policy at that time in Washington was totally focused on Communist expansion wherever it took place. The Soviets could not really match up with us for they clearly didn't have the resources that we did. However, they moved wherever they saw the opportunity, and Central America was fertile soil.

Thus, when Jack Peurifoy arrived in Bangkok, we were nervous. He was characterized in the U.S. press as a free-swinging interventionist. Well, within six weeks, we were all in love with Jack Peurifoy. He was a great leader of men. He worked that embassy like no ambassador I've ever seen. He was constantly walking around, sitting down on your desk saying, "What are you doing today? What can I do to help? I'm going in to see the foreign minister this afternoon, is there anything you'd like me to raise with him?" He'd visit and raise your issue with Prince Wan, the foreign minister, and then come back and report to us on what Prince Wan had said. I would then write a telegram reporting on what "we'd" done. It was his constant openness, and availability, and respect that we admired. He knew he didn't know much about the area, but he had people on his staff like John Farrior, for example, who knew the Chinese situation; and

Al Moscotti (my colleague in the political section), who had a Ph.D. in Thai studies from Yale, a very bright man, bilingual in Thai. Our embassy had topnotch officers, and Jack Peurifoy knew how to use them. He also had a superb deputy (Deputy Chief of Mission, or DCM), the late Norbert Anshutz, a true career officer's career officer. He was courageous, debonair, smart, outgoing, and articulate. Anshutz was a terrific man with a wonderful wife who was a true "house mother," a great Foreign Service wife. The Peurifoys and the Anshutzes turned that embassy around. Before then we had been suspicious of what the CIA was up to.

Tool of Diplomacy: Trade Fairs

The other big event in my year as an economic officer was the first Constitution Trade Fair. This was the first program under the Eisenhower International Trade Fair program, which was designed to help promote U.S. exports to the world, a harbinger of what has become a major U.S. policy. My job was to coordinate U.S. business participation in the trade fair. It was a great success. Ambassador Peurifoy had a terrific sense of stage management, and he weighed in back in Washington to make sure that we had good corporate participation. Opening night we had a panoramic screen called Cinerama (since then well known in this country). It was the first time Cinerama had ever been used in that part of the world particularly, and it was breathtaking. Peurifoy invited Sihanouk, the king of Cambodia, to come for the opening; Sihanouk and King Bumiphol of Thailand officially opened the trade fair. With Peurifoy in a white silk suit and his attractive wife, the two kings and their beautiful wives, it was a great, high-profile operation. A critical role in putting this event together was played by the Embassy's public affairs office and particularly the outstanding cultural attaché Steve Sestanovich.

I was involved in recruiting American companies and assisting them in putting together their exhibits. We had one of the first Thunderbirds from the Ford Motor Company and a Chevrolet Corvette. They were the hit of the exhibit. Ironically, at the end of the fair, Ambassador Peurifoy, with General Motors' assistance, donated the Corvette to Prime Minister Phibul Songgram as a gift, which was extremely well received. Phibul was a car buff. And Peurifoy persuaded his wife to give him the Thunderbird for his birthday present. Ironically, it was in that Thunderbird that Peurifoy was subsequently killed in an automobile accident in the southern part of Thailand. It was his own fault; he was going much too fast over a bridge that narrowed to one lane from two. He didn't see an oncoming truck and ran head-on into it.

With Peurifoy's arrival, things had come together. When he was killed, Norbert Anshutz became in charge (acting ambassador), and he was superb. However, after six months, Peurifoy's replacement, a man named Max Bishop, arrived. Max had been a career officer, and a Japanese language officer. He was the only career Foreign Service officer to

testify against the Chinese language officers in the period of the McCarthy witch hunt. He was extremely unpopular among career officers: reactionary, and paranoid about China. He came out from his position as special assistant to Deputy Secretary Herbert Hoover, Jr., and Secretary Dulles.

Personally, I found Bishop to be very dedicated. He was not in any way lazy or corruptible. He just had a skewed vision of things, in my judgment. He immediately started trying to get his hands around the embassy, which he claimed was perceived in Washington as left-leaning. That was a ridiculous thing to accuse Jack Peurifoy and his deputy of, especially given Peurifoy's high-profile record of anti-Communism.

Reflecting Ambassador Bishop's paranoia, on one occasion when I attended the country team meeting for the political section, we were talking about what to do for the upcoming SEATO (Southeast Asia Treaty Organization) exercises. The economic counselor said something about the Colombo Plan, which was an economic plan put together by Britain, India, Ceylon, Malaya, and others as a sort of economic counterpart to SEATO, but not run by the United States. Bishop blew up and said, "The Colombo Plan is a bunch of damned Socialists, that's a terrible thing, and we should be focusing on SEATO. That's the anti-Communist instrument that we should be focusing on, to the exclusion of the Colombo Plan." And then he got really carried away and said, "You know, I'm fed up with all this talk about the Colombo Plan and the British. Nobody had done anything about SEATO until I got here. I'm the one who has put SEATO on the map in this country."

Norb Anshutz, who recognized this as perhaps unwitting emotional criticism of the late Jack Peurifoy, quietly said, "That's a damn lie, Mr. Ambassador, and you know it." And everybody in that room said a silent vow that, wherever he went, we would support Norbert Anshutz. It was a very heroic thing to do. It deflated the ambassador completely, and of course Bishop never forgave Anshutz for it.

Soon after this, we received a new DCM named George Wilson who was appointed by Dulles from Senator Bill Knowland's staff, a conservative Republican from California. Wilson was also paranoid about China, and anti-State Department. He was convinced that a State Department cabal was responsible for "losing" China.

Bertie McCormick's Wife Puts Her Stamp on the United Nations Association

Bishop was subsequently pulled out of Bangkok after an intriguing incident. Robert McCormick, the publisher of the *Chicago Tribune*, had died, and his wife was left owning the newspaper. She was interesting, intellectually engaged, well informed and, as it turned out, interested in Asia, China in particular. When she arrived in Bangkok, we didn't know any of this. And, because she had known the British ambassador when he was consul general in Chicago (in fact he had courted McCormick's daughter), there was a close family tie there. She chose to stay at the British ambassador's residence, instead of the American ambassador's. Max Bishop, being an ambitious, arch-conservative officer, was very upset that he was denied the opportunity to host the owner of the arch-conservative *Chicago Tribune*.

The British ambassador, Sir Barkley Gage, hosted a dinner for Mrs. McCormick. "C" was a friend of Sir Barkley's wife (who was a good deal younger than he was, and had been a student at Northwestern University when he met her). At the dinner party, a discussion started about China. Mrs. McCormick had decided she was going to go into China. Americans were discouraged from traveling to the mainland, and certainly a high-profile American such as the owner of the *Chicago Tribune*, Bishop felt, would be giving political recognition to the "gang of rogues who were running Red China." At dinner, in front of everybody, he said, "I forbid you to go to China." Mrs. McCormick looked at him like he was out of his mind and said, "I find that amusing. Who the hell are you to tell me where to go? You work for me, I don't work for you: you're the ambassador and my taxes pay your salary, and don't you forget it, young man." Bishop was undaunted by this and continued to argue the case.

In the final analysis, of course, she went to China, and when she arrived back in Chicago a front-page article she wrote for the *Tribune* began, "The American ambassador in Bangkok might be a good plumber, but he's a lousy diplomat." Not long after that, Bishop was out of Thailand. For me, it was a fascinating episode to observe as a young Foreign Service officer.

Eleanor Roosevelt Puts Her Stamp on the United Nations Association

At about this time, I was shifted to the political section of the Embassy. I then had a marvelous experience with Eleanor Roosevelt in Bangkok. The World Federation of United Nations Associations, which is still extant, holds an annual conference, and this particular year they held it in Bangkok. Because Eleanor Roosevelt was regarded as the "Mother of the United Nations," she was held in tremendous universal respect and affection for her role in promoting the United Nations after her husband died. She was invited to be the number-one guest at this event. The U.S. delegation, which was always a "Presidential delegation," appointed by the White House, was, as usual, full of political contributors, most of whom didn't have a whit of knowledge as to why they were going to the conference. They were just going out to buy silk from Jim Thompson and see Thailand. In short, the U.S. delegation was weak. The Communist Chinese sent a delegation even though the United Nations was officially still at war with China in Korea. They were allowed in because the third-world countries were already trying to cut deals with the Chinese, and this was not an "official" government event, in theory. The instructions our embassy received were to assist the

American delegation in any way possible, but not to get involved.

I met the delegation and briefed them on what was going on in Bangkok, and told them a little about the conference. I met Mrs. Roosevelt and expressed my admiration. And she said, "You know I'm not part of the American delegation, but I appreciate your support." On the first day of the conference, it was clear the Chinese had organized a lot of support among so-called neutral states, including the Indonesians and the Egyptians, and were seeking to be voted in as full members of the World Federation with the Taiwanese Chinese being forced out. This would have been a major step toward the recognition of the regime. This was potentially an important setback for American policy.

I went to see Norbert Anshutz and he said, "By all means, get in the middle of it, ignore your instructions, get into it." So I met with the American delegation and early on decided they were pretty hopeless. But I did go to work on the various friendly ambassadors who were in Bangkok, the Belgian, the Israeli representative, and the German, and the Frenchman; I put together a little coalition of delegations that would speak against the Chinese maneuvers, and try to head it off. Well, it came down to the third day to a vote on the subject, and it looked as if our opponents had the votes and we didn't.

Operating without any instructions, but with Norbert's blessing, I went to see Mrs. Roosevelt, who was sitting in a panel of academics. I called her out of the meeting, and we sat down on a bench in front of the meeting place. I explained to her what was happening, and she looked at me very coolly and said, "Well, what do you think we should do?" And I said, "Mrs. Roosevelt, I have no right to ask you to do this, I have no authorization from the State Department to do it, but if you agree with me that this would be a setback for the United States, and would damage the United Nations and its reputation in the United States, particularly at this tense time in the United States when critics are denouncing the UN as being a bunch of Communists anyhow, I would like to suggest that if you would proceed down to the General Assembly meeting and ask for the floor, out of deference to you personally, they would give you the microphone."

She said, "I see that and I agree, and what do you think I should say?"

So I said, "You might want to consider the following because I think you might be able to move these delegations to support you. I have already lined up the Thai delegation [the deputy foreign minister was a good friend of mine], as well as the Belgians and the Israelis, and several others to lead an effort to bring about an amendment that would strike this proposal to make the Red Chinese members. But it would take a catalyst like your personal intervention."

And she looked at me and said, "Young man, take my arm."

It was 1955, and Eleanor Roosevelt was seventy-one years old. Heavyset, she was feeling the heat. I took her arm and we carefully wended our way down the stairs, and Mrs. Roosevelt worked her way toward the front, and waved to the podium, and said, "I wonder if I might have a word?" The chairman immediately lit up and said...of course! At this point all the men who were engineering the effort to bring the Red Chinese in realized what might be happening and scurried around trying to persuade him not to let Eleanor Roosevelt speak. Well, there wasn't any way that they were going to say no to Eleanor Roosevelt. She kept right on walking toward the podium. She was such a dominating figure in the United Nations' culture that she got the microphone. She gave a hell of a barn-burning speech.

She denounced the Chinese for continuing to remain in a state of war with the United Nations, and rejected as ridiculous any suggestion that the World Federation of United Nations Associations should accept them into their membership. At which point the Thai representative stood up, followed by the Israeli and the Belgian and the German, to support Mrs. Roosevelt. And finally the American delegation leader (a producer from Hollywood), stood up and said, "Yeah, we agree, we agree."

The Red Chinese initiative was killed, thanks to Eleanor Roosevelt. I cherish the photograph I have of her with me at that time. She was a great American, and a great political figure. That was an exciting thing to experience, and I got a nice commendation from the Department for ignoring their instructions, and a big pat on the back from Norbert, which I also cherish because I continue to feel that Norbert Anshutz was a great Foreign Service officer.

Our Airedale provided an unusual insight into Thai officialdom. He had to be trimmed regularly to keep him from being terribly uncomfortable in the heat. The only place I found where we could have this done was the Thai army cavalry veterinarian. I would take him over to the stable where two sergeants and I would take big clippers (the ones used to trim horses), and give him a haircut. I developed a special friendship with an unusual group of military men.

Bangkok Politics

The political situation in Bangkok was interesting throughout my assignment. Phibul Songgram, the prime minister, had been a general who seized power in a coup. He replaced an admiral who had come to power as the result of an earlier coup. Phibul was a small, delicate man, and very pleasant. He was prime minister and remained prime minister only because the two real power centers, the police and the army, both found him acceptable. They were each determined to keep the other one from power, so Phibul was propped up by competing political forces. They were political competitors, but not in the sense that one was liberal and one was conservative. Neither was particularly soft on Communism, or tough on Communism. They were "businessmen," somewhat like today's mafia. Our CIA was heavily involved with the director of the police, General

Phao, who among other things ran the opium business. Our large army military assistance group was providing equipment and training for the Thai military, again going back to the days of Wild Bill Donovan, who tried to create an effective army to contain Chinese aggression. The army was headed by General Sarit, whose power came from his control of the whorehouses, the pork business, and the liquor business. Thus each faction had its "economic bases," each had a lot of bodyguards, and each had—thanks to CIA—its own armed forces. They were two competing military forces, both milking the United States for all the assistance they could get, competing with one another while supporting Phibul in the middle. At the same time, the Thai were extremely cooperative with us in regional planning and in the United Nations. They supported our anti-Chinese policy, although in fact they maintained their own channels to Beijing. And they kept a very strong public association with Taiwan. They hosted SEATO, whose headquarters was established there. And they did basically what the Thai have been doing for centuries—they collaborated with whomever they had to collaborate with to remain independent. Thailand means "land of the free," and even though they were nominally occupied by the Japanese in World War II, they maintained their own government. They played along with the Japanese while at the same time cooperating with the OSS, notably Jim Thompson. They were clever that way. It was interesting for a western-oriented Foreign

Service officer to see the subtlety, and the Byzantine nature of politics and power in Thailand.

The Communist terrorist threat along the Thai-Malay border area was a serious challenge. I traveled down to the border and rode along in helicopters with the CIA-trained border police who were trying to prevent the Communist terrorists in Malaya from using Southern Thailand as a base of operations.

I had good relations with the British officers assigned to the Malay border police unit, and worked to develop cooperation between the Thai and the British. Our CIA team deserves a lot of credit for this, and I made a small contribution. What with the shooting going on down there, I should have gotten combat pay. But I enjoyed it, I learned a lot, and I saw a lot.

Vietnam was even more ominous for U.S. interests. My wife and I drove in our convertible Ford to Saigon and stayed with friends there. We stopped at Phnom Phen, and we visited the Angkor Wat ruins. At that time Ngo Dinh Diem was running South Vietnam, and it was taking off economically. During this brief interval, the countryside was peaceful. I think Diem's success, and the dramatic success of the private sector business economy that was organized there, drove the Vietminh in the North to launch their attack because they clearly were losing the economic contest. They saw that the tide of history was running against them and had to intervene to reverse that. Not long after we left

Vietnam, real shooting broke out. Intense, dramatic, political "backing and forthing" was going on in our Saigon embassy, where we already had a large delegation.

Joseph "Lightning Joe" Collins, who had been a general in World War II, was made ambassador to Saigon by General Eisenhower. He was subsequently replaced by Henry Cabot Lodge, who made serious misjudgments and contributed to the eventual morass into which we slipped. Our direct participation in the Vietnam War was one of the great disasters in our history.

Collins understood the importance of maintaining a clear wall between permitting American forces to engage in combat and having them there just as advisors. He deserves great credit for that. Subsequently Robert Kennedy, with Defense Secretary Robert McNamara's active support, pursued policies that led us into combat and eventually to defeat. I think history will treat them harshly for the arrogance they displayed in dealing with Vietnam and the strategic defeat that followed.

I had several friends in our embassy in Saigon, which was badly divided about our policy. The main thrust had been established by Collins' predecessor as ambassador, Donald Heath. Anything we needed to do to keep the French in NATO (the North Atlantic Treaty Organization), we should do, and if ignoring the Vietnamese and talking to the Vietnamese only through the French was necessary, that's what we should do. The DCM was a courageous FSO named Edmund Gullion. Ed was pushing very hard for directly engaging with Vietnamese nationalists who, many specialists believed, were on the fence at that time. They wanted very much to have a relationship with the United States. I think history has proven that they were not in China's pocket but rather independent-minded. Gullion had figured all that out. Agreeing with him were the CIA station chief and the AID director. But Heath and Bill Leonhart, who went on to be ambassador to Yugoslavia, were opposed to any independent action. Leonhart and Heath dominated the process; they had the rank. However, the minute Heath went home on consultation, Gullion started firing off policy telegrams questioning the wisdom of where we were headed. He never did succeed in changing the policy. An interesting novel about this episode called *Forest of Tigers,* by Robert Shaplen, dramatizes this dispute within the embassy. It's a gem.

Travel in Thailand

I found the whole time in Bangkok instructive. I did a good deal of upcountry traveling. We were engaged in an anti-Communist program called the democratization drive. We would go out with our Thai local employees in Jeeps, and provide pictures of the king and the U.S. Constitution. It was fairly simplistic, and I think the Thai were all some-what bemused by our actions, although they were hospitable and always enjoyed parties. So I had a lot of interesting dinners with governors. Chicken was the up-market thing to be eating, so they'd always have some chicken and rice, and we'd drink a lot of rice wine. They were enamored of refrigerators, and German beer. So a governor would typically have in his living room a Westinghouse refrigerator full of German beer or Danish Carlsburg, which they called "Catchyburg." After dinner we'd all drink cognac. That was another big favorite; the French influence was very significant in that sense. Cognac was very popular. We'd be sitting around having cognac and in would come four or five Chinese dancing girls. After a few dances and more cognac, we were supposed to go off to a bedroom with our Chinese girl. That was part of the dinner, "the dessert." I was always able to wiggle out of that, but it wasn't easy—it took some diplomacy. I would be sick or come up with all kinds of excuses. "C" used to tease me about whether I was enjoying "dessert."

Unfortunately, I contracted typhoid fever while traveling upcountry. Typhoid was no joke—I damn near died and went down to 120 pounds before the doctors finally diagnosed it properly. A couple of good Harvard-trained Thai doctors stumbled onto the diagnosis while looking for dengue fever. Once they did that, a new antibiotic called chloromycetin was administered, and within twenty-four hours it broke the fever. Then I had four months of recovery. It was a tough time for me. I arrived home in June 1956 at the ripe old age of thirty, weighing about 125 pounds.

Thailand was a charming country. In those days the government had not paved over all the *khlongs*, or waterways. I gather it has pretty well changed its cultural identity since then. The after-effects of the Vietnam War, which had enabled Bangkok to become the rest and recreation center for tens of thousands of American troops, were severe. But the Royal Bangkok Sports Club remains a happy memory in my mind, plush and attractive, with a race course, tennis courts, and golf course, set up very much in the British tradition— linen-jacketed waiters, barefoot, and brass buttons. Playing golf there was unique. We had a caddy carry the bag, and then we had a so-called *khlong* caddy. Half the time you were going in the water because the golf course was laced with canals and the place was full of snakes. The *khlong*-caddy's job was to kill the snakes and make sure you could address the ball without stepping on a cobra. Coming out of five years in Germany, it was a whole new experience.

It was in Bangkok that our second child, Michael, was born. Nothing remarkable about having a baby, but the process in Bangkok *was* unique. Michael was born in the Seventh Day Adventist hospital in Bangkok—a remarkably efficient, super-clean setting. Adventists do not eat animal products, which meant that "C" subsisted on soy burgers and soy milk for the week that she was confined.

The Adventist experience raised the general issue of the political propriety of Western missionary activity in Budd-hist Thailand. In practice, the general open tolerance of Buddhists removed much of the resentment toward foreign missionary activities that one confronts in Islamic and Hindu countries. The excellent Adventist hospital benefited all of Thailand. Several dozen individual Catholic priests were solidly entrenched, doing God's work throughout Thailand, particularly in the infertile impoverished northeast where Communist infiltrators were most active. They worked with the poor, providing medicine, supporting local schools, and stimulating local government efforts to broaden education. I visited several of them in various up-country outposts and found them universally beloved. They were, for me, invaluable sources of information about local attitudes and Communist activity in Thailand's poorest regions.

Thus, while American missionary efforts may be seen as arrogant intervention in some societies, in Thailand they were warmly received and enhanced Thai appreciation of the U.S. because of this charitable work.

And as an aside, Michael's Thai birth certificate offers him the choice of Thai citizenship, should he so choose.

SEATO

As a part of the Eisenhower administration's efforts to reinforce Thai independence and resistance to China's influence, Secretary Dulles seized upon a proposal to invent an Asian NATO. Thus was SEATO (the Southeast Asian Treaty Organization) created in 1955 to provide a multinational military partnership, with Thailand at its center. Together with Ambassador Donovan's build-up of U.S. military assistance and CIA activities in Thailand, Burma, and Malaya, SEATO was supposed to provide a major military obstacle to Chinese encroachment. Given the strategic shift encountered when Mao conquered China, Ho Chi Minh defeated the French, and Malaya came under siege, the concept of a military alliance of the U.S., France, U.K. together with free South Asian forces, Pakistan, Thailand, and Australia, made eminent sense.

It was hoped India would join, but this hope ran head-on into the emergence of the third-world anti-colonial grouping. The Pakistanis came in because they wanted Western support against India, and SEATO would set them apart from India. It ensured a close military partnership with the U.S., and Pakistan was a military-run country. Burma, on the other hand, was with India. Pakistan provided the most military muscle to SEATO. Insofar as SEATO had any Asian substance, I would say it was the Pakistanis who provided it. Obviously the British, Australians, and Americans provided military strength, but for an Asian ingredient, it was Pakistan; their military officers were splendid, Sandhurst graduates.

We had an operation in Bangkok to launch SEATO's existence, called Operation Firm Link. Firm Link combined airdrop and naval landing exercises to demonstrate SEATO's ability to inject force onto the Asian mainland if needed. Five thousand U.S. paratroopers came from the Philippines. The Pakistanis had a couple of airborne battalions. U.S., British, and Australian jets arrived and swooped over Bangkok. U.S. and British Navy units came into Thai ports, along with the New Zealand Navy. And Australian units parachuted into the airport without accident, a highly effective operation. Big parades were held through Bangkok with lots of press coverage. But when we thought about how we were trying to impress the Chinese with their millions of men, it was really rather thin. We had doubts as to whether it was going to have any impact. Certainly the Thai were heartened, and it reinforced their commitment to stay with the West. The Pakistanis were desperately trying to stay with the West any way they could. The Malays were excellent. Cambodian and Vietnamese were associated with SEATO, although not active participants, and they sent a lot of observers. Given the state of the world at that time, it was a reasonable and effective thing to do.

Although the Chinese controlled business and much of the finance of that part of the world, they never seemed to make a concerted push to get control of politics. If the mainland Chinese had invaded, local Chinese would have collaborated with them to a large extent. It was always a concern that the Thai not feel that time was on China's side and begin to adapt in advance. We used to say that political reed-watching was the order of the day. If the wind was blowing in a certain direction, then they would be there. We tried to maintain a prevailing breeze in our direction, and to some degree we succeeded with things such as Firm Link, the SEATO operation. There was a lot of historic anti-Chinese sentiment. The Thai would complain socially and privately to you that the Chinese controlled all the money, but they didn't hesitate to collaborate, to accept directorships, marry Chinese, to get their hands on the money. Not very noble, but realistic in a sense. The Thai have always felt that they were a small country, that they were impotent but clever, and that they would survive through being clever. That was how they dealt with the Chinese.

My second CODEL (Congressional visit) event occurred in Bangkok in 1954, about a year after the election of President Eisenhower. A powerful Republican Congressman (Chairman of the State Department Subcommittee of the Appropriations Committee) visited to review the work of our embassy, now characterized as a Cold War frontline mission facing Communist China, the Viet-Minh, and Malaya's threat. The congressman arrived and made no bones about his suspicions toward the State Department, which he saw as "completely Democrat oriented." We made some progress in convincing him that we were career professionals, dedicated to the national interest, not the Democratic Party. But this was the McCarthy era and from Secretary John Foster Dulles down, there was little public expression of confidence in the Foreign Service. In fact, back home, very few Republicans were willing to eschew the populist appeal of bashing the State Department, which Joe McCarthy had accused of harboring Communists.

Thus it was somewhat ironic when this outspoken "patriot" required my assistance in bailing him out of an embarrassing "situation" at a local high-class whorehouse. It was more than ironic when we learned subsequently that on arrival back in the U.S., he introduced a "private bill" to allow the young lady to emigrate to the U.S., even though she had been earlier rejected for a visa because of her "profession."

With this exception, however, my experience with CODELs in Bangkok was essentially positive. I was in fact proud to have had a part in the visits of two distinguished senators, Everett Dirksen and Theodore Green, ranking members of the Senate Foreign Relations Committee. Both men contributed importantly to our relations with the Thai government and made every effort to seek advice and provide specific support for our efforts to bind the Thais to U.S. efforts to build an effective barrier against Communist expansion into Southeast Asia after the collapse of the French regime in Vietnam. SEATO paled in comparison to NATO, but it nonetheless proved a major serious initiative to build a "coalition of the willing."

Dirksen and Green were particularly effective in bringing home to the Thai government that the U.S. commitment was reliable and that their continued freedom depended heavily on close collaboration with the U.S. This congressional effort was directed by Ambassador Peurifoy, whose long Washington experience had allowed him to build strong support in the Congress.

Indochina Crisis

On leaving Bangkok I thought that we had made progress, that support for the Thai was truly effective. The

Thai were desperate to maintain their independence, and recognized that we were available and probably reliable. What was clear by 1956 was that things were coming unraveled in Indochina, gradually but clearly. That was distressing. In Saigon, for example, half the city was Chinese, all working with China. What most senior policymakers seemed not to appreciate (the few true expert analysts who did were ignored by the Secretary of State John Foster Dulles and his brother, Alan Dulles, who was director of CIA, and the administration) was that the Vietnamese hated and feared the Chinese and vice versa. It didn't matter whether they were Communists or anti-Communists; there was a historic attitude and mentality. That was true in Thailand and true in Burma. It's still true throughout Southeast Asia, and it's logical. It shouldn't have been too hard for us to figure out that nationalism, not ideology, was driving politics. For ideological reasons, however, the Dulles brothers were, in historic perspective, off the mark.

Donovan was creative and aggressive, but we missed the opportunity not only to undercut Communist influence in Southeast Asia by dealing with and exploiting the nationalist thrust, but by ignoring the fact that within China itself, nationalism was a key element. The Chinese language officers, many of whom were deliberately driven from the Foreign Service, were right; they had the courage to say it, and they paid a terrible price. I'll never forgive President Eisenhower for caving in to the Joe McCarthy fear mongers who were dominating our domestic policy, even though

COLD WAR SAGA

Eisenhower certainly was a great leader in World War II. John Foster Dulles, to his credit, had an agenda. It happened to be wrong because his picture of the enemy was wrong. He saw the Soviets as ten feet tall, and us as five foot four, but it was exactly the opposite, and history has confirmed that.

I felt that Thailand was on a pretty good track, and I left feeling that things were going to move ahead. In fact, as you look at it, Thailand has not yet suffered a serious reversal. Even the loss of Vietnam didn't really damage the Thai. They are remarkable survivors. They made a lot of money out of the Vietnam War, and they got a lot of commitments out of us. Their military received massive equipment support, they got a lot of jobs, they paved a lot of roads, and a lot of bordellos made a lot of money. The net result of the whole thing was that while Vietnam was destroyed and we created a tremendous domestic crisis in our own country, nobody ever laid a glove on the Thai!

The U.S. response to the strategic crisis that arose in Asia in 1950 provided a model for subsequent crises as we faced Soviet and Communist Chinese advances in the Cold War. As I noted in the beginning of this chapter, while we had moved in admirable fashion and with great foresight to mobilize leadership and resources under President Truman to confront and counter Soviet efforts to expand in Europe, the collapse of Chiang's nationalist government in China, and of France's control of Indochina five years later, shocked the U.S. The new Republican administration of President Eisenhower also responded forcefully, but with focus distracted by a sense that someone must be at fault. "Who lost China?" This proved divisive and led to some initiatives that became historic mistakes, taking over the failed French effort to hold onto Vietnam, Laos, and Cambodia most notably. In this process, the exploitation of fear, evidenced by the entire McCarthy episode undercut our national effectiveness and cost us dearly.

The U.S. response to these strategic challenges was instructive. In Thailand, we dramatically increased our military assistance, expanded our CIA covert activity role a hundred-fold, sharply increased the staff and resources for our information activities (USIA), and built up a major economic development (AID) program. The size of the U.S. presence exploded.

Because the Thai people had never been colonized, they did not suffer from the anti-colonial revolutionary attitude that dominated Indochina, Indonesia, Malaya, Burma, Pakistan, and India. And the Thai were fundamentally pro-American: the northeast area of the country, which had been briefly occupied by the French in the 1930s, was freed by the personal efforts of an American attorney, Francis B. Sayre (subsequently Assistant Secretary of State under Truman), who was revered in Thailand; King Bhumipol was born in Boston and held pro-American views; and hundreds of young Thai were educated in the U.S. On top of this historic, cultural empathy for the U.S., Thai officials recognized that we were the only insurance policy available to deflect the

Chinese imperialist expansion. Thus, our sudden, massive buildup was not resented.

The friction, waste, and misjudgments as we adopted an aggressive policy to block Chinese expansion were probably inevitable. The coordination of these efforts presented a major challenge. Ambassador Donovan, with his profound experiences in intelligence in World War II, and in transforming the war-time OSS into the CIA, effectively created covert political and military capability in Thailand (and in Burma). However, while he succeeded in a rapid injection of U.S. capacity, he was less interested in the need to manage, balance, and maintain Thai support for our long-term objectives in the area. In fact, I doubt and certainly never saw evidence that any serious consideration was ever given to a strategic area policy other than a somewhat panic-driven "defense."

Thus, our massive military assistance program, while effective in traditional military buildup terms, was also quickly exploited by the military leaders into personal gain (widespread corruption) and to build a political platform. The CIA provided a substantial injection of assistance to the Thai police, who also diverted funds into political power bases and built a competing military structure.

The CIA's efforts were remarkably successful in many ways. The Thai police developed an effective aggressive capability to project force into the Malay border area and reduce Chinese terrorist activities in Southern Thailand and

Malaya. Thai police helicopters provided an immense technical advantage, thanks to the CIA's program. Several Thai police officers were trained by the agency and developed into a strong, pro-America cadre; one of them, Colonel Siddi Sithani, in fact, became prime minister a decade later, to our clear advantage.

The U.S. efforts quickly evolved into what has become a classic challenge to managing a U.S. mission—usually an embassy headed by the U.S. ambassador. Few ambassadors—Peurifoy was an outstanding exception—especially political appointees as contrasted to career Foreign Service officers, were able to harness the extensive package of U.S. programs together.

A special complication in this "management challenge" arose because the CIA station in Bangkok, dramatically expanded by Donovan, became an operational unit and had extensive regional directives. "Sea-Supply," a "private" airline that the CIA directed, flew supply missions to Burma, Laos, and Cambodia, which brought into play the U.S. ambassadors in all three countries. They were often unaware of these U.S. government activities ("no need to know?"). While these were not "rogue" activities as the recent book on CIA, *Legacy of Ashes*, by Tim Weiner, charges, they did not comprise an integral coordinated U.S. effort in the area. In short, Donovan effectively created a major "surge" of U.S. activity, but did little to create a clear regional policy to exploit the surge. For the past two decades there has been a clear Presidential directive on the books that the U.S.

ambassador is the direct representative of the President in his host country, and all USG activities in that country are subject to his direction. Even in 2009 that sensible policy is seldom exercised in full.

Legacy of Ashes, while often tendentious and critical, does provide many examples of the inevitable frictions and waste that our missions abroad suffer. This challenge is very much with us today.

Home leave is meant to be a time of regeneration, and it was; especially for me, returning to the U.S. from Thailand at 125 pounds after suffering from typhoid fever. "C"'s family was marvelous, filled with supportive people and grandparents who loved their grandchildren. There was a cold-shower impact on us, however, to feel the palpable suspicion among "C"'s old school friends and their families towards the State Department and us—a sour note left over from Senator McCarthy's empty but scurrilous attacks on the department.

CHAPTER V. WASHINGTON AND HARVARD

On leaving Bangkok, we received the good news that my application for Russian training had been accepted. After the month with my wife's parents in Lake Bluff, Illinois, we moved down to Washington for nine months of intense language training. I was honored, on the one hand, for having been selected out of a large pool of applicants, but a little unsettled by the need to find housing for such a short period. "C" was responsible for two (one in diapers) very young boys and while in Washington gave birth to our third son. We did luck into a nice Dutch colonial house in Bethesda for a very reasonable rent—the owners had a Foreign Service son—walking distance to the Giant grocery store. A special benefit for my deserving wife was the fact that our next door neighbor was Mischa Schneider, the Budapest String Quartet cellist who practiced with his window open. He and June, his wife, became our close friends.

I launched into a demanding daily routine: carpooling to the State Department followed by six hours with three colleagues in a small, windowless room listening to a native speaker instructor. Mrs. Malin was a refugee from the war and had been an English teacher in Moscow before the war. The routine was quite exhaustive. All day we would repeat over and over words for the pictures Mrs. M. would present; she would correct and repeat until we got it right. Before long we learned to "palletize" our sounds (thus *Putin* becomes *Poutyin*). We also became increasingly irritable and contentious with one another.

Thus, by the time I arrived back at our home each night, I wasn't the best company for my harassed wife, three boys, and Tigger. And I had to do another one or two hours of study at home. However grinding the experience, we all survived, and I did make very good progress in Russian. We prepared to pack up and move on to Harvard. A poetic handoff occurred when I introduced my close colleague Frank Meehan to our special landlord. He enjoyed the special friendly rent rate for another year and inherited Mischa Schneider!

It was at my school, Bowling Green, in 1946, that my interest in Russian had first been sparked. In my senior year I had, on a whim, enrolled in a two-semester course on Russian history taught by an elderly German refugee, Dr. Hans Nordmann. Like most of us (if we're lucky) a professor will strike an interest that can open a career path to his student. Nordmann was a brilliant teacher and analyst. By the time I graduated, I was more or less hooked. Government would be my objective, and the rapidly evolving Cold War and Russia's role my special interest. My subsequent graduate work at George Washington University had put me directly on the route to the Foreign Service. I had earlier also attended midshipman school at Notre Dame for a semester while in the Navy.

Thus between Bowling Green, where I was first assigned in the Navy officer's training program (V-5), Notre Dame, and then George Washington, where I did my Master's in International Law, I was a fairly well traveled student.

Russian Studies at Harvard

On September 1, 1959, we moved up to Cambridge for a year in "Russian Studies." Here, I had the great opportunity to study with men like Marshall Shulman, who had been Dean Acheson's special assistant in the Department when I first started in 1950 and returned to be President Carter's principal advisor on Soviet affairs. Marshall was a fascinating and wonderful man, and I learned a great deal from him. I also had two semesters each with Zbigniew Brzezinski and Richard Pipes, both of whom became National Security Council Advisors; William Langer, one of the premier historians in the United States, who taught a magnificent two-semester course on the history of the Ottoman Empire; and the very impressive dean of professors on the Soviet economy, Abe Bergson.

I also benefited from courses taught by Merle Fainsod, who was the unquestioned dean of the academics who specialized in the Communist Party of the USSR; Martin Malia, a wonderful teacher and specialist in Russian history; and Barrington Moore, the leading U.S. academic expert on the theories of Communism.

On those occasions when we had a spare moment, my fellow students and I were also encouraged to host informal dinner parties at the alumni club where, for example, we spent evenings with Henry Kissinger. All in all, our group of four Russian language students had a fascinating and very productive academic year at Harvard.

Shulman's special genius allowed us to study the Soviet mentality and connect the historic plans of the bizarre blend of brutal Russian tribal politics with the cultural richness of Russia, the subsequent emergence of what became the most oppressive political regime, and its first world nuclear weaponry.

Brzezinski was a brand-new, brilliant young specialist in "Communism in Eastern Europe Between the two World Wars." He was a unique and very provocative professor. He held a small seminar in which we spent two hours, twice a week, arguing and debating his shock therapy propositions. The four of us from the State Department each had almost a decade of overseas experiences and we were older than "Zbig." The other "civilian" graduate students also came with interesting experience. Brzezinski's brilliant insights to Central European history and their perspective on Russia proved invaluable to us. I keep in touch with Brzezinski and admire his public efforts to cut through the romanticized and unrealistic policies we are now bogged down with in Iraq, for example.

Professor Bergson was a particular treasure. As the reality of the global confrontation with Moscow became clearer, understanding the reality of Soviet economic behavior, its accomplishments, and staggering deficits became even more critical. Bergson was the undisputed master of the study of the Soviet economy. Ever since the revolution, the Soviets had been obsessed with secrecy in all fields. In things economic, this was essentially to mask the failure of Marxist economics as practiced by Moscow. They annually released economic statistics to "prove" their achievements and developed a sophisticated system of reporting to support this. Bergson worked from a massive collection of internal Soviet economic reports that the German troops had captured when they overran Smolensk in western Russia in World War II. The Smolensk collection, held at Harvard, proved just how inflated Soviet economic claims were.

Just as valuable for us was the intellectual awakening we experienced in Langer's two-semester course on the Ottoman Empire. To ingest and appreciate the centrality of the Ottoman influence in Russia, and on Russian political thinking, was a true eye-opener. Of course, appreciating Ottoman history remains critical today as we struggle to understand the Middle East, the Balkans, and the Caucasus. Few in the country comprehend the central role that the Ottomans played in Russian history, not to mention the reality that today's bizarre Middle East map was created arbitrarily out of the ruins of that empire after World War I.

Richard Pipes, who authored the definitive history of Soviet expansion and absorption of its "near abroad," *The Formation of the USSR,* was another brilliant and stimulating Harvard asset for me. Each one of his seminars was a new adventure. His unique scholarship, together with Langer's Ottoman course, equipped his students with a deep appreciation of the historic fault-lines in the seeming solid Soviet empire, fault lines that continue to erupt even in the twenty-first century.

For Pipes, I researched and produced a paper on the oddity of the three UN votes for the USSR; the Russian (USSR) Republic, the Byelorussia Republic, and the Ukrainian Republic each were recognized as charter members of the United Nations. The history of how this came to be was intriguing and little understood, I wrote:

The decision was made at the infamous Yalta Conference in 1944. Ever since, arch-conservative Republicans have charged that the Yalta Conference was a "give-away" by President Roosevelt who, was purportedly outfoxed by Stalin. The charges were principally that FDR (and Churchill) sold out the peoples of Eastern Europe who fell under Soviet occupation, and that we had acquiesced in giving Moscow three votes at the UN.

The reality, of course, was quite different. Soviet forces occupied Eastern Europe because they, at massive human cost, had driven the Germans out of Eastern Europe. At Yalta, Western leaders simply recognized the reality on the ground, while attempting to win Soviet pledges to allow free democratic elections in the Eastern European countries—a pledge freely given and promptly ignored.

The lesser charge—three votes for Moscow in the UN— was a product of Churchill's determination that Canada and India be recognized as charter members because of the contribution to the Allied cause. Stalin did not resist this Churchill request, but agreed if Byelorussia and Ukraine (which had suffered the greatest losses in World War II) also be recognized as charter members. Stalin then offered to accept Alaska and Hawaii also for balance. (Stalin clearly did not place great strategic interest in the UN, which was Roosevelt's top priority.) The U.S. delegation accepted India, Canada, the two so-called Soviet republics, but declined to add Alaska and Hawaii. It is interesting to note that within the U.S. delegation, only Alger Hiss opposed granting Stalin's request.

During my Harvard appointment, the Soviets launched Sputnik and set off a national debate on the adequacy of our education system. Khrushchev played this breakthrough in the "space race" to the hilt. Sputnik seemed to confirm the inflated false Soviet claims of economic progress, and Khrushchev bragged that the Soviet Union would "bury us."

The reality, of course, was quite different, and Bergson's stark portrayals of the shortfalls in the Soviet economy were correct. But, in the charged political atmosphere in 1958, it was difficult to calm political leaders who were affected by those who insisted that we were losing. This mentality, stoked by domestic partisan politics, created a picture of the Soviets being ten feet tall and on a roll. Hard-line inheritors of the McCarthy culture accepted this Khrushchev myth and, as so often happened in the post-war period, turned to fear-driven policies to respond. There can be no question that our consumer-driven policies stoked Soviet aspirations. Sputnik led to a more vigorous national effort in space, military preparedness, and education.

There was a subtle, but very real tension in the Harvard world focused on the Soviet Union. All agreed that we, the U.S., had to get serious, redirect our power, and build our national structure to confront a dangerous enemy who by dint of brutal national sacrifice was a real threat. However, some eschewed a fear-driven response to this threat while calling for new efforts. Shulman, Fainsod, and Malia were proponents of engage and confront, without fear, reflecting their belief that Soviet power was fragile. Others, Pipes particularly, persisted in a Paul Revere-like campaign that lacked the skepticism that history has shown we should have had about Soviet pretensions. Brzezinski, driven by his deep Polish aversion to all things Russian, also supported boycott and isolate policies, which, while they coincided with Pipes', were obviously drawn from distinctly different motivations.

The Soviet threat had been and remained real, but our capacity to confront and stare down Soviet challenges was always present; the Soviets were only five feet four inches tall!

There is a myth that Americans are naïve, that our embassies are not professionally staffed to represent our great country, and above all, that we do not handle foreign languages. This *is* a myth. The fact is that U.S. embassies in Moscow, Beijing, Tokyo, and in non-occupation situations in the Middle East come very well staffed with language officers with outstanding academic backgrounds. No country does better than the U.S. in this regard. Hopefully it is apparent from this chapter that the core substantive embassy officers, political and economic, are remarkably well-trained. Our embassy in Moscow completely overshadowed others in language and area training. Our major European allies had a few well-trained counterparts (UK, France, and Germany) but most friendly embassies relied heavily on our assessments, not only in political, economic, and military attaché areas. We alone had a bilingual expert agricultural attaché, plus a full team of press and cultural language officers. Japan's big contribution to the Allied effort was their Russian-speaking fisheries attaché!

These U.S. Foreign Service training programs in Russian were begun after World War II (George Kennan, Chip Bohlen, Llewellyn Thompson, Foy Kohler, Jack Matlock were products) and continue in 2009. They are rigorous, competitive, and effective. More could be done to train spouses and non-substantive officers—administration and consular—but the core program is right on target. It is also true of our Chinese and Arabic programs.

CHAPTER VI: BERLIN: COLD WAR CAULDRON

Setting

Little did I know that arriving in Berlin in June 1958, I was stepping into the middle of what was arguably the most dangerous confrontation between the U.S. and the USSR of the entire Cold War. By the summer of 1958, a consolidation of the Cold War status quo had emerged. Stalin's death in 1953 produced a fundamental shift in the power structure in Moscow. The imperialistic dictator disappeared, and the uncertain transition in Moscow initially led to a more cautious Soviet role in the outside world. Georgy Malenkov, who emerged briefly as Stalin's successor, was a consensus leader, selected because he was viewed as less threatening to the other members of Stalin's inner circle. Lavrenti Beria, the feared head of the KGB, posed a constant threat and before long produced a violent confrontation within the new leadership. Nikita Khrushchev, in a Shakespeare-like drama, cobbled together enough of a coalition to provoke a Politburo leadership meeting, at which Beria was assassinated and Malenkov unseated and sent off to a remote Siberian power-station in Ust-Kamenogorsk as manager, leaving Khrushchev firmly in charge of the Soviet Union.

The Soviet drive to absorb Western Europe had slowed as Stalin's efforts to promote local Communist parties in West Germany, France, and Italy sputtered. With Khrushchev's ascension to power, priority was shifted to consolidation of Soviet hegemony of Eastern Europe and especially East Germany. The U.S., British, and French presence in Berlin, 110 miles inside the Communist border with West Germany, became a growing source of instability for Moscow—the principal barrier to Soviet consolidation of its Eastern European empire.

Meanwhile, Communist regime consolidation was also the dominant reality around the world. Mao Tse Tung's control over mainland China hardened, with the exception of Taiwan, which, while an embarrassment, did not threaten Mao's total power over China. The U.S.-supported opposition tribal groups in Burma on China's border were never successful enough to affect Mao's control. They remain today an interesting but irrelevant irritation to Burma and Beijing.

By 1958 the volatile Korean peninsula had also become a relatively stable confrontation with U.S. and South Korean forces dug in and confronting North Korean troops along the 38th parallel—a confrontation that remains fifty years later.

In Vietnam, Ho Chi Minh consolidated his control over the North and developed his underground Viet Minh structure in the South. The South, having instilled the pro-Western Catholic Diem as leader, was making impressive economic progress, aided by an influx of U.S. and European support. Already it was apparent that the magnetic appeal of competitive prosperity was a threat to Ho's aspirations.

Hundreds of thousands of North Vietnamese had fled to the south, especially the better educated Catholic population.

And in Cuba, where the U.S. efforts had proved impotent, Castro also was consolidating his control, causing a flood of Cubans to flee to the U.S. Again it was the professional, more educated Cubans who fled to nearby Florida.

Lest this portray a simple, quiet solidification of Moscow's new post-war empire, and a stable relationship between the West and Moscow, it is well to recall that in 1956 serious unrest occurred in Poznan, Poland, and Hungarian students sparked a revolt against the Soviet occupation that quickly erupted into a countrywide outbreak. Khrushchev was clearly stunned by this dramatic violent uprising and ordered Soviet tank-led troops into Budapest to put down the Hungarians. For six days Hungarian groups and their military, led by the heroic General Pal Maleter, held out, exacting a large price on the raw Soviet soldiers. These troops, like the Soviet leaders, were astonished by the bitter resistance of the Hungarians. Hungarian pleas to the U.S. and the U.N. to intervene and support them went unanswered. They subsequently claimed that U.S. radio broadcasts by Radio Free Europe had urged them to rise up. This was an exaggeration, but not without some foundation; particularly since Secretary of State John Foster Dulles and the Eisenhower administration upon coming to office had pledged to "roll back the Iron Curtain."

Hungarian calls fell on deaf ears, not only because of the reality of Soviet power on the ground, but also because the Western alliance and U.S. leaders in particular were paralyzed by the rift that occurred when the British and French, with Israeli participation (or, more realistically, leadership), had invaded Egypt to reverse Nasser's seizure of the Suez Canal. The U.S. condemned this Anglo-French initiative and threatened our closest allies, the British, that we would bankrupt British banks unless they withdrew their troops.

Nasser had established himself as the virtual leader of the Arab world after seizing control in Cairo. Initially the British, French, and Americans attempted to win him over with aid, support for his massive Aswan dam project, and military equipment. However, Nasser cleverly played off his Western "friends" against Khrushchev who leapt at this chance to promote Moscow's influence in the strategic Middle East. The dam was finally built with Soviet assistance.

One must ask why the U.S. could not deal with two admittedly unexpected crises at once. We missed a very brief but real opportunity to inject a prominent mission, perhaps a U.N. team into Budapest. Recently opened Soviet records confirm that there was ambivalence among top Soviet officials, some of whom worried that the U.S. and U.N. might inject a presence into Budapest. And, we suffered a major setback in our influence in the Middle East, to Moscow's advantage.

Arrival Berlin

Thus, as "C" and I arrived in Berlin in July, 1958, there was indeed a seeming settling-down between East and West, but the dramatic explosion in Budapest, and the Soviet coup in Egypt reminded all that the struggle was still on and it was world-wide.

My assignment to Berlin was a story on its own. After Harvard, I had been assigned back to the State Department to the Bureau of Intelligence and Research (INR) in May. INR is the research base for the operational desks for each country in the Department. Usually, mid-career officers and language training officers would be assigned for two to three years to INR to build on their knowledge (in this case of the USSR) prior to going on to Moscow. "C" and I were disappointed but resigned to this delay in going into the USSR. We were delighted when, as we were departing Cambridge, we were notified that the INR assignment was cancelled and we were going to go directly to Berlin. This surprise occurred because John Baker, a good friend and outstanding political officer in Moscow was suddenly expelled by Soviet authorities for committing "unlawful espionage activities." John's real "crime" was that he had successfully joined in with a Moscow university student basketball team and was developing genuine friendships. This action was part of an established expulsion practice by the Soviets called "PNGing" (*persona non-grata*). The State Department, as always, promptly "PNGed" a Soviet diplomat in reciprocity.

This event occurred just as the Soviets shot down an American U-2 flight, captured CIA pilot Gary Powers, and opened a major show trial in Moscow. The State Department immediately tapped one of our best bilingual officers, Vlad Toumanoff (also a good friend) for Moscow, where he covered the Powers trial. Toumanoff (who finished his Harvard training a year ahead of me) had been on his way to Berlin. And, with the Berlin slot open, I was shifted, in part because of my four years of German experience.

For us, Berlin was a highly prized assignment. Professionally, the city was reorganized as the point where Western vital interests conflicted head-on with Soviet expansionism. Khrushchev had been quoted as stating that "Berlin is the testicles of the West. Every time I want to make the West scream, I squeeze Berlin." West Berlin was a defenseless outpost with two million Berliners 110 miles inside Soviet-occupied East Germany. Highly vulnerable access routes—three air corridors and three highway routes—were "guaranteed" under the four-power occupation agreement. But Soviet occupation forces had overwhelming superior power surrounding some 30,000 Allied troops in Berlin.

Personally, in addition to the fact that Berlin was the center of the Cold-War confrontation, it was a very vibrant and satisfying city in which to live. "C" and I, by virtue of our earlier four years in Germany, were both quite fluent in German. On arrival in Berlin we were briefly quartered in the Harnack Haus, a turn-of-the-century house that had been the home of a prominent Nazi official and converted into the

U.S. Army's guest house, until our own house was available. The story of Harnack Haus illustrated the practice under our occupation of seizing housing throughout Germany that had housed Nazi officials. We were assigned such houses earlier in Munich, Hannover, and Hamburg.

The Division of Germany and Berlin: How Did it Happen?

Allied rights in Berlin were established by the defeat of the Third Reich in 1945 by the USSR, U.S., France, and United Kingdom, which assumed supreme authority in all of Germany at that time. The division of Germany into occupation zones for the victorious allies reflected the realities on the ground at the time of the German surrender. Soviet forces occupied Eastern Germany up to the Elbe River, including Berlin, the capital, while British, U.S., and French forces occupied Western Germany. On June 5, 1945, the four allied powers met in Potsdam and agreed to the four occupation zone borders and to four-power control over Berlin, the German capital. Greater Berlin was to be treated as a distinct and separate area of administration to be governed by the four-power governing authority. As was Germany itself, Berlin was divided into four sectors. On June 18, 1945, the USSR and Western allies, in response to President Truman's initiative, agreed to guarantee Western access routes across the Soviet Zone into Berlin: air lanes, highways, and rail lines.

Thus, the division of Germany, and Western presence in Berlin, 110 miles inside of the Soviet zone of occupation was a right based on the victory over Germany. Critically, it was formally agreed to by the USSR and established Western rights to be in and have access to Berlin.

The U.S. Mission in Berlin: A Unique Outpost

The U.S. mission in Berlin was an organizational anomaly. The three Western missions in Berlin operated in fact as normal embassies would, with typical political, economic, consular (passports and visas), and cultural staffs. However, because the legal, treaty-based rights in Berlin flowed from the quadripartite occupation agreement between the Soviet Union and the three Western powers, the Western presence in Berlin was under the authority of the U.S., French, and British generals who dealt with their Soviet military counterparts. The U.S. commandant during 1958-1960 was a major general, Barksdale Hamlett. General Hamlett was a solid and politically sophisticated officer who went on to become a "four-star," and his top-staff colonels were also most impressive; Col. Fred Wyant, who was one of my tennis partners, went on to become a four-star deputy commander in Vietnam. Thus, we operated as an embassy, but our line of command was nominally to Hamlett. In substantive terms, we also were under the authority of the U.S. Ambassador to Germany, who sat in Bonn, the capital of West Germany. While we were in constant communication with Bonn, reflecting Berlin's actual strategic position, we also reported directly to the Secretary of State in Washington with "consultation and copies" to our embassy in Bonn.

This somewhat convoluted organizational arrangement, however, operated smoothly, largely because of the excellent teamwork with General Hamlett in Berlin and our experienced counterparts in Bonn; the deputy Chief-of-Mission (DCM) in Bonn was Martin Hillenbrand, formerly division chief in Berlin, who in fact was the top German expert in the U.S. government—highly respected by both Secretary Dulles and Secretary Rusk. He subsequently became U.S. ambassador to Germany.

The mission also had another unique element; the political section was responsible for relations with Mayor Willie Brandt and the city government, a larger second political section: the eastern affairs division (EAD), to which I was assigned as the resident Russian-speaking specialist. The EAD was responsible for coverage of developments in the Soviet zone, within Eastern Germany (the German Democratic Republic) and for policy recommendations dealing with the Soviets in Germany.

The de facto ambassador of our Berlin mission when we arrived was Bernard Gufler, a seasoned German/Eastern-European affairs veteran who had taken his Russian training with the celebrated Chip Bohlen, ambassador to Moscow. That "training program" in the late 1930s was a harbinger of the excellent training program I described in the previous chapter. The U.S. had established a small elite training operation in Latvia—independent at that point before the Stalin-Ribbentrop Pact enabled Moscow to absorb Latvia, Lithuania, and Estonia.

Gufler was soon replaced by E. Allan Lightner, another top German affairs veteran. Lightner had an excellent relationship with General Hamlett and Marty Hillenbrand in Bonn and improved on the already solid collaboration between our division and the embassy in Bonn.

Lightner had two outstanding deputies: Findley Burns, whose skill in dealing with the intensely involved elements in Berlin and Washington (CIA, Defense, State, and Congress) was of utmost importance; and Howard Trivers, a remarkable Harvard Ph.D who also had a doctorate from Heidelberg University in Germany prior to the war. His book on the German philosopher Karl Jaspers remains a classic. Trivers directed the Eastern affairs division and was my direct supervisor. In my judgment, the team of Lightner, Trivers, and Burns was truly outstanding.

Eastern affairs followed and developed policy recommendations on the internal situation in East Germany, as well as Soviet policies and action in East Germany and Berlin. And though we were prohibited from traveling in the Soviet zone of occupation, we were able to travel throughout East Berlin, the Soviet sector of Berlin, which was legally under four-power control. We regularly interviewed particularly interesting East German defectors as they poured into the

Berlin refugee camp, Marienfelde (from which they were flown to West Germany after being vetted in Berlin). Through these interviews we were able to gauge in some detail the efficacy, or lack thereof, of the oppressive Soviet occupation of East Germany.

U.S. Intelligence Agencies: Massive Presence

The U.S. intelligence activity in Berlin was somewhat less harmonious. Given Berlin's strategic importance and the unique access to developments in the Soviet zone, it is not surprising that Berlin drew intense interest from all the elements of the intelligence community. Many creative and courageous activities were very productive—especially the management of the refugee flow, and subsidies for West Berlin media and exploitation of the pro-Western students in East Germany. Others were less successful, e.g. the highly publicized (and from the beginning, Soviet penetrated) project to dig a tunnel into East Berlin to tap the telephone system. Above all, the bureaucratic turf battles between the large intelligence staffs from the Army, Air Force, and even Navy were wasteful and distracting. A fascinating account of the struggle between Western and Soviet intelligence activities in Berlin was produced by the U.S. station chief Bill Harvey (CIA head) and Sergei Kondrashev, his Soviet counterpart (see Bibliography).

Battleground Berlin: The Soviet Zone's "So-Called Democratic Republic"

The vast, Soviet-occupied area of eastern Germany was perceived by Stalin originally to be a launching pad for Soviet expansion to the West. As the massive Soviet occupation took hold in 1945, the twenty million inhabitants were quickly organized into the full range of Communist organizations—political parties, secret police, youth groups, and centralized industrial and agricultural organizations. Farms were forcefully collectivized and industries quickly harnessed to insure that their production flowed into Moscow's overall economic five-year plans. This creation of a mini Soviet Union out of East Germany was led by several hundred German Communists who had fled to the USSR during Hitler's rise to power. They spent a decade or more working and training in Moscow and other Soviet cities. Some perished in Stalin's terror-trials, but most survived. They were the vanguard as the Red Army swept into Germany in 1944-45. And as soon as security conditions permitted, these German political operators created a Communist regime and economic system throughout the Soviet zone of occupation. Resistance to the communization of the Soviet zone was quickly repressed. These avid old-time German Marxists were overshadowed, of course, by the overwhelming presence of Soviet occupation forces (450,000 heavily-armed men among a population of only 18-19 million).

Soviet control was total. Many viewed the Soviet zone Communist returnees as more Communist than those in Russia. Just as total, but with German efficiency, and bolstered by the absorption of former equally totalitarian Nazi remnants. In a predictable response to the Western Allies' recognition of the new Federal Republic of Germany and establishment of a separate Western based currency, the Soviets declared their zone a new separate state, the German Democratic Republic. They converted their occupation puppet regime into a full-fledged government structure with a Marxist flag, new GDR passports, a foreign ministry, financial ministry, health ministry, and a massive new GDR military structure. By 1958, when I arrived in Berlin, the GDR armed forces included a 100,000-man army, 100,000 border police and special forces, and a 300,000-man militia (Kampfgruppen) force—all trained and overseen by Soviet occupation troops. These forces, who were never considered by NATO forces as effective and reliable combat units were, however, a useful instrument for Moscow to mobilize and control the East German population. By this means, the Soviet occupiers converted the Nazi military remnants, blanketing them into the Soviet-led GDR armed forces. It was noteworthy that these units were lightly armed, reflecting Moscow's lack of confidence that these "allied forces" might turn against them, given the chance.

Co-opting remaining Nazi SS structures, the Moscow returnees organized a Soviet zone-wide police and intelligence system that penetrated every corner of the German population. University facilities were reorganized and "party trustees" promoted to control the historically respected and, even under Hitler, largely autonomous academic institutions.

Both the Evangelical (Lutheran) and Catholic Churches were assigned trustworthy Communist overseers. Throughout history, the churches—Catholic and Lutheran—had dominated social and political life in Germany. A cardinal development in Germany's historic evolution has been the impact of the Protestant Reformation, Martin Luther's revolt against Rome. Luther's church in Wittenberg is in what was East Germany, on the Elbe River. Ironically, Wittenberg is only a few miles from Torgau where advance units of the U.S. Army joined up with advancing Red Army units from the East as the defeat of Germany was consummated. The new Soviet masters struggled to control and eventually exploit both churches. Outstanding church leaders, both Lutheran and Catholic, resisted the Soviet policy of diminishing their influence. Lutheran bishops Dibelius and Not were a constant challenge to the Sovietization of religion. Many less prominent ministers and priests were inspired by Dibelius and Not in their efforts to sustain their "flocks." However, it was largely a losing battle, and Moscow successfully turned several church leaders into collaborators. Lutheran bishop Mitzenbaum became Moscow's leading supporter in undermining the independence of the church.

East Germany had historically had a very productive agricultural sector—the bread-basket of the Reich. Under the new Moscow-controlled German leadership, Soviet-style collectivization was imposed and, as in Russia and Ukraine, formerly productive farms began to deteriorate and production fell sharply.

In short, the Soviet zone of Germany became drab and repressive, with stagnant productivity, Stalinist political controls, and disaffected populations. Not surprisingly, with an open gate through Berlin, thousands of East Germans fled to the beckoning vibrant West Germany. By 1958, when we arrived, the refugee flow had swollen to 2,000-3,000 per day, a flood that was decimating East Germany's economy and undermining Soviet control of its westernmost puppet state. More than three million East Germans had fled to the west, and the flood continued. In retrospect, it was predictable that the Soviets would have to act to stop this flood—as they finally did in 1961.

Meanwhile, the pressure on Moscow to stem the refugee flow mounted, their efforts to promote reorganization of their puppet regime—the German Democratic Republic— accelerated, and they stepped up efforts to undermine the Western presence in Berlin, all designed to consolidate their hold on the post-war westernmost outposts.

The refugee flow loss, of course, also reflected the contrast between the growing West German economy and stagnant Soviet zone economy. One of the most damaging factors for the East German regime was the severe loss of doctors who were fleeing to the West.

In short, Moscow's consolidation of its zone in Germany was deteriorating and Soviet efforts to shore up their grip were soon to lead to the second major Berlin crisis. As I arrived in Berlin in June of 1958 the first signs of an impending confrontation between the West and Moscow were emerging. On October 10, 1958, the Soviet East German puppet, Walter Ulbricht in a major address, declared that the legal basis for the Allied presence in Berlin had expired. My division chief, Dr. Howard Trivers, immediately recognized that Ulbricht's speech was a dramatic step that could only have happened with Moscow's direction. We flagged this to our embassy in Moscow and Washington and warned that the lull in Berlin was over.

On November 10, 1958, Khrushchev followed up with a major speech, placing his seal-of-approval on Ulbricht's declaration. Unknown to the outside world at the time was the fact that Khrushchev's decision to launch a major confrontation in Berlin created a sharp division within his leadership. The "dean" of the Politburo was Anastaf Mikoyan. He made a major effort to force Khrushchev to draw back with the assistance of KGB chief, General Serov. However, Gromyko waffled and the Kremlin's top ideologue, Sulov, backed Khrushchev. Mikoyan failed. Having overcome internal resistance, Khrushchev then moved to step up the pressure. In December 1959, he deployed twelve R-5 medium range nuclear-tipped satellite missiles into East Germany, from where they could threaten Britain and France. Khrushchev's politburo confrontation is detailed in the Fursenko-Naftali book *Khrushchev's Cold War* (see Bibliography) and is drawn from documents that became available after the collapse of the USSR.

Crisis after crisis cascaded from that time. East Germans began to substitute for Soviet officers at checkpoints in an effort to force the U.S. to recognize their sovereignty and the division of Germany. Harassment of our convoys in the Berlin corridor increased regularly. The elevated train system, which ran throughout the city in one of the anachronisms of the otherwise divided Berlin, was maintained in East Berlin. The S-Bahn trains, as they were called, began to appear in West Berlin with flags of the so-called East German Democratic Republic on them. This led to action on our part to stop the trains and remove the East German flags before they could proceed. Guards at the checkpoints in the presence of the Soviet officials would attempt to stamp East German visas into our passports. While these may seem petty, they were all part of clearly calculated policy to "salami-slice" the Western presence in Berlin.

One of my responsibilities was to monitor the refugee flow and especially the flow of doctors. I was helped in this by the opportunity to interview former Soviet zone doctors who were living in West Berlin and by the presence of the fiancée of the *New York Times* reporter David Binder in East Berlin's top hospital. There were entire states in the Soviet zone of Germany that were virtually without doctors. You can imagine the psychological impact on the population to see all their doctors leave. In a desperate effort, the Soviets even began to import Vietnamese and Bulgarian doctors as an emergency measure, which had an even more dramatic negative effect on the morale of the East German population (given its historic racist instincts about Asians and Slavs).

While our office concentrated on alerting Washington to the dramatic changes we saw unfolding in our exposed position in Berlin, we also tried to stay on top of attitudes in general in West Berlin and in the East German population in every way possible in addition to monitoring the flight of doctors. Together with my British colleague, the late James Bennett, and my French colleague, Xavier De Nazelle, we would attend open-air district political Communist rallies in the parks in East Berlin where we witnessed the population attacking party spokesmen for the dramatic deterioration of the situation and the contrast between their situation and the steadily rising standard of living in West.

On one occasion, when Bennett and I walked into an outdoor restaurant where the local party was holding such a rally, the security goons who always tailed us as we went into East Berlin stepped to the dais, where an East German party leader was speaking, with a note. He read it, stopped, and said, "I understand that we are honored by the presence of representatives of the U.S. and British missions tonight. I wonder if they would like to come forth and contribute to our conversation." It was indeed tempting, but "exercising uncharacteristic restraint," Bennett and I decided it was better to sit tight, drink our beer, and wait for the program to go on rather than to take this unsolicited opportunity to present Western views to the audience, which would have led to our being physically thrown out!

Our freedom to move around in East Berlin, after going through a checkpoint, even though we were followed, led to many interesting experiences. When Khrushchev came to Berlin on November 28, 1958, to reiterate his ultimatum to the West and turn up the heat on our presence in West Berlin, he spoke at an open-air gathering of tens of thousands in Alexander Platz. Once again, Bennett and I had driven through the checkpoint and then taken to foot to walk to where the rally was going to occur. There were East German police everywhere, controlling access to the event and questioning the right of people to attend. We feigned ignorance of German and kept emphasizing that we were there from the United States and England to witness this historic event. We finally had worked our way to within a few hundred yards of the platform where Khrushchev would speak when a particularly hostile police guard stopped us and said, "No one may pass beyond this point without special identification." As a lark, Bennett and I took out our PX cards and held them up to the man who, to our astonishment, displayed the traditional German respect for documents and without understanding what he was observing, waved us through. The result was that we stood in the front row right in front of Khrushchev and observed the interplay between Ulbricht and other officials on the platform as Khrushchev spoke. Khrushchev was a dramatic and even theatrical speaker. His voice was shrill and threatening as he denounced the Western presence in Berlin as no longer legal and declared that the West had six months to depart or to suffer consequences. The nervous excitement of the East German minion on the dais with Khrushchev was palpable. Needless to say, this made for interesting reporting telegrams back to Washington and London.

Perhaps the most dramatic confrontation of this period occurred slightly later when East German guards, in an effort to force our acknowledgment of the so-called German Democratic Republic and its sovereignty over West Berlin, instead of just harassing our Army convoys, actually seized one on the autobahn. Since each of these convoys was equipped with a radio, we received word in the mission almost immediately. The convoy leader reported that instead of just being delayed, the East Germans were attempting to take actual possession of our six-truck convoy. General Hamlett instructed the officer in charge of the convoy to sit fast in the truck and refuse to leave. The East Germans stood on the running boards outside the truck, but did not attempt to use force to evict the American soldiers who were driving them. This deadlock continued for several hours. Meanwhile, General Hamlett and Minister Al Lightner were on the phone to Washington and Bonn, as were their French and British colleagues to their respective capitols.

From where we sat in Berlin, this was clearly one more desperate effort by Moscow to frighten us out of our legal position in West Berlin. In Washington, the situation quickly created near panic and anxiety that general war could erupt over such an incident. General Hamlett called together the mission team and we debated for a short time what to do. Meanwhile, the "call of nature" was having a predictable effect on the beleaguered American soldiers in the trucks, and it was clear that they could not hold out indefinitely. Abandoning the trucks would constitute the first acceptance by the West of the suggestion that we did not have a full legal right not only to be in West Berlin, but to traverse the autobahn from West Germany to West Berlin to sustain our presence there. It was decided that Findley Burns, Lightner's deputy in the U.S. mission (a career diplomat), should go to Karlshorst at Soviet headquarters with two military officers and a Russian-American enlisted man, as an interpreter, to present a démarche to the Soviets: if the trucks were not released within two hours, we would use force to retrieve them. And, bless his courage, while Washington continued to debate nervously, General Hamlett instructed our tank units in West Berlin to load up with live ammunition, start their motors, and begin to assemble to drive down the autobahn to free the U.S. convoy. This action, arming the tanks with live ammunition and moving them out of their assembly point toward the autobahn, was of course closely observed and reported on by Soviet spies who monitored all of our military activities in Berlin constantly. Faced with the threat of the use of force, the Soviets backed down, the trucks were released, and the convoy continued. Subsequently, we filed a very strong protest with Karlshorst, in Moscow, and with the Soviet embassy in Washington warning them against such irresponsible and dangerous activity in the future. For the time being, our point had been made. The Soviets had to allow for the possibility that we might actually risk war in order to maintain our rights. It was this perception that was central to our ability to remain in Berlin over subsequent years until in fact the wall eventually came down.

Throughout the two years I was in Berlin—notwithstanding the high quality of U.S. and allied officials throughout our governments—the mission, Bonn (and more so Washington) as well as our British and French colleagues and their respective foreign offices at home, each did develop significantly different perspectives. We were convinced that the name of the game in Berlin was willpower. If the Soviets were persuaded that we could be threatened and forced out of Berlin, or that we would lose our determination for the long pull, they could, by salami-slice tactics, wear away our rights and our determination to maintain our position. The net result, if they were successful, would have been the permanent advance of the border of the Soviet empire and raise doubts among our allies that our commitment to Europe would not stand the test of time. We saw several policy debates in Washington, particularly when John Foster Dulles was the Secretary, that led us to fear that the reliability of the U.S. commitment to Berlin was in question. Dulles, an astute corporate lawyer, seemed to be always seeking a legal means of reducing our engagement and eventually extricating ourselves from an indefensible position.

One of the tactics that the U.S. mission in Berlin evolved almost by happenstance to deal with this issue was to develop our own parallel channels of communication. In my case, I built a very close friendship with Dr. Otto Frei, a highly respected Berlin reporter for the equally highly respected *Neue Zuericher Zeitung*, a Swiss newspaper that is probably the most respected paper in Europe. Among other things, we knew the *NZZ* was read first thing every morning by Germany's Chancellor, Konrad Adenaur. We might occasionally have trouble persuading our own government in Washington and the British government under Selwyn Lloyd (this was before Lord Home became foreign minister) to stand tough. Our French colleagues were never quite certain where de Gaulle was standing (although it was usually very solid and very helpful). At least we were able, by working with Otto Frei, to communicate our views about developments in Berlin directly to the German chancellor. This may seem a bit irreverent, if not worse, but we of course did not divulge classified information, while we did engage in mutual discussions with Frei about our assessment of Soviet and East German intentions and activities. In return we received from Frei very impressive and timely assessments of the attitudes in West Berlin and among Western correspondents. The net result of this was that when a four-power discussion would take place on how to deal with the latest salami-slice initiative by Moscow, Adenauer would always be up to speed on our view and assessments of those actions and vigorously defend standing fast in the face of the Soviet threat. This was heady stuff. We, of course, kept our direct supervisor informed of the discussions we had with Frei, and it was in many ways the most effective communications channel that we had.

One other unorthodox ally in our campaign to stiffen the spine of the Eisenhower administration's dealings with Berlin was Eleanor Dulles. Eleanor had been given a special portfolio in the State Department by her brother, John Foster. She was in charge of recruiting private-sector investment in Berlin. Her crown jewel in this effort was a new U.S.-built and supplied hospital. Eleanor was extremely proud of her hospital and visited Berlin regularly to oversee the project. Bright and concerned as she was, it wasn't long before she was converted into a dedicated supporter of the mission's "no compromise of Western rights" position, and a strong advocate within the State Department (and presumably with her compromise-minded brother!). We endowed her with the title "Mother Berlin." During one of her visits to Berlin, after a policy meeting with her, Ambassador Lightner asked me to entertain her for the evening. On a lark, I took her to an infamous night club, the Racy Bar, where we had drinks and enjoyed the boisterous scene. "Racy" featured several dozen tables with a number and phone on each table, designed to enable men to spot a woman "of interest" and phone her table, seeking an invitation to join her. With a small monetary gesture, I had a young man phone Eleanor and join us. She was thrilled!

One of the great luxuries of living in Berlin, in addition to the excellent restaurants and the very hospitable and friendly population and first-class cultural activities, was the existence of two top-flight tennis clubs. As a tennis enthusiast, I always tried to actively participate in a tennis club at each of my assignments. Throughout my German assignments this was a very successful way to know an unusual slice of German society. In Berlin I joined the Rot-Weiss Tennis Club and became a member of the club team, with whom I journeyed to Western Germany to play matches against other teams. The members of the team and I became close friends, and I had the pleasure of regular tennis at one of the premiere tennis clubs in Europe.

Earlier I had done this in Munich, Hannover, and Hamburg. In Hannover where the club rank list began with Baron von Cramm and included three other Davis Cup historic players, I landed at number eight. I always had to explain that there was a tremendous gap in quality between number four and number five and even between seven and eight, but nonetheless I was on the ladder with four famous German players. There, too, we had great fun traveling to matches against other clubs and had the pleasure of playing on first-class facilities.

In Berlin, I also knew a lot of people in the British intelligence section because they were all dealing with East Germany and I was a source of information for them, and they for me. Oddly enough, there was a famous British turncoat whom we knew, and whom we once entertained in our house, George Blake.

Blake was subsequently caught, arrested, and jailed in England and, in a dramatic helicopter escape, spirited out of the jail by KGB agents. He went off to Moscow and wrote a book. It was a major scandal (see *Bibliography*). Like Burgess and McLean, he came from a highly structured British society where if you were not in, you were out. The story goes that because his mother was Lebanese, he felt he was not socially accepted. He suffered from this at university and in society. He had also been captured by the North Koreans during the Korean War and subjected to intensive pressure to "convert." He had a very nice British wife, who was a friend of my wife. He was a handsome fellow, wore a military uniform, but was really working for Sandy Goshen, the head of British intelligence in Berlin. Blake caused the death of dozens of covert agents in East Germany by identifying or "fingering them" to Soviet authorities.

Our best personal friends in Berlin were a British captain in the tank corps and his wife, who went on to become a military advisor to the Queen, Major General, Sir Michael Palmer. Mike and I have remained close friends, we visit back and forth, our children are friends, and his youngest son, Jonathan, is my godson. (Jonathan was a major in charge of a tank unit in "the desert rats" in the Gulf War.) So we had a great exposure to British regimental life, and enjoyed that very much. Palmer, like many military officers in Berlin, was intensely interested in the politics of the Berlin crisis and, like Hamlett and his U.S. staff, felt completely part of the political struggle in Berlin.

We also had many friends in Berlin among young journalists and lawyers. The city was very pro-American and welcoming. When I received orders to go to Moscow in 1960 and went out to buy supplies for the Moscow assignment, I always encountered a warm reception. I took an old Harris Tweed overcoat in to a furrier to see if I could get a fur lining for it, to wear in Moscow. I walked in to this tailor, with whom I had dealt, but didn't know particularly, told him that I had been posted to Moscow, and I wondered if I could have a rabbit skin lining. He said, "Absolutely." He did a beautiful job and when I went to pay for it—it was going to cost $100, a lot of money in those days—he refused to accept payment. He said, "You have defended my city. You're going to Moscow to continue to defend my city, it's my contribution."When my wife went in to buy some costume jewelry, the same thing happened to her. When merchants learned that we were going to Moscow, they often refused to accept any payment. They were right. We were all "saving Berlin."

I had direct relations with the Soviets in my role as U.S. mission official overseeing U.S. involvement in the air-traffic center (ATC) control, which formally was a very sensitive four-power body controlling the air corridors. The air corridors were one of the three critical routes by which we maintained our position in Berlin. Once Khrushchev had established the German Democratic Republic, the Soviets more or less abandoned their ATC operations, and we operated by using it to notify them of flight plans. Subsequently, as the Soviets stepped up their harassment of our air corridor access, the ATC became more sensitive.

We also had regular meetings with the Soviets, including social dinners, at the Soviet headquarters in Potsdam. These events in the summer of 1958 were lively, often very pleasant, and quite opulent with caviar and vodka toasts, and occasionally with wives included. Potsdam was and still is a fascinating site. I visited Potsdam recently in 2006 and it is beautifully maintained. I was impressed by the historic photos of Truman, Stalin, and Churchill throughout the Soviet headquarters. However, once Khrushchev followed up Ulbricht's speech in November 1958 with an ultimatum declaring that our rights in Berlin had expired, there was no more socializing in Potsdam.

While we were closely restricted by the Soviets and their East German minions, we found many occasions to enter the Soviet sector of Berlin and observe their efforts to dominate the repressed East Berlin population. Because travel between East and West Berlin, while "controlled," was in fact quite free, we aggressively attended cultural events in East Berlin and underwrote major cultural activities in West Berlin, which attracted thousands of East Berliners—adding obviously to the format that undercut Moscow's efforts to consolidate the so-called German Democratic Republic. The U.S. helped to construct an ultra-modern symphony hall and our cultural affairs officer recruited Leonard Bernstein for the opening, a smash success that drew several hundred East Berliners. In East Berlin we regularly attended the opera and symphonies that inevitably drew widespread friendly attention from the East Berlin population.

The U.S., British, and French missions also maintained large cultural centers. Our *Amerika Haus* was immensely popular. I created a regular political roundtable discussion group in *Amerika Haus* where we had lively discussions about development in the U.S. It attracted dozens of East Berlin students. I also organized an East Berlin-U.S. mission basketball team that was very popular. These activities provided us with valuable contacts and insights into East Berlin attitudes.

In an example of the effective, close collaboration with our British colleagues, the British mission learned in advance of a dramatic defection, which allowed us to stage a very high profile press conference in West Berlin to the embarrassment of Moscow and the Ulbricht regime.

Jena University reached its 700-year anniversary in 1959. One of the world's oldest and most respected universities, Jena University was the crown jewel of the GDR education system. As the anniversary approached, the GDR propaganda machine launched a major effort to publicize the event to demonstrate that Moscow's puppet-state was, in fact, a respected state in its own right. Distinguished foreign academics from all over the world were invited and a massive media campaign to build up the importance and respect for the Soviet zone institution was launched. My British colleagues came to see me two days before the event with the news that the prominent rector of Jena, who was to be the center-piece of the anniversary, had defected and was being processed at the Marienfelde refugee center. Together, we intervened and "sprang him" from the processing center to star in a major international press conference in West Berlin. The press conference was a huge success. The rector totally deflated the Soviet zone effort, presenting a devastating account of how academic freedom in East Germany had been destroyed.

Another longstanding Soviet propaganda effort in Germany was to convince the world that the remnants of the Nazi regime were coddled in West Germany (and West Berlin), while the Soviet zone authorities had stamped out residual Nazi elements in East Germany. In 1960, the winter Olympics were held in the U.S., and the German Democratic Republic, as a key part of building its prestige in the world, fielded a separate GDR team. Like the USSR, East German authorities had created a strong state-controlled, year-round training program to prepare East German athletes to make a strong showing. As the Olympics approached, the GDR media built up the excitement about their team that would show the world that there was a *new* democratic German state in contrast to "the Nazi-ridden West German regime."

In Berlin, at the end of the war, the Allies had taken possession of the central Nazi party files, the Berlin Documents Center. With typical German efficiency, these files were

complete. As the GDR Olympic campaign un[
researched the officials of the GDR sports ministr
"coaching staff" for the Games, which predictably ...included
dozens of political commissars to protect against defections
of GDR athletes. Lo and behold, which we had been confident would be true, eighteen of the GDR officials leading the
Olympic delegation had been Nazi officials, including
several SS officers. We organized a very successful media
conference to present this material, and announced that the
18 would not receive U.S. visas. European media, especially
the West German press turned this story into a major event,
complete with photos of the GDR officials in their SS
uniforms. The GDR athletes did well, but the attempt to
exploit their performances into political legitimacy for the
so-called GDR was a total failure.

Berlin: A Psychological Beachhead

As mentioned at the beginning of this chapter, from the
beginning of the post-war occupation of Germany, Berlin
had been a serious running sore for Moscow and Soviet
efforts to convert the Soviet zone of Germany into a viable
Communist state. They had developed in the USSR during
World War II the experienced political commissars who led
Soviet forces in setting up the Soviet occupation of East
Germany. Reinforced by the massive Red Army occupation,
Moscow clearly expected they would be able to quickly
convert the Soviet zone into an efficient economic, and
politically stable base in the westernmost salient of their

new empire. By 1958, it was clear to one and all that they had failed, due to Western steadfastness in Berlin as well as the courageous Berliners who refused to buckle under. In this situation, the morale of Berliners was the critical factor. Had they lost confidence that the West was resolved to keep Berlin free and risk military confrontation with Moscow, it was obvious that our position would collapse.

Therefore, every action by Washington, London, and Paris that could be read to reflect the Western commitment to Berlin was scrutinized and worried over by Berliners. The first Berlin crisis, the 1948 blockade, and the airlift that broke the blockade, had given Berliners great faith that even Stalin's military effort would not break the Western commitment to Berlin. Here, in 1958, ten years later, Khrushchev made the second major initiative to close down the Western outpost and cure the disease of a free West Berlin in the center of Moscow's puppet GDR.

Berliners were initially confident that our airlift-proven commitment was dependable and that Moscow would once again have to back down. The two speeches in the fall of 1958 by Ulbricht and Khrushchev were crystal clear: Western rights in Berlin had "expired," and we would have to accept GDR sovereignty over Berlin. And Western rejection of these claims was also crystal clear...initially.

However, as Moscow's salami-slice pressures mounted, the U.S. especially and Britain began to suggest that we would be receptive to negotiation of a compromise. Therefore, when Secretary John Foster Dulles, renowned for his anti-Communist rhetoric (it was Dulles who spoke of rolling back the Communist takeover of Eastern Europe) in an ill-fated lawyer-like statement, suggested that perhaps we would accept a compromise under which Western access would be controlled by GDR officials, who we would consider to be acting as "agents" of the USSR, it was a serious blow to the Berliners who clung desperately to Western guarantees. They recognized that a new crisis over Berlin had erupted. And above all, they saw this as a new psychological test of Western willpower.

A period of plummeting morale among Berliners followed. Random statements by American congressmen, and especially British foreign minister Selwyn Lloyd, increased the despair among Berliners. Thus, when Dulles died suddenly and was replaced by Christian Herter, Herter's early visit to Berlin was seen as a critical test of the West's commitment to Berlin. Our mission team convened and worked at length to put together a positive program for Secretary Herter's visit that would ensure that the U.S. commitment to Berlin was solid. We were quite stunned, therefore, when an advance text of Herter's proposed speech arrived and completely failed to provide any reassurance. Herter's staff had put together a rather routine restatement of the Allied position, but with more emphasis on the need for compromise than for standing firm.

Our mission chief, Ambassador Alan Lightner, and General Hamlett were aghast, agreeing that the Herter draft text would be disastrous for Berlin morale. We prepared an irreverent response, stating that such a text would render his visit useless. We laid out what we considered an effective statement. To Lightner and Hamlett's great credit, they cabled our recommendations and added that the secretary's visit should be cancelled if his proposed text were to be delivered! Herter came and gave our speech. Berliners were reassured that this quintessential New England blueblood was a very tough man in a crisis.

Thus, as I left Berlin in June for a month of home-leave and then directly to the U.S. embassy in Moscow, the tectonic fault-line plates between East and West Berlin continued to grind away. The morale of Berliners held firm; the three U.S., French, and British brigades remained, serving as a tripwire defense against "Soviet takeover in Berlin." The Soviet hold over their zone continued to erode as East Germans continued to flee to the West, through the open gates of Berlin.

CHAPTER VII. MOSCOW 1960-1962: THE EYE OF THE STORM

Confrontation in Full Bloom

In August 1960, the global Cold War confrontation with the USSR was in full bloom. Berlin was indeed the central neuralgic focus of the struggle, but Khrushchev's adventurous erratic lunges into fragile and uneasy crisis areas of the world created mini-crises in virtually each continent. Under his aggressive, hyper leadership, the Soviets developed and propagated a major campaign to support so-called "wars of national liberation" across the world. Khrushchev built up a role for the USSR to accelerate the end of colonialism, and so-called economic imperialism in Indonesia, the Arab world, Latin America, and Africa. He, with some success, joined in with Indonesia's Sukarno, Nehru in India, and Nasser in Egypt to persuade the world that Moscow was on their side and that the "third world" needed Moscow's help to throw off the shackles of colonialism and economic exploitation by "the Western powers."

In short, in 1960, the Cold War confrontation was indeed worldwide. This year was, as it turned out, the high-water mark of Soviet imperialism and Khrushchev's ambitions. Soviet astronauts ("cosmonauts") outpaced the U.S. space program. As mentioned in the previous chapter, Soviet influence had replaced the Anglo-American domination in Egypt, and "wars of liberation" were thriving in Laos, Cuba, and Africa. Khrushchev had begun to unfreeze the Stalinist structure internally and launched an ill-fated initiative in agriculture—the "new-lands" program to produce massive increases in cotton production. When he bragged that he would bury the West, he probably believedit!

In the background, the U.S. presidential campaign unfolded as Jack Kennedy ran against Vice President Nixon. The election, which was to provide Kennedy with a narrow victory in November, saw Kennedy run as the candidate of change, focusing especially on young voters, while Nixon attempted to persuade the country that Eisenhower's prosperity programs needed to continue. Soviet citizens were fascinated by the campaign. Their initial enthusiasm for the youthful Kennedy was dampened when in the debates he insisted that the USSR had opened a significant lead in nuclear weapons and the U.S. had to "catch up." In fact, history has revealed that there was *no* missile gap, and that Khrushchev's inflated claims masked the weakness of the Soviet arsenal, as well as their dysfunctional economic programs.

Moscow Arrival

Mid-day in August 1960, our family arrived on a flight from Copenhagen to Moscow's Sheremetyevo International Airport; my wife "C,"Peter, now seven years old; Mike, five; and four-year-old Tim --, and, in the hold of the SAS plane, ourAiredale, Tigger. Approaching Moscow we were very excited. This was the culmination of two years of intensive training and the dramatic two-year assignment in Berlin where Soviet power had been at the center of our lives. From the sky, as we descended, it was truly beautiful; vast pine forests, occasional lakes, with groves of white birches interspersed. This distant view from the air only heightened our surprise as we landed and immediately were struck by the run-down, shabby nature of the airport and its surroundings. "It's so drab," my wife commented. We knew that the USSR was a "drab" place, but expected their principal international airport would have been designed and maintained to impress foreign visitors. Later travels within the USSR revealed that in fact Sheremetyevo was indeed relatively spiffy in comparison to the truly shabby local airports and cities across the USSR. For the first time we began to absorb the reality that the USSR was indeed a "third world country," with a "first world" nuclear weapons capability!

We were met by an embassy officer and escorted through customs and security, a laborious procedure that introduced us to another reality of Soviet life: the incredibly stifling bureaucracy and wide-spread underemployment; there were at least five uniformed men for every procedure. Once in the airport and through customs, we faced our first "crisis": extracting Tigger from the baggage/customs official who insisted there was no dog! In addition to the fact that I could see Tigger's crate and hear him whining, I had his "ticket" in hand. After much back and forth, the Soviet official allowed that there did indeed seem to be a dog. He then stated that we would need approval of the Soviet agricultural officials to admit the dog into the USSR. After a lengthy argument, with the help of the U.S. embassy officer who met us (fortunately it was Bill Horbaly, the agricultural attaché whose Russian was fluent), we persuaded our adversary that Tigger was not an agricultural product, was fully vaccinated, and very friendly. All this took almost two hours, but finally we freed Tigger and, with him on his leash, proceeded to the main gate to meet "C" and the boys and load into an embassy van with Tigger and our luggage for the drive into Moscow. Just outside the airport, Horbaly pointed out to us the stark, eerie memorial of massive tank-traps that marked the utmost point of Nazi troop penetration during the ill-fated German invasion of the USSR some twenty years earlier.

We drove into Moscow to the Hotel Ukraine, our temporary quarters. We walked up to the desk with the Airedale on the leash and our three boys and put our passports down. They confirmed that yes, they did have a reservation for us, a "suite" of two rooms back-to-back. And then the woman in charge looked up and said, "Of course, we do not allow dogs in the hotel." This was a real challenge and I must say, in my entire career, I handled this perhaps more diplomatically than anything I ever faced. I decided okay, this is the land of non-sequiturs, here we go. I replied to the woman, profusely, "I am so impressed. Do you know on the entire European continent, the Soviet Union is apparently the only country where dogs are not allowed in hotels? You are so progressive, that's so sensitive to sanitary considerations. I really take my hat off to you." And she nodded and smiled broadly and said, "That's right. No dogs allowed in the hotel." We picked up our passports and the keys and the dog and went right up to our room. She never said a word. And as we came back out about two hours later to take the dog for a walk along the Moscow River, she looked up and wagged her finger and said, "Remember, no dogs." And I said, "Yes, I do remember. I can't wait to tell my friends." And she beamed and nodded. For six weeks, every day she would say, "No dogs." And I'd answer, "Absolutely."

During what seemed like eternity, our six weeks in the Ukraine Hotel, we had one other flare-up with the dog. We were walking Tigger, and I didn't normally keep him on a leash because he was very well trained. We were right along the edge of the river, and there was about a three-foot drop down into the river, and occasionally there would be stairs going down where boats could tie up. Well, all of a sudden the dog saw a fish, and he jumped in. The Moskva River was filthy, covered with an oil slick. I eventually got him back out again, up one of those little stair platforms. We took him back into the hotel. The woman at the desk didn't happen to be looking. We got him up in the room and then called the embassy doctor to advise us as to how we could get the oil off his coat. There were three days of bathing, and not a happy Airedale. It did introduce us to Alex Davidson, the embassy doctor who in fact was a native Russian speaker and had a key role in handling Oleg Penkovsky, arguably the singlemost important Soviet defector in the entire Cold War. (More about Penkovsky later.)

Our Embattled Outpost

The U.S. Embassy in Moscow was truly embattled. Soviet KGB forces placed a top priority on sealing off the embassy to the fullest extent possible from contact with the people of the USSR. Paranoid about the possibilities that the disgruntled Soviet people would reveal "security information" to us, or even just reveal the appalling weaknesses in the Soviet economy, the KGB left no stone unturned to prevent contact by us with the population at large, and especially intellectual, scientific, and military personnel, whose cynical attitudes about the regime were almost universal.

The entrances to the embassy building, the ambassador's residence, and the three apartment buildings where our diplomats and journalists were housed, were tightly controlled; the entrances were under round-the-clock guard by burly Soviet "militia men" who prevented Soviet citizens from entering and carefully controlled our own traffic. Efforts to befriend these poor watchdogs were always rebuffed.

The atmosphere was hostile, designed to discourage both us and curious Soviet citizens. It is hardly surprising that the Soviet population was easily discouraged and very careful, given that Stalin's regime of terror had ended only six years earlier when he died in office, amid his latest brutal purge, which had targeted Jewish doctors.

Our objective, on the other hand, was to "push the envelope" and exploit every crack in the KGB cocoon that they had in place to contain us. And there *were* cracks in the seemingly impenetrable shield. Soviet priorities also included a number of goals that conflicted and often compromised their efforts to screen us off. For example, from the inception of Soviet control under Lenin, Soviet authorities mounted a full-scale propaganda campaign to imbue Soviet citizens with the grandiose (and usually ineffective) concept of a new "revolutionary man" indebted to the State. This program, Agitprop, remained a central element in the regime's program until the collapse of the Soviet Union in 1989. Thus education was promoted (literacy levels did reach 90%) to ensure the population could imbibe the regime's propaganda. ("Agitprop" translates out as "agitation propaganda," or "the party line.") Newspapers, radio, and TV (when it arrived) were all harnessed to a central purpose; editors received daily topic lists to be covered, and often exact texts that were to be used verbatim. Furthermore, all across the Soviet Union (and subsequently in Moscow-ruled Eastern Europe), regular programs of "lectures" were held by Communist Party spokesmen directed at every level of society—including military audiences—to promote the Party's theme of the day. These lectures were open to the public and thereby allowed us invaluable opportunities to get "the line" and, more importantly, hear the often cynical argumentative responses of the audience.

On one memorable occasion, I attended an advertised lecture at the Frunze Military Academy where the Berlin crisis and German policy were addressed. Obviously, I was followed by a "tail," but no effort was made to block my entrance. Some 200 Soviet officers were present to hear a Soviet colonel lecture about the illegitimacy of the Western garrison in Berlin and describe the "degenerate, corrupt West German regime." My "tail" passed a note to the speaker, obviously warning him that a U.S. embassy officer was present, but he seemed to ignore it. After his blatantly propagandist presentation, a storm of argument and questions ensued, but was summed up by one officer who ridiculed the speaker by stating that if the Soviet sector of Germany was so great, why did the West Germans have such a superior standard of living. "You see," he said, "I was stationed in Germany and the picture you have drawn is totally false!" It was apparent that many of the officers present had also served in East Germany, and several weighed in, complaining that the East Germans lived much better than Russians. "Who won the war?" one asked, to general applause. This lecture was perhaps the most dramatic one I attended, but there were dozens of others that embassy officers "covered" during 1960 to 1963.

The KGB program to control our movements and frighten away curious Soviet citizens worked, to a point. They worked primarily by ostentatiously observing us, so that Soviets were always aware that *they* were being observed, too. Six years earlier, in Stalin's era, people were sent to prison camps for less. It didn't take long, however, before we found that, while frightened, Soviet citizens on the whole were very curious about us and were inclined to be friendly. Older residents rarely failed to recall our alliance in World War II.

Each day we ran up against the reality of the totalitarian and hostile nature of the Soviet world in which we lived. We were always aware of the fact that we were constantly photographed, overheard, shadowed by our ever-present "tails," and subjected to efforts to entrap us. All embassy officers and their dependents were regularly reminded of the realities we faced, and we were thoroughly inculcated with the warning that this was serious business; "Do not fool around or play games with your 'tails!'"

Soviet security forces studied carefully our family relationships; any suggestion of marital difficulties and the diplomat in question would find an attractive young Russian woman bumping into him at the theatre or suggesting a rendezvous. The KGB had an ample stable of "swallows" that they would deploy. We all encountered those. On one of my rail trips, I found my compartment occupied by a very attractive young woman who spoke excellent German and grilled me on my experience in Berlin, offered to share her vodka bottle, and slowly proceeded to disrobe! These incidents were called "provocations" and were fairly standard procedure on train trips.

A humorous reminder of this ever-present control occurred on a picnic outing that our family took. There was a well-known writers' colony at a village named Peredelkino, about twenty miles out of Moscow. Boris Pasternak, author of *Doctor Zhivago*, lived there. The dachas (summer houses) there were particularly appealing with their bright colors and natural gardens. We drove out to a field adjacent to this colony and unloaded our basket and blankets, while Tigger raced around investigating the grove of trees that bordered the field. All of a sudden he flushed out three Soviet militiamen bearing machine guns! We waved at them, recalled Tigger, and proceeded to have our picnic while they glowered at us from fifty yards away. A reminder!

We were also always aware of the wired nature of our own existence; we knew there were cameras in our apartment, listening devices ("bugs") in our offices, and that any hotel room we were allowed to use on our travel was always prepared (bugs *and* cameras) for "foreign guests." Each time we departed in our car from our apartment building, a "tail-car" would follow us out. Anyone who was inclined to scoff at all this would be completely persuaded when the periodic "sweep" of our offices discovered electronic listening devices in radiators, under carpets, or furniture.

Perhaps the most convincing evidence of the totalitarian nature of this paranoid Soviet regime was when we discovered the KGB was radiating our embassy windows. After consultation with security officials in Washington, we learned that a battery of radiation cameras across the street was focused in on the ambassador's windows and the political section of the embassy (my office). And it was explained to us that by beaming in on our windowpanes, they would be converted into transmitters so that all sounds—our conversations and the "music of our typewriters"—within the office could be overheard in the KGB office across the street. Finally, we were told that with their modern computer capability, the typewriter sounds could be easily and automatically transcribed and the messages revealed. It seems that each typewriter key is configured uniquely and, by running the sound through a computer, can be "translated." Our Washington security people confessed that they knew this worked because we obviously did the same thing to the Soviet embassy on 16th Street in Washington!

Faced with the reality that our conversations and even our typewritten telegraphs to Washington were subject to radiation monitoring, our embassy as well as the British, French, and Canadian embassies had constructed clear plastic rooms, on Lucite stilts, surrounded by the product of a sound machine to provide us with at least one truly secure workplace. We held our weekly staff meetings in "the box," as we called it, had all sensitive telegrams typed up in the box, and met with our key allies in our box or theirs. Presumably the Soviet embassy in Washington had a counterpart.

There was, in fact, a basic commitment to reciprocity of treatment that was fundamental to our relations with the

USSR. We were less effective in applying controls over Soviet diplomats in Washington because of the very open nature of our society, while the Soviet Union was constructed upon a fundamental commitment to control, secrecy, and suspicion; characteristics that were historically also a part of Czarist Russia, but now reinforced by the police state efficiency of the KGB. In his penetrating foreword to *The Penkovsky Papers* , the renowned British expert on the Soviet Union, Edward Crankshaw, described the pervasive pressure of the KGB as follows: "Having lived so long in the shadow of Soviet security services, I have come to take many of these thing for granted. I am not outraged by the presence of microphones in any room in which I happen to find myself in the Soviet Union; I expect them to be there even if they are not. I am not shocked by the knowledge that some of my pleasanter and most intelligent Russian acquaintances are members of the KGB in plain clothes, or at least part-time informers; if they are not, I expect them to be ... I am not appalled by Penkovsky's statement that at least 60% of all Soviet diplomats are employees of the KGB or GRU (the GRU was the military intelligence organization working in fierce rivalry with the KGB with parallel objectives). It never occurred to me to expect anything else."

The effect of this atmosphere—which we all accepted as reality in Moscow—did weigh on us. But, given the historic importance of our efforts, it also provided us with a sense of drama. We were "under pressure" and constantly reminded of it. However, like front-line Marines in battle, we also were inspired and even uplifted by our efforts. We did find ways to see behind the curtain, escape from the KGB cocoon, and learn about the frailties of the USSR. We partied among our colleagues and friendly embassy staffers with real enthusiasm and were reminded each day how important our insights and work were in the nuclear-tipped Cold War confrontation of our world. In short, our morale was, with very few exceptions, excellent.

Our family had an early but dramatic experience with Soviet determination to not only control but penetrate our mission. On leaving Berlin, we had hired a young German nanny to help us with our three young boys. She was the daughter of a Lutheran minister who was also a personal friend of ours in Berlin. She was very good with the boys, and having grown up in divided Berlin, we assumed she would be politically savvy about the nature of the Soviet Union. We were wrong. Soon after our arrival, she announced to us that she had met a "very nice young Russian," who invited her to take a trip to the Black Sea! Recognizing the move for what it was, we put her on the next plane out to Copenhagen. The KGB regularly worked over the household staff personnel of Western embassies and occasionally successfully converted a nanny into a household source.

The Embassy Team

The high quality of the U.S. embassy staff in Moscow was fundamental to this "good morale" and critical to the security of the mission. It was led by career ambassador

Llewellyn Thompson, who was on his third tour in Moscow. During World War II, as the Germans approached the Soviet capital, Stalin evacuated most of the Soviet government to Kuibyshev, a provincial city behind the Ural Moun-Mountains. "Tommy," then a young officer, remained behind in Moscow to maintain our mission there. Fluent in Russian, Tommy collected reports from Kuibyshev, added his own observations as the Germans reached the outskirts of the city, and kept Washington informed. Prior to returning to Moscow in 1959 as ambassador, he led the long, grueling negotiations with the Soviets over Austria, which succeeded in winning the withdrawal of all Soviet forces from Austria, a singular diplomatic achievement. In a word, we were led by a true superstar.

Tommy's deputy (DCM) was another veteran, Ed Freers, who, like all the embassy team, was fluent in Russian, and very cool under our daily pressures. As DCM, Ed presided over what must have been the most skillfully selected U.S. embassy in the world; for each key issue in the U.S.-Soviet relationship, our embassy had an accomplished Russian-speaking expert:

1. Moscow's relations with China were already beginning to unravel and the strategic importance of this so-called alliance was each day becoming more fractious; my colleague, Culver Gleysteen, in the political section was bilingual in Chinese and had spent his career monitoring developments in China. He was raised in a missionary family in China as a young boy and was able to divine

from Soviet agitprop materials and public lectures the clear deterioration in the ties between Beijing and Moscow.

2. Soviet intentions in Afghanistan, India, and Pakistan reflected the historic Russian efforts to expand into South Asia. The successful coup by the Moscow-dominated Communist party of Afghanistan was a major breach in the "containment policy" of the U.S. and our allies; my colleague Adolf "Spike" Dubs was a veteran of our embassy in Kabul and worked effectively with friends in the Afghan, Indian, Pakistani, and Iranian embassies to monitor and interpret the fast unfolding events in Kabul. Dubs was subsequently sent to Kabul as our ambassador to Afghanistan and was murdered by a Communist terrorist team in Kabul. Dubs was also responsible for the critical negotiations on nuclear proliferation, a fascinating and immensely important field. When Dubs was transferred, I took over this area as well as Berlin negotiations.

3. Frank Meehan, a third colleague, was our expert in NATO and European defense issues. A brilliant linguist, Frank also had particular responsibility for former French colonies in Southeast Asia when Khrushchev's wars of national liberation were boiling up and Moscow-directed Communist forces strove to take over from the French in Laos, Cambodia, and Vietnam. Frank went on to serve as the U.S. ambassador in East Germany, Czechoslovakia, and Poland.

In addition to this outstanding team dealing with global issues, the embassy also had equally expert language officers dealing with Soviet economic performances, the internal political situation that was evolving from Stalin's absolute control into a slow but perceptible unfreezing of the process, and a two-man team that travelled widely in agricultural areas to monitor the crop production. The economic section was led by an outstanding economist, Bill Morrell, who was on loan from CIA, where he headed the 500-man division that monitored Soviet-economic performance. (It's reassuring that at that time CIA knew more about the Soviet cement production than the Soviets did!)

We also had a team of brilliant military attaches who, taking advantage of the appetites of Soviet military leaders for respect in the West, were able to develop a range of official relations with top Soviet generals and marshals. Marshal Vershinen, commander in chief of the Soviet air force, engaged in an exchange of visits with our USAF chief, General Twining, arranged by one of our attaches. The top U.S. defense attaché was an air force colonel, Mel Nielson, who not only spoke Russian well, but also had a PhD in nuclear Physics.

It was odd, but a reassuring factor that the Soviet military leadership, even as we confronted each other in Berlin, and in Cuba, cherished their contacts with their U.S. counterparts. In my experience around the world, there is an almost mystical attraction of "mil-to-mil" relations, potentially a critical element in avoiding war. This is an activity, again in my experience, that the U.S. Defense Department very intelligently exploits.

Dissent within this totalitarian police state frequently could be found in cultural activities and publications. And dissent there was! Playwrights, film producers, poets, and the top of Russian classical musicians and dancers were very likely to be thirsty for contact with the West and approbation by their Western counterparts. The embassy had a small but superb team of cultural attaches from the U.S. Information Agency. The top man in this section, Hans "Tom" Tuch, was an extremely capable officer who had widespread experience in Germany in directing cultural visits of top American groups. He was also a decorated paratrooper in World War II who parachuted behind German lines on D-Day. Tom had two assistants, both veterans of our massive "public affairs" program in Germany. This unit arranged for series of exchange visits that were carried out under our U.S.-Soviet educational and cultural agreement, which was renewed every two years. From Moscow's point of view, the agreement provided an opportunity for young Soviet scientists to study in the U.S. and to showcase the Bolshoi Ballet and the Moscow Philharmonic Orchestra. From the U.S. point of view, the exchange agreement provided a chance to place an exactly equal number of U.S. academics and artists in Moscow and Leningrad to study Russian literature, history, and medical developments.

The agreement also established an exchange of a handful of literary figures from both sides. During our tour in Moscow we received John Updike and Edward Albee and showcased the Philadelphia Philharmonic, Benny Goodman (who was a huge success in Moscow), and the University of Michigan marching band. All these activities put Tom Tuch and his team in working relationships with Soviet cultural and academic leaders. One would question why the Soviets would allow this kind of "penetration" of their closed society, or ever accept an exchange program at all. In fact, their willingness to do so reflected the genuine inferiority complex of the regime and popular attitudes with which they had to cope. Paranoid as they were (and still are!) about security and control, they are equally paranoid about being acknowledged as accomplished and deserving of respect and acclamation. Their world-class orchestras, violinists, authors, and above all ballet dancers were, and continue to be, Russia's greatest assets. Thus, they eagerly grasped at the chances the exchange agreement offered, while deploying thousands of security people to try and contain U.S. exchange activities in the USSR. (More about this in the next chapter.)

We were particularly fortunate when a new Foreign Service officer, Jack Matlock, arrived to join our mission. Jack had been a professor of Russian literature at Dartmouth before entering the Service. Like all his colleagues at the embassy, he spoke Russian well. Assigned to the consular service, as a "new boy," he was stuck dealing with U.S. tourists and visa problems. But, we also recruited him as a part-time political officer monitoring the cultural media. And, as dissent grew, released by Khrushchev's reduction of

Stalin's brutal control over the Soviet population, there was a surge of fascinating, encouraging expression in intellectual circles. With his refined knowledge of Russian literature, Jack was able to grasp the political protest and pressure for more artistic freedom often expressed in literary parables. His reports on this historic evolution were commended by President Kennedy personally. Jack Matlock subsequently returned on a second tour in Moscow as DCM, and then was appointed by President Reagan as ambassador on his third tour. He finished his career as President Reagan's top Soviet affairs advisor and in retirement at Princeton, has authored several acclaimed studies. His *Autopsy on an Empire* describing Gorbachev's era and the collapse of the Soviet Union stands as a classic.

My responsibilities in the embassy included, first and foremost, the Berlin crisis. But I was also charged with covering Soviet activities directed at Latin America, especially Cuba, and I inherited arms control negotiations when Dubs was transferred. Berlin obviously was very consuming. But, as Khrushchev grew more and more frustrated by our blocking his campaign to remove "this Western cancer" in the middle of the Soviet empire Berlin, the Soviets accelerated their activities in Cuba.

Lumumba University: Soviet Training Camp

Before moving into the Berlin negotiations and the intelligence battles in Moscow, it behooves me to outline the value of our engagement with other members of the diplomatic community. The Soviet effort to break out of the containment that the U.S. and its allies had established by means of supporting "wars of national liberation" and courting third-world countries, opened up valuable opportunities for us through cooperation with key diplomats from these countries. While in many countries around the world "anti-Yanqui" attitudes had become instinctive, when cast into the oppressive controlled atmosphere of Moscow in 1960, their diplomats became *very* pro-American. The ambassadors and top political officers of the Brazilian, Mexican, Argentine, and Uruguayan embassies were courted, awkwardly, by the Soviets, but took every opportunity to cooperate with us. They regularly reported Soviet efforts to win their support and defection efforts by the KGB. And they looked to me to provide them with our insights into internal Soviet politics, agricultural production, and our views about the Soviet campaign to support "wars of liberation."

With the establishment of Lumumba University in 1960 in Moscow, our diplomatic colleagues became more valuable. Lumumba University constituted a major Soviet initiative to infiltrate third-world countries around the world. Several hundred Africans, Latin Americans, and Asians were recruited and brought to Moscow for an all-expenses-paid university education that in theory would produce legions of pro-Soviet activists when they returned to their homelands. It was largely a colossal failure. The students on the whole were shocked to encounter the almost universal racism of Russians whenever they went "off-campus." They were stunned to find the prevalence of poverty and regimentation. A few did acquire the revolutionary spirit that the Soviets had anticipated, but many left "turned off" by their experience. Our cultural center library, which was blockaded by KGB militiamen for Soviet citizens, became a true "hot spot" for Lumumba students who were not fazed by the guards. They became a powerful distribution system for our *Amerika* magazine, a superb glossy publication by the United States Information Agency (USIA), *Time, Newsweek,* and *Life.* But most valuable to us was the steady flow of reports from the diplomatic representatives of the countries from which the Lumumba University students came. They, of course, regularly visited their own embassies and unloaded their unhappiness and disappointment—which in turn our friends in the embassies shared with us. A very useful insight into the techniques used as Moscow sought to create an army of third-world revolutionaries. Over the years of the Cold War, we became increasingly convinced that if we could but send Western Communists to live briefly in Soviet reality, the Communist movement would wither on the vine—as it subsequently has.

Our Key Allies in Moscow

A particularly valuable resource for us, of course, was our colleagues from the British, Canadian, French, German, and Israeli embassies. While not as completely staffed by Russian language officers with graduate level training in the history and economics of Russian as we were, each of our major allies' embassies had several outstanding officers from their own diplomatic service, with whom we worked closely and from whose judgment and observations we benefited greatly. We cemented this collaboration by very close social relations (some of them remain close friends with me even today, 50 years later), and through extensive sharing and comparing of information.

As is often the case around the world, we had an especially close special relationship with our British colleagues. The British ambassador, Sir Frank Roberts, was a brilliant, seasoned professional who was particularly close to our Llewellyn "Tommy" Thompson. They made an odd pair; Sir Frank, only 5' 2" tall, was dwarfed physically by lanky Tommy. But their mutual admiration and decades of experience strengthened the superb cooperation we shared. My counterpart, Sir John Fretwell, who rose to the top of the British diplomatic service, was equally brilliant, and with his beautiful wife became our closest friends as well as my full partner on Berlin. As we will discuss below, our intelligence officers were equally close.

The French embassy also included several outstanding officers; it is fair to say, the best of their own diplomatic service. My counterpart, Jacques Andreani, went on to become ambassador to the U.S., and top foreign policy advisor to French President Mitterrand. At the level of ambassador it was a different story. Ambassador Maurice

Dejean was less committed than Tommy or Sir Frank, and intensely interested in Russian cultural activities. Therein lies a tale!

Following his tour in Moscow, Dejean returned to Paris as the personal foreign policy adviser to the French president. A few years later, a mid-level KGB officer defected to the West and told a bizarre and fascinating story: he had been the "case officer" who set up Ambassador Dejean with a ballerina whom he had admired at the Bolshoi. The young lady was a KGB "swallow" who launched a passionate affair with the married Dejean. The defector laid out, so to speak, all the lurid details including how the KGB attempted to exploit Dejean's elevated position with the French president. His book became a bestseller in Paris! Notwithstanding Dejean's vulnerabilities, we benefited greatly from his superb staff, especially the flow of information they provided us about Soviet efforts with Algerian, Moroccan, Vietnamese, Lao, and Cambodian Lumumba students and embassies in Moscow.

The German embassy was very strong obviously on Berlin, East Germany, and also on all trade issues. Soviet trade with the Federal Republic of Germany was the Soviet's most important trade relationship. My colleague on the Berlin team was Jorg Kastl, a Harvard graduate with great political insights. However, the German ambassador, Hans Kroll, was a serious problem for our allied efforts. Kroll was a powerful political figure in Bonn, a political appointee to Moscow who suffered from an overblown sense of self-importance. We came to the conclusion that his dialogue with Khrushchev muddied the question of Western determination to never abandon our embattled position in Berlin. Kroll, at the end of World War I, had lived on what became the new Eastern border of Germany and Russia. He became fluent in Russian. He then joined the German diplomatic service and became fascinated by Russia. After World War II, he became active with the Free German Democratic Party (FDP), a second-tier party, and subsequently was recruited by Chancellor Adenauer to be ambassador in Moscow. Kroll was convinced that he had a special understanding with Khrushchev, who was all too ready to "play Kroll like a fiddle." Notwithstanding Kroll's malevolent influence, our cooperation with Kastl and other German diplomats was very valuable. We were also gratified by Kastl and his colleagues' candor with us about Kroll's freelancing efforts.

The small Israeli embassy was also superbly staffed—all "language officers." They had widespread relationships throughout the Jewish community in Moscow. Rarely allowed by the Soviets to travel, they received a steady stream of Soviet Jews and garnered very valuable information about conditions and attitudes in the provinces. That embassy was closed down after a few years as the Soviets' paranoia overcame their policy of engaging the world as though they were actually respectable.

The Latin American embassies—Brazil, Mexico, Argentina, Uruguay, and Ecuador—were also staffed by the best and the brightest of their diplomats. However, few of them knew Russian or had special expertise about the Soviet Union. What they did provide was an invaluable channel back to their governments, which enabled us to influence these governments to support the containment policy of the U.S. and our NATO allies.

The Brazilian embassy was the most valuable. It was led by a very capable career diplomat, Leitao de Cunha, who went on to become the foreign minister of Brazil and included particularly helpful colleagues of mine who were courted by the Soviets, who recognized Brazil's stature in Latin America. The Soviets never gave up their vision that leftist Brazilian politicians who often sounded like radical Marxists would become genuine allies of Moscow. Whatever the popular anti-American flavor among Brazilian trade unionists, Brazil's diplomats—who were all well-trained career officials—were among our closest collaborators. Every trade mission from Brazil, or cultural delegation, provided us with rich accounts of Soviet efforts to romance or even recruit them. And Brazil's Lumumba University students were among the most disenchanted.

Ambassador Leitao de Cunha became a special friend of mine as a result of a bizarre athletic incident. Tommy occasionally would organize an all-day picnic at our country house (dacha), which the Soviets provided us in exchange for their being able to enjoy a similar "dacha" on the Chesapeake for the Soviet diplomats in Washington. On this day, he invited several of our friends in the diplomatic community and in the Western press corps. Bloody Marys were served to all and we commenced a pick-up soccer game with great enthusiasm. Unfortunately, early in the play, our naval attaché tripped Ambassador Leitao and he broke the ambassador's leg! I volunteered to drive him back into Moscow (fifteen miles or so) to see our embassy doctor, Alex Davidson. In real pain, he gritted his teeth and reassured me that while it really hurt, when the press in Brazil reported that the Brazilian ambassador had broken his leg in a *futbol* (soccer) game, he would be an instant hero!

Davidson set his leg nicely. Davidson was playing, unbeknownst to most of us, a key role in handling the defection in place of KGB colonel Oleg Penkovsky—arguably the most important CIA/British MI6 espionage victory in the entire Cold War.

The Argentines, Mexicans, and Uruguayans were equally cooperative, though not as well staffed. It is noteworthy that the Soviets used Uruguay as their "base-camp" for activities throughout Latin America. While Uruguay was represented in Moscow by one very pleasant diplomat (who spoke little Russian) the Soviet embassy in Montevideo, Uruguay had 113 accredited diplomats. They traveled freely throughout Latin America, taking advantage of Uruguay's relaxed posture on reciprocity.

Soviet efforts in Latin America were sparse. With the exception of Cuba, where Castro was determined to be accepted as a Communist and an ally of Moscow, the hemisphere-wide offensive yielded little. Ecuador was in continuing unrest, but Soviet efforts there were not decisive. To everyone's surprise, however, a self-proclaimed Marxist, Carlos Julio Arosemana Monroy, was elected president. In response, Moscow moved in with military assistance and promptly invited this new ally for a state visit in Moscow. Agitprop material trumpeted this new advance for "international socialism" and his visit was given extensive coverage. However, after a dinner and tour of Soviet achievements, what does one do with the president of Ecuador? On his final night, his Spanish-speaking KGB "minders" took him to dinner at the Sovyetskaya Hotel, the official foreign guest hotel in Moscow. The Sovyetskaya was just a little less seedy than Moscow's other hotels, but did serve rather better food than most.

Because of this distinction, I also went to the Sovyetskaya for dinner that same night, unaware that the KGB was fêting Arosemana there. Our group was having a farewell dinner for my closest colleague, Frank Meehan, who was on his way back to Berlin. We had also invited our mutual British friends, the Fretwells. As fate would have it, we were seated directly next to Arosemana's party. After cocktails—multi-vodkas and caviar—it dawned on us that Arosemana was next to us. He obviously was bored to death and his KGB handlers had run out of things to talk about by the time he had had several vodkas.

The evening became a total disaster for the KGB officers when Mary Fretwell—a gorgeous woman who was fluent in Spanish (her father had been a businessman in the Philippines when she was a child)—leaned over and inquired of Arosemana how he liked Moscow in her excellent Spanish. Arosemana promptly stood up and moved over to join us at our table, next to Mary! We had a great time; both Frank and I also spoke Spanish. His KGB escorts repeatedly urged him to leave with them.

Japan's embassy was also very professional, with several language officers, including a "fisheries officer" who was the only Allied diplomat observing this important Soviet industry. Our embassy staffs were very close, aided by the fact that the Japanese ambassador was also a graduate of the Harvard Russian studies program.

And, we had valuable individual friendships with the U.S.-educated Ghanaian ambassador, a Sudanese military attaché, and others.

Given the strict controls on our contact with the Russian people, the relationships with allied third-world embassies and the press corps enhanced our information and evaluations of the Moscow and the Soviet regime. I had to become quite inventive in our social activities, and I never missed a chance to find athletic activities. The *dacha* soccer game was unique, but I did find ways to stay in shape, and in the process develop tighter bonds with my diplomatic colleagues, and occasionally Soviet athletes. For example, the Indian embassy had a squash court—unheated, but a squash court. We put together a small group of racquets devotees, including the Indian first secretary and his deputy, two

Britishers, two Australians, and myself, and played Sunday mornings. Often it would be below zero weather and the court was really cold. We would arrive all bundled up with a bottle of cognac, take a swig and then start; shedding clothes as we heated up. The squash got better and better as the cognac flowed, and by the end we would all be in shorts and t-shirts! Great fun. In the process we would learn a lot about what the Soviets were trying to entice out of our Indian friends.

We also were able to play tennis on the Soviet courts under Dynamo soccer stadium and came to know several Soviet tennis enthusiasts. Tennis, at that time, was a very limited sport in the USSR (in contrast to today when Soviet stars dominate world tennis) and these young Soviet players were eager to play with us, try our racquets, and learn more about the game.

Basketball provided us with a third opportunity. Our petition to the Foreign Ministry to rent a court at Moscow University once a week was approved. And after a few weeks of playing amongst ourselves, university students who were playing on adjacent courts started drifting over; soon we had a group that was half Russian and some excellent games. Eventually we had matches between our embassy team and a team from TASS, the official Soviet newswire service, and a Moscow University team. In these circumstances the conversation flowed and their curiosity overcame their caution, lubricated by our sweat and vodka!

The Press Corps—Another Valuable Resource

Along with the productive and gratifying personal ties with our diplomatic colleagues, the bond we had with Western press representatives in Moscow was equally valuable. BibliographyOnce again, because of the high priority given to a Moscow dateline, the Western press corps was comprised of outstanding men and women, many of whom have gone on to TV anchor-stardom. As in all Western activities in Moscow, the Soviets maintained a large string of journalists in Washington, New York (to "cover the UN"), and Western capitals. We suspected and now know, thanks to several Soviet defectors, including Penkovsky, that most TASS (wire service) and other Soviet journalists were in fact KGB agents, an access Moscow valued.

Thus, on a reciprocal basis, several U.S. papers and networks, as well as British, French, Italian, and German media outlets had "Moscow offices." And, as in the case of the diplomatic corps, these journalists were often very special. ! There were several who had historic ties and unique access as a result. Marvin Kalb, of CBS (who wrote the *Forward* to this book), had a graduate degree in Russian studies and both he and his wife Madie spoke excellent Russian. Henry Shapiro, chief of the three-person UPI bureau had survived in Moscow for twenty years. NBC TV stars Frank Burgholzer and John Chancellor, as well as Pat Ferguson of the *Baltimore Sun* and Seymour Topping (subsequently managing editor of the *New York Times*), were matched by the education and quality of their British, French, and Italian colleagues. And as a group, with their distinct access and contacts with Soviet officials who were in charge of controlling the Western press in Moscow, they gave us insights into this key aspect of the Soviet regime.

Journalists were exposed to the same KGB pressures as we were, and did not enjoy the protection we had as accredited diplomats. They were assisted by the knowledge that should they be abused or expelled, the U.S. government would immediately retaliate against a Soviet TASS reporter in the U.S. Notwithstanding this limited immunity, they were constantly under pressure—and rarely, but occasionally, compromised. A *London Times* reporter and a *Time* magazine reporter both became entangled, compromised, and stayed on in Moscow. Valuable to us, again for their insights, even though they were sadly entrapped. The UPI bureau enjoyed a unique advantage over its competitors in that Henry Shapiro had been in Moscow for more than twenty years. One of Shapiro's team, a very bright woman named Aline Mosby, was a victim of one of the KGB's most flagrant actions: meeting with students, someone drugged her coffee; she was taken to an "official" drying-out station and photographed before being freed. Shapiro, determined to protect his superior access, discouraged the expected outburst of outrage about this treatment, and his colleagues reluctantly agreed to mute their coverage.

Shapiro's team also included Nick Daniloff, whose grandfather had been a famous revolutionary, who was banished by the Czar to Siberia in 1825. Nick's unique historic tie opened a rich vein of access until he was arrested by the KGB on a cooked-up charge of espionage. He was released after high-level U.S. interventions. His book *Of Spies and Spokesmen* about his adventures provides a fascinating insight into the KGB paranoia about "relationships" between Westerners and Soviets. Shapiro's obvious determination not to ruffle Soviet feathers worked in terms of his reach into the system, but also made the embassy hold a certain reservation about his reporting, which seemed to sometimes serve Moscow's ends. We had no such concerns about Daniloff and Mosby, who were very valuable partners for us.

Beyond Ed Stevens of *Time*, Ralph Parker of the *London Times*, and Shapiro's special access, we also met the most extreme case of a Westerner who had been co-opted: Wilfred Burchett, an Australian Communist sympathizer who had covered the Korean War from the North Korean side. He was the author of the canard that U.S. forces had used germ warfare in the Korean War. This "story" was seized on by Moscow and Pyongyang to launch a major propaganda campaign. Burchett was widely considered a KGB-controlled agent by the small Western community, but also made himself interesting by providing "inside information" about Kremlin politics—obviously directed, but intriguing.

However, with those few exceptions, the Western (and especially the U.S.) press corps were invaluable partners and considered very much family by the U.S. embassy. Several remain among my closest friends today. All of this illustrates

162

that in spite of the KGB's massive efforts to seal us off from the real world of the USSR, and its efforts to penetrate and influence other embassies, we were able to reach into that sad society and learn a great deal about it. It is fair to say that although we and our Western colleagues recognized the threat that the nuclear-armed Soviet Union posed to us all, it was, at bottom, an empire built on sand; thus validating the wisdom of our "containment" policy.

As noted in earlier chapters, visits by congressmen – CODELS—were demanding but also offered excellent opportunities for us to interact with local officials who hosted the delegations. Above all, such a visit provided us with an in-depth opportunity to impress and befriend the senators and congressmen. During our tour in Moscow, I had two excellent CODEL visits. Senator Jack Javits (R-NY) and his wife Marian arrived for a four-day visit. We went to special pains to impress the Soviet Foreign Ministry with the influential role Javits had in Congress. He was a senior Republican member of the Senate Foreign Relations Committee and had been particularly active on U.S.-Soviet relations. Highly respected in Congress and at the White House, he was perhaps the most effective Congressional voice on the plight of Soviet Jews. He was also, as Kissinger once described him, "the fastest brain in Congress." His wife, on the other hand, was a handful! An active player in New York society and entertainment circles, she told me that people often confused her for Jacqueline Kennedy. She made a splash at Moscow's fanciest restaurant when she took the floor during a musical interlude to demonstrate the new rage in New York, "the twist"!

Javits himself was a truly effective visitor and effectively presented the U.S. position on Berlin and Southeast Asia to Soviet Foreign Minister, Anotoly Gromyko, and other Soviet officials. He became a valuable friend for me and on my subsequent assignment as Kissinger's man with Congress, Javits was of inestimable help to us.

My second memorable CODEL was an outstanding three-man group from the House of Representatives: Congressman Al Quie of Minnesota, Charles Goodell of New York, and John Brademas of Indiana. Again we had valuable contributions from them in their official meetings. All three were very well informed and influential "members." Quie went on to become governor of Minnesota; Goodell became a senator and active member of the Senate Foreign Relations Committee; and John Brademas was one of the most influential leaders in the House. He became chancellor of New York University. "C" and I entertained all three one night with our British colleagues, John and Mary Fretwell, and our French friend Jacques Andreani. During a great evening at the Aragvi restaurant (Georgian food) and after several vodkas, the congressmen began to tease us because we had made a point of pointing out to them that we were always followed by KGB officers. In the relaxed atmosphere of the Aragvi, they found it hard to believe that we lived under surveillance. However, after dinner we accepted John and Mary's invitation to visit their apartment and drove off, the three congressmen with me. En route, I became slightly confused and ended up going one block the wrong way down a one-way street. Out of nowhere we immediately found ourselves blocked front and rear by two Soviet cars, confronted by obviously KGB officers who inspected our documents in a gruff manner before allowing us to proceed to Fretwell's apartment, a block away. Skepticism about surveillance ended!

Exploring the USSR

One of my responsibilities in the embassy was to chair the interagency "travel program." Although we were very restricted in our ability to travel, officially the Soviets maintained that only 25% of the USSR was "closed" to foreign travel. In fact, they virtually closed about 50% of the USSR by travel requests from foreign embassies on transparent grounds, such as "there are no hotel rooms available at this time." We worked to maximize trips by embassy staff, convinced that a realistic picture of Soviet conditions was essential to our ability to evaluate Soviet power and attitudes. We mapped out the "open" areas we were supposed to be able to visit and sent teams of embassy officers—diplomats and defense attachés alike—across as much of the USSR as we could. While the Soviet's security forces would have preferred practically no travel in the USSR, they were equally interested in seeing as much as they could of the U.S. and NATO countries in Europe. Then we played real hard-ball in terms of strict reciprocity. If the Ministry rejected a request for one of our travel plans, we immediately had the State Department reject a Soviet request in Washington.

In spite of Soviet limitations and harassment, we did learn a lot of strategically important information and a great deal about popular discontent within the Soviet population.

I personally had two unforgettable trips while in Moscow, as part of our travel program. We always travelled in pairs to minimize KGB efforts to entrap us.

One special trip was a rail visit via Leningrad (St. Petersburg) to Murmansk, the terminal port city above the Arctic Circle where our massive lend-lease material was shipped to counter German U-Boat attacks during World War II. Murmansk was a dreary, dirty city with a miserable hotel and a very active port. My colleague and I walked the city, visited the port facilities, noting several Soviet submarines, and called on the mayor. We retired to our hotel and went down for dinner. Miserable food and a lot of drunken Soviet diners. As we left to go out for a walk, one diner who seemed particularly drunk came up, embraced me, and planted a sloppy kiss on my face. He exclaimed that we looked like Americans and he had to thank us for our support during the war. "We would not have won without your Dodge trucks!" The next day we went to a local barbershop for a sort of haircut. While sitting in the chair, we noticed the razor-strop was stamped with a big "Made in USA" imprint. The barber admitted, with tears in his eyes, that the U.S. "had saved us" in the war.

The train trip to Murmansk ran through what had been part of Finland prior to the Soviet invasion of Finland in 1940. It was remarkable for the fact that here, fifteen years after the war ended, what clearly had been "Scandinavian neat" productive farms were still in ruins.

My good friend and WWII paratrooper, Tom Tuch, and I made a long trip through Alma Ata (then the capital of the Kazakh Republic), Frunze (then the capital of Kyrgyzstan), Odessa (the Black Sea port), Kishinev (capital of the Autonomous Republic of Moldova), and Lviv (in northern Ukraine). Each republic had its own historic significance.

Alma Ata was a run-down, but still appealing town with unique architecture and filled with apple orchards. It is replaced as capital today by a new, singularly unattractive city at Astana.

Frunze was a grim town with no architectural interest. It was home to a large collection of German settlers (found throughout the USSR) who as *Volksdeutsch* had been part of a significant expansion effort during Czarist Russian days. We called on the editor of the German language local paper, who was touched by our German language and remarkably candid about how miserable conditions were in Frunze. We walked in the main square still adorned with a massive statue of Stalin (Khrushchev had denounced Stalin only five years earlier). We also took the opportunity to pluck a handful of pine needles for our defense attachés. It seems that pine needles absorb nuclear fallout and a major Soviet nuclear base was some fifty miles north of Frunze.

Odessa was a run-down but beautiful city built on the Black Sea coast during Catherine the Great's rule by a French architect. The cascading steps down to the shore remain an architectural gem today. Odessa was also a principal center for Russian Jews. We visited the local temple and had several interesting talks with religious figures who were intrigued by Hans "Tom" Tuch's Berlin background. While enjoying the sea-coast we also had a chance to observe Soviet submarines and a cruiser tied up at the port, of interest to our defense attachés.

Kishinev and Lviv were of less interest. Kishinev was a forlorn city with Stalinist architecture. Bored, we decided to try and recapture some of the area's checkered history; under Orthodox European rule for centuries, it became part of Romania after World War I, then was occupied by the Germans in World War II, and finally gobbled up by the Soviets after the war. On a whim, we walked out to the cemetery at the edge of town. Lo and behold, reflecting Kishinev's bitter history, it was clearly divided up into Ottoman, Romanian, German, and Soviet sections; the latter distinguished by the awful headstones that featured tractor steering wheels instead of religious symbols. It was a particularly sweet moment to observe our "KGB tails" scurrying around the graves, no doubt wondering what in hell we were up to!

The Espionage War: The Great Prize

The blanket KGB control program described above was a dominant psychological reality in our lives. Any sign of fragility in personal behavior was likely to be seized upon to attempt to seduce the foreigner and co-opt him—be it the wandering eye of the French ambassador or our young nanny. While we looked upon fleeting friendships with Soviets via basketball games as chances to gain an insight into the closed Soviet society, the KGB saw these meetings as chances to mount a "provocation" to compromise us. In fact, the non-Communist country embassies were all locked in a game with the KGB that devoted thousands of officers to the contest.

Within this all-encompassing struggle, there was a deadly serious project underway while we were in Moscow that most of us were unaware of: the greatest strategic espionage coup of the Cold War, the incredibly successful recruitment of GRU colonel Igor Penkovsky. (See *Penkovsky Papers* in the Bibliography.)

Truly significant intelligence operations in the Cold War were few; Penkovsky stands above all others for our side. On the Soviet side of the ledger, obviously, compromise of French ambassador Dejean was a coup, but probably of less value than the successful recruitment of the Swedish defense attaché, Colonel Stig Wennerstrom. The Swedish colonel is a clear example of KGB sophistication. Reeled in, not by money or women, Wennerstrom was recruited by exploiting his ego. KGB operations persuaded the colonel that he could play an historic role in preserving peace by providing the Soviet Union with critical information about "the aggressive plans" of NATO. Sweden, not a NATO member, was regarded by NATO members, including the United States, as an unofficial NATO member and received extensive briefings, stimulated by the hope that Sweden would, in turn, initially join NATO. Wennerstrom's contributions while in Moscow (prior to my arrival) were limited. They became valuable, however, when he was transferred to Washington as defense attaché, where he continued to be wooed as an unspoken but valuable ally. Eventually uncovered by Swedish authorities, he was convicted and jailed in a high-profile case that, in fact, resulted in stepped-up Swedish cooperation with the U.S. and NATO. The Wennerstrom case is described in detail in the book *Agent of Choice* by Ian Hamilton.

Penkovsky provides the opposite side of that coin. Again, it was ego, fueled by disgust with Khrushchev's erratic adventurist activities, and total disillusion with the Soviet regime's squandering of post-World War II opportunities to build a peaceful, prosperous Soviet Union.

Igor Penkovsky had been a decorated combat tank battalion commander in World War II, and became the protégé of General (later Marshal) Varentsov. In the 1958-1962 period, Varentsov rose to command all Soviet missile forces, which provided Penkovsky with access to information about critical nuclear forces of the Soviet Union. Penkovsky was also descended from a line of Soviet general officers. This elevated "golden boy" position was enhanced by his marriage to the general's daughter and his subsequent transfer into military intelligence (GRU). In his *Penkovsky Papers*, he describes at length the bitter rivalry between the GRU and the KGB, and the resultant waste of vast resources and dysfunctional performance by the two competing organizations. Penkovsky, in his "Papers," which were acquired by the joint British/U.S. team which "handled" Penkovsky, devotes most of his writings to condemning Khrushchev's adventurism, his proclivity for nuclear brinksmanship, and his rejection of professional military warnings to be cautious. Top Soviet military leaders in whose circles Penkovsky moved were universally alarmed by Khrushchev's nuclear confrontation with the West over Berlin, and his subsequently desperate gamble to place nuclear warheads in Cuba to force the West out of Berlin. Penkovsky was also obsessed by the idea that the West did not begin to appreciate the massive KGB/GRU intelligence network that dominated all Soviet diplomatic missions and press representatives around the world. He was wrong about the latter; we in fact assumed that Soviet "diplomats" and media people were all involved to one degree or another in espionage activities.

Igor Penkovsky was not singled out and then aggressively recruited by the West; he was a "walk-in." Following enhanced training in Moscow, he had been assigned to one of the elite and most choice organizations for espionage activity: the State Committee for Coordination of Security

Research. Combining top scientists with star intelligence officers from both the KGB and GRU, the committee functioned as a full cabinet department. Headed nominally by a renowned scientist named Rudnev, the real power in the committee was Dzhermen Gvishiani, the husband of Soviet President Kosygin's daughter. Gvishiani's father had been a KGB general and relative of Stalin's. Thus, Penkovsky came from a general's family, married another general's daughter, attracted the top Soviet missile general as a "sponsor" (based on their World War II combat experience), and graduated into the state Committee dominated by President Kosygin's son-in-law. In short, a perfect pedigree.

The Committee was created and evolved in form from Lenin's pre-war project to steal industrial technology from the West. In a subsequent assignment as assistant director of the U.S. Information Agency, I had an early defector from the "committee" in post-war years, Alexander Barmine, also a KGB "general." Barmine tutored me at length about Moscow's massive efforts to catch up with the West industrially by stealing industrial technology. The Committee left no stone unturned in this quest; each Soviet embassy had a section of "Committee" officers (usually KGB and GRU officers), no international trade fair went uncovered, individual trade missions sent abroad were first and foremost designed to collect critical industrial information.

It was in this latter function that Penkovsky first came to travel to Europe. Before long he was recognized for his outstanding trade mission work and became a regular leader of such missions. The head of military intelligence General Ivan Serov, who had previously headed the KGB, personally called Penkovsky to commend him for his work. At the same time, as he travelled in the West, he also was increasingly impressed by Western industrial superiority, and by the standard of living in the West. Finally, he gradually was captivated by the easy freedom that he observed and enjoyed in his dealings with British businessmen. The more he experienced the West, the more he capitalized his frustration and slowly but surely, his sense of hostility toward Khrushchev—a feeling that in his "papers," he insisted, was widespread among senior Soviet military officers.

At one of these trade fair events, Penkovsky came into contact with a (legitimate) British export-import businessman, Greville Wynne. Actively pursuing sales of British industrial electrical equipment to Moscow, Wynne periodically visited the USSR. As his acquaintance with Wynne grew, Penkovsky was also reaching the end of his patience with his own regime. Wynne had, in the meantime, established contact with British intelligence and described his increasingly warm friendship with the GRU colonel. When Penkovsky made his fateful decision to turn, and actively work against Khrushchev and his "dangerous" policies, Wynne was ready. On Penkovsky's trade mission to London in the spring of 1961, he told Wynne he wanted to meet with "appropriate" British officials to collaborate with them. Wynne arranged a meeting for Penkovsky at a London hotel where he was introduced to British and American officials (Rory Chisholm and Alex Davidson) who in fact were both intelligence officers assigned to their respective embassies in Moscow. Penkovsky had already provided through Wynne some preliminary written material that persuaded both the British and Americans of his access to critical strategic information about Khrushchev's intentions, Soviet missile capabilities, and dissent among Soviet military leaders. Penkovsky had several additional such meetings while in London where he was trained in the use of Minox cameras and provided with a list of priority information. He was able to move freely in London because of his leadership role in the Soviet trade union and recognition by the KGB and GRU officials in the Soviet embassy that he was indeed a "golden boy" within their service.

Arriving back in Moscow, Penkovsky embarked on a historically unmatched espionage run, providing critical information to the U.S. and UK about the capabilities, production, and mode of operation of the nuclear missile forces of the USSR. Through his family connections and favored position within the GRU, he had virtually unfettered access to this information. In a bizarre but highly effective operation, he would photograph this information on his Minox and then walk in the park and give candy to a child who was being pushed in a pram in the park by Janet Chisholm! For almost two years, 1961 to 1962, he carried on this activity. Managed on the ground by British officer Chisholm and his American partner, Alex Davidson, the program was virtually flawless. Wynne revisited Moscow to purchase Soviet industrial equipment, but had really fulfilled his role. Eventually Wynne was picked up by KGB agents, recorded tapes of Wynne's conversations with Penkovsky were discovered, and the trail followed back to Penkovsky and they were both arrested. On May 7, 1963, a show trial was held at the Supreme Court of the USSR in Moscow. After four days, the two were convicted. Wynne, who really was a legitimate businessman, was released in an exchange for an imprisoned Soviet agent in London in 1964. Penkovsky was shot. The trial was "public" to allow the regime to portray how effective their counter-intelligence efforts were. However, it also posed a serious problem for them because Penkovsky was so tied into prominent military families and President Kosygin. The public trial was therefore very awkward for the Soviet authorities. They went to great lengths to fabricate an image of Penkovsky as a playboy, and to insist that he had no information of importance.

The Penkovsky project was clearly the most important espionage victory for the West, perhaps ever. His information enabled the U.S. to accurately assess Soviet nuclear weapon capabilities and deployment modes of operation. It confirmed that the Soviet Union lagged behind the West in quality and accuracy. And, historically most important according to a friend of mine who chaired the joint-agency photo-intelligence unit, he provided critical information to us as Khrushchev's dangerous initiative to place nuclear missiles on Cuba unfolded.

Penkovsky's operation occurred while we were in Moscow. And, to the credit of our CIA team in the embassy and their British colleagues, we never knew at the time. We did know our people involved, but not that they were "intelligence" officers. Rory Chisholm and Janet, his wife, were social friends, and Alex Davidson was an excellent general practitioner who served as well as the embassy doctor!

Soviet espionage efforts in the U.S. and around the world were indeed massive. And some KGB recruitment initiatives were costly for us: George Blake in Berlin who cost the lives of dozens of Western agents in East Germany; subsequently, CIA officer Aldrich Ames who "fingered" several CIA agents for Moscow; and FBI agent Hansen who provided Moscow with a stream of information about FBI activities. But none of them produced the critical strategic intelligence that altered the course of the Cold War. Penkovsky was the prize!

Daily Life in Moscow: A Struggle for Average Citizens

Penkovsky was a dramatic critic of the depressed state of the Soviet economy as well as the most important source of military intelligence. In his "papers" he writes with passion about the inefficient squandering of resources and wasteful military equipment spending while the life of Soviet citizens, as he described it, remained grim. In fact, by any standard, it *was* grim!

In the harsh climate of the USSR, housing, medical care, food supplies, and clothing were hard to find, and of shoddy quality. In 1961-1962, there was an average of eight adults per toilet in Moscow, which enjoyed by far the best living standard in the USSR. My family "enjoyed" a combination of two apartments in the run-down, but relatively opulent apartment building at 45 Leninsky Prospekt. An average of ten Soviet citizens occupied similar spaces in the two "non-foreign" wings of "45." The building had been built, along with a dozen similar units, along Leninsky Prospekt in 1958-1960. The complete absence of any incentive in the Soviet economic system produced an equal disinterest in any quality control over construction. Thus windows did not close truly, doors hung irregularly, toilets were unreliable, and both shower tiles and exterior brickwork regularly fell off—bad enough in any weather, but in Moscow's sub-zero weather a real disaster. We met some of these challenges with embassy supplied duct tape and putty rolls—items that were not available on the Moscow market.

An incident in our courtyard one afternoon brought home to us just how severe the cost of this poverty was. Our boys often played soccer on the bare ground of the courtyard, frequently with Soviet children from the other wings of the building. One day, on hearing a ruckus, I went out on our sixth-floor balcony and from afar witnessed a tragic event; there stood a totally drunk Soviet father beating his eight or ten-year-old mercilessly. After some five minutes of this sickening scene, some of the boy's friends had had enough.

They jumped the man, dragged him to the ground, and beat him until he was bloody. The boys then ran off, home to their apartments, with their poor friend. One sees many disturbing scenes living around the world; poverty, filth, illness, and even starvation. Somehow this event, for us, was especially disturbing. Life in the Soviet Union, after two devastating wars and Stalin's brutal regime, was almost unbearable in many ways. But, on reflection, we considered this courtyard incident as especially revealing: there was no privacy in daily Soviet life. Not only coping with toilet traffic jams, but on average two or three couples lived in a shabby room divided by hanging old blankets and one stove. Alcoholism was (and reportedly still is) rampant. From where we sat in Moscow, it appeared to us that Soviets drank themselves into a stupor, as the courtyard father did, to achieve internal "privacy." Hard to believe that a nation that produced world class musicians, ballet companies, writers, *and* a world-class nuclear weapons force could be so backward and incapable of providing minimum standards for daily life. It is true that the totality of Stalin's police state control allowed him and his government to allocate its resources without taking popular needs into account. But it was difficult to believe the totality of the control.

Shopping for food in Moscow was also a grim process. Stores (*magaziniy*) were broken down into product categories. There was a meat store, a bakery, a vegetable store, and a dairy store—sounds fine except there was rarely any meat that we would consider edible. Other than potatoes, which were irregularly available, no vegetables were available except turnips throughout the eight-month winter. Milk ran out by noon, and fish was occasionally available in cans. Only the bakery was appealing. Excellent multigrain bread at very low cost was almost always on the shelves.

Gallows humor was widespread in Moscow, especially about food shortages. While we were in Moscow the Soviets successfully launched Gherman Titov into space. Predictably they made a major propaganda event out of this success. The joke which swept Moscow intellectual circles at the time described a radio broadcast back to Earth by Titov. Asked by a Moscow radio "anchor" when he would return, Titov replied 48 hours and 30 minutes. Titov then asked the anchor whether he could speak with his mother. The reply was "we can't be sure when she will be back— perhaps tomorrow—she is looking for potatoes!"

Given this shortage-dominated process, black markets were vigorous and expensive. It was noteworthy that these semi-legal operations were often run by Chechens and other "Orientals," as Russians commonly called them. Not surprisingly, this activity was reflected in the strong racist hostility of most Russians for these "foreigners," reflective of the historic anti-Semitism directed at Jews in czarist Russia. It is striking that this prejudice remains in today's Russia where the richest of Russian and Ukrainian oligarchs are reviled as Jewish and Moscow's violent suppression of Chechen efforts for independence is universally popular among the Russian population.

One aspect of daily Soviet life that we found charming was to be found on occasional street corners in the summer: the neighborhood *kvas* wagon. These "wagons" were large tanks on wheels that held sweet fermented fruit juice. An old woman with one glass and one grubby towel would wipe out the glass and draw a *kvas* for five kopecks and serve it to the children, who would come running when she arrived. "Good Humor" truck it was not, but it seemed to serve the same purpose. The *kvas* wagons also reflected the universal disregard for the most basic hygiene.

Between alcoholism, universal cigarette smoking, and lack of hygiene, it is no surprise that the average life-span of Russian men even today is twenty years shorter than that of Americans.

Berlin and Cuba Heat Up

The pressure on Khrushchev to act on Berlin became unbearable in the fall of 1960. The outpouring of East Germans into Berlin, en route to the West, became a flood. In the month of July 1960, over 30,000 refugees fled the German Democratic Republic. Ulbricht's regime was losing control. The sense of popular resignation of the downtrodden East German population was converting into outright hostility. Ulbricht (post-Soviet era documents reveal) became more frantic and demanding that Moscow had to act. He insisted that Khrushchev follow through on his 1958 threat to sign a separate peace treaty with the Soviet-sponsored GDR and turn over control of GDR borders in

Berlin and with West Germany to Ulbricht's forces, backed by the massive Soviet occupation force in theGDR.

While Khrushchev was indeed erratic and prone to gambling, Western efforts to persuade him that we would not abandon our rights and position in West Berlin gave him pause. The developments in the "German Democratic Republic" as the refugee exodus continued pointed to some sort of desperation action by Ulbricht's regime with Soviet support. Post-Cold War Soviet documents confirm that Ulbricht was barraging Moscow with demands that Khrushchev act on his threat to unilaterally turn over control of GDR borders, especially with Berlin, to GDR forces that could block the refugee outpouring.

Having witnessed first-hand the flood of refugees and the impact of the loss of critical professionals, especially doctors, it was increasingly clear to me that some form of Soviet blockade was inevitable. In scouring Soviet public statements in the press, in "public lectures" and individual reports from our press friends, foreign embassy staff (especially our Indian friends), and the borderline journalists who were used by the Soviets to promote their line, a steady buildup in Moscow's threatening over Berlin was clear. I prepared a full review report of the "evidence" and predicted that Moscow had to act soon to stop the hemorrhage. It was our view that the egress route for East Germans would be blocked, probably by creating a barrier around the entire city of Berlin— East and West—thereby avoiding confronting us over our four-power rights in the entire city.

Adding to Khrushchev's frustration and embarrassment over Berlin was the steady deterioration of relations between Beijing and Moscow. Mao was openly critical of Khrushchev's demonization of Stalin and ridiculed Moscow's reluctance to "resolve" the Berlin question. Chinese attacks on Moscow for abandoning Stalinist policies were conducted at first through Beijing's puppet regime in Albania. Daily public calls for firm action against the West in Berlin and denunciations of Khrushchev's criticism of Stalin's cult of personality began to appear in the Albanian media. Led by a hard-line Stalinist, Enver Hoxha, Albania openly broke with Moscow early in the 1950s and was embraced by Mao. While not generally noted in Western media, our Chinese specialists—especially Culver Gleysteen in our embassy—seized on the "Albanian" role to confirm that Beijing and Moscow's alliance was unraveling.

Meanwhile, U.S focus on Castro sharpened. In October 1960 the U.S. imposed an embargo on trade with Cuba and ended the tentative policy of "trying to do business" with the Castro regime. By April of 1961 it had become obvious that Castro's revolution was not simply a popular revolt against the corrupt, U.S.-supported Batista dictatorship. To Moscow's surprise, Fidel Castro had announced to the world that his new regime was "Communist." Under heavy domestic pressure from the Cuban diaspora (largely educated Cuban refugees from Castro's revolution), in April, President Kennedy launched the ill-fated Bay of Pigs invasion, which had been prepared by President Eisenhower's administration. Its dismal failure stunned the new Kennedy administration and had a major effect on them as they faced Khrushchev's blusters over Berlin.

The Bay of Pigs stands as a dramatic example of intelligence gone wrong. There was virtually no support for our invasion among Cubans, and without a sympathetic popular reaction, the adventure was doomed from the beginning. It was also a clear case of the danger of allowing diaspora populations in the U.S. to shape U.S. foreign policy—a problem that continues to plague us in the twenty-first century. In this case, the invasion was ardently supported by the Cuban refugee population in Florida that had cultivated key members of Congress and the administrations of Eisenhower and Kennedy.

Our failure at the Bay of Pigs was a serious embarrassment for the U.S. presence in Moscow as well. Khrushchev and Soviet colleagues were reinforced in their dangerous underestimation of our commitments, especially in Berlin. The Soviet population and Soviet military leadership began to think that perhaps Khrushchev was right; the U.S. had feet of clay. Needless to say, our Western friends and allies in Moscow were deeply concerned—to virtually all of them, U.S. power was perceived as the rock on which their own security was based.

Khrushchev Confronts Kennedy in Vienna

President Eisenhower had been scheduled to meet Khrushchev in Paris in June to attempt an overreaching agreement on nuclear weapons and reset the dial in the U.S.-Soviet relationship across the board. The Paris meeting followed and Khrushchev's visit to the U.S., which had initiated a widespread hope that the dangers of continued confrontation of the world's nuclear powers could be redirected. The Paris summit was suddenly aborted when a U.S.-U.2. flight over the Soviet Union was brought down by a Soviet missile. Khrushchev demanded that President Eisenhower publicly apologize and blame the penetration of Soviet air-space on rogue military operations. "Ike" refused to do so and Khrushchev cancelled the summit meeting.

As Kennedy became president, there was genuine hope that he could revive the summit process and resume talks to ease pressures with Moscow. Once again the plans to develop a dialogue with Moscow were threatened—this time by our abject disaster at the Bay of Pigs. Our embassy obviously had reservations about a Vienna meeting on the heels of our defeat in Cuba, but the tension over Berlin made it essential that Kennedy meet Khrushchev to attempt to defuse the very dangerous confrontation in Berlin.

On April 24, 1962, Khrushchev, according to now available Soviet records, arrived in Vienna reinforced by our Cuba failure, determined to force the U.S. and its allies to begin abandoning our Western outpost. The meeting went badly. Khrushchev bullied, blustered, and reiterated his insistence that we acknowledge that our post-war rights in Berlin had expired and East German control of access to the city would take place—renewing the ultimatum first laid down by Khrushchev in November 1958.

President Kennedy, according to eye-witness accounts, was shaken by Khrushchev's performance. However, at the end, he firmly defended our position in Berlin, but included several indications that he would like to find ways to negotiate access issues and what Khrushchev called "Cold War activities" in Berlin. The free radio in West Berlin, RIAS, was a powerful voice throughout the Soviet zone of Germany, and Radio Free Europe and Radio Liberty, CIA-controlled stations, also used Berlin as one base of operation to penetrate the Warsaw Pact nations and USSR itself.

Encouraged by his "victory" at Vienna, Khrushchev stepped up the pressure on Berlin. A growing pattern of "incidents" were directed at Allied access to Berlin. Allied convoys from West Germany were harassed as they moved on the autobahn to Berlin. Air access was tightened as the Soviets insisted that Allied aircraft were restricted to the narrow corridors—always limited in width—to fly only between 8,000 and 10,000 feet. MIG fighters tracked the Allied flights closely and occasionally feigned attacks. The most dramatic of these air corridor harassments occurred on April 12, when a Soviet MIG closed in on a British military transport plane carrying the British ambassador, Sir Kit Steele, and actually brushed the wing of the British plane. There was only superficial damage, but it was clearly that only by a matter of inches that Steele's plane avoided crashing. In Moscow, the British ambassador, Sir Frank Roberts, called Ambassadors Thompson and Dejean and agreed that we had to protest immediately in the most dramatic terms. My British and French colleagues (Fretwell and Andreani) and I drafted a very direct and threatening note that was delivered within two hours to Gromyko. Our respective capitals had only time to instruct us to protest, the language was left to us. It was heartwarming that the Soviet reply was an "apology," and Lord Home complimented us on the "directness" of our note. The affair was illustrative of the complete understanding our three embassies had achieved as the Berlin crisis mounted, cementing our bonds.

Any sense of reassurance that Khrushchev was becoming more predictable was blown away on July 2; at a Kremlin reception that day Khrushchev cornered British ambassador Sir Frank Roberts in a bizarre threatening exchange, and reiterated that the Western position in Berlin was no longer legally valid. He ridiculed the addition of another NATO division. He warned Roberts that "only six of his H bombs would be enough to annihilate the British Isles, and nine would take care of France."

Given the blatant threat to Sir Frank, Khrushchev's decision, two days later, to personally attend our July 4th Independence Day party was a dramatic reminder of Khrushchev's unpredictable behavior. We were astounded when he led a large delegation of top Soviet officials to attend the annual event at Spaso House, Ambassador Thompson's residence in Moscow. His gesture was unprece-

186

dented. For decades, the July 4th reception was largely ignored by Soviet officials. A token, mid-level handful of representatives from the Ministry of Foreign Affairs would appear briefly.

This year, however, Khrushchev personally attended along with the fabled wise-man Bolshevik, Anastas Mikoyan, Foreign Minister Gromyko, General Serov, chief of OGPU (military intelligence), and several other ministers, generals and Politburo members. The arrival scene was truly melodramatic. Khrushchev greeted Tommy and his wife Jane warmly. Then Mikoyan stepped up. Jane, gowned in a low-cut dress reached out and embraced the diminutive old Bolshevik (perhaps five feet tall) and his face disappeared in her bosom. Khrushchev roared with laughter as Mikoyan emerged red-faced.

The Soviet leadership stayed on for more than an hour, giving embassy officials a rare opportunity to talk at length with them. I was particularly intrigued by my chance to engage General Serov (Colonel Penkovsky's boss) who was known *inter alia* as the Butcher of Budapest for his leading role in suppressing the Hungarian revolt in 1956. He was quite engaging and repeated the ultimatum line on Berlin, while I strove to impress on him that the West would *not* surrender its position on Berlin. He listened attentively when I described my two-year Berlin tour and the deterioration of the Ulbricht regime as the GDR population fled west.

Disarmament Negotiations

Meanwhile, Khrushchev authorized opening bilateral talks with the U.S. on disarmament. There had appeared to be basis for agreement on this issue. Khrushchev for more than a year had been ratcheting up his public international campaign on behalf of "general and complete disarmament." The Western allies from the very beginning were dubious about his sincerity and assumed that he was playing a propaganda card only. He knew that the West would never accept a proposition that would leave massive Soviet ground forces in Central Europe (more than 500,000 in the Soviet zone of Germany) while U.S. forces in Germany, which provided the core of NATO, would be required to depart. As this campaign unfolded, Khrushchev refined the Soviet position to agree that Soviet forces would retreat into the USSR but remain poised to threaten Germany while we retreated across the Atlantic. Like the Khrushchev campaign to pose as the champions of anti-colonialism and wars of "national liberation," his General and Complete Disarmament (GCD) campaign was viewed as an attractive propaganda instrument. The continuing growth of nuclear weapons on both sides did in fact frighten the rest of the world, and GCD did achieve a certain resonance.

President Kennedy fully recognized the dangers over the growing accumulation of thousands of nuclear warheads. Kennedy was determined to continue to press every opportunity to reverse this nuclear arms race. When, in spite of the growing crisis over Berlin, Khrushchev agreed to open bilateral talks on disarmament, President Kennedy invited Khrushchev to send Gromyko to Washington to see whether there was a basis for opening arms control negotiation. Kennedy personally met with the principal Soviet arms control negotiator, Valeriy Zorin, Gromyko's deputy. Out of this meeting came agreement to open talks on Moscow. The president sent John J. McCloy at the head of a powerful interagency task force to meet with Zorin and his team on July 17, 1961. The McCloy delegation included "Butch" Fisher as deputy. Fisher was the legal advisor of the State Department and was personally close to President Kennedy. Top weapons systems experts from the Defense Department and Intelligence officials were included.

Since Spike Dubs had just left Moscow, I was assigned to be the embassy officer on the team. We met in the Soviet ministry "guest house" for twelve days—long, laborious and unproductive meetings. No apparent progress. Again surprising all observers, however, Khrushchev suddenly invited McCloy with his wife and daughter (who had accompanied him to Moscow) to Sochi on the Black Sea. At this surprise visit, Khrushchev broke through the stalemated discussions we had had with Zorin to present a full set of basic principles proposal for General and Complete Disarmament. The proposal included a commitment that "both sides realize their resolve that until a treaty on GCD is concluded, they will refrain from acts which may increase international tension ..."

It is quite mind-boggling that Khrushchev would put forward such a proposal, when within weeks he would revive the confrontation over Berlin, replete with threats to use force if necessary. However in retrospect, it fit into the regular pattern of his erratic behavior.

The Berlin Wall Stops the Hemorrhaging

Soviet and East German desperation to deal with the hemorrhaging of refugees from East Germany finally culminated in mid-August. On August 13, 1961, Ulbricht's forces cut off subway traffic between the Soviet sector and West Berlin. Barbed wire began to appear, foot traffic was halted, and the construction of the wall began. Berlin was hermetically divided. The wall skirted an immediate conflagration by running between West Berlin and the Soviet-controlled East Berlin and permitting controlled access by Allied officials into East Berlin. The German population, however, was blocked; the refugee flow was over. A bold and dangerous initiative by Khrushchev, but not unexpected given the collapsing population in East Germany.

In the Western capitals, the Allied governments struggled with how to respond. The Kennedy administration, and the president personally, recognized that the Soviets would inevitably have to stop the refugee explosion. Debate raged. Predictably there were those who argued that Allied forces "had to tear down the barbed wire and growing wall." General Lucius Clay, an advisor to President Kennedy, spoke out publicly to that end. However, it was clear that the three

Allied brigades, some 30,000 troops, would be no match for the Soviets. The Allies denounced the Soviet/GDR action as dangerous and illegal, but acquiesced in its reality.

President Kennedy recognized, however, that the unilateral division of Berlin was a psychological defeat for the U.S. and posed a serious threat to the credibility of the Western position in Berlin. As an immediate response, Kennedy sent a battle group—another brigade of U.S. troops into Berlin. This visible movement of the force over the autobahn corridor did reassure West Berliners and underlined U.S./Allied determination to protect its Berlin position. Kennedy also sent Vice President Lyndon Johnson to Berlin.

Meanwhile, President Kennedy personally directed his advisers to step up work on a plan to draw Khrushchev into a new negotiation about access into Berlin. Khrushchev's repeated harassment of our access and the division of Berlin were heightened by his announcement that he was resuming nuclear testing. Secretary McNamara countered this by announcing the deployment of 40,000 additional U.S. troops to Europe. And President Kennedy decided to send General Lucius Clay, the hero of the Berlin airlift, back to Berlin as his personal envoy. The drumbeat of war-like initiatives was ominous.

Throughout his reign as First Secretary of the Communist Party—and ruler of the USSR—Khrusuchev had proven over and over that he was unpredictable and a gambler.

Therefore, when at the height of the Berlin showdown, reveling in the fact that he had staunched the collapse of the East German regime and the wall had been tolerated by the Western powers, we were relieved, but not shocked, when in October he seemed to relax the pressure on Berlin.

In the tightly managed press in Moscow, the exact language used to describe Soviet policies was handled as scripture. A changed word often reflected serious policy changes. In our embassy we followed the terminology used in *Pravda* and *Izvestia* very carefully. Thus, when I caught the absence of "on that basis" in a lead editorial about Berlin, it was immediately clear that the Soviet insistence since November 1958 that Western rights in Berlin had expired was being dropped. Khrushchev subsequently confirmed this in a public statement, "If Western powers show a willingness to settle the German problem, we shall not insist absolutely in signing a peace treaty [with the GDR] before December 31st, 1961." He lifted the ultimatum that had threatened peace over Berlin for three years!

The reference to "a willingness to settle the Berlin problem" reflected the fact that agreement had been reached by Gromyko in talks with Secretary Rusk and President Kennedy to reactivate talks about Berlin. The stage was set for the historic talks between U.S. ambassador Llewellyn Thompson and Soviet foreign minister Gromyko.

President Kennedy, following the Vienna meeting with Khrushchev, the subsequent construction of the wall in

August, and gradual acquiescence of the West to the division of Berlin, had decided with cautious Allied agreement that the West had to present some new formulation of Western rights in Berlin to Khrushchev in order to validate those rights and define the very dangerous confrontation which Khrushchev had initiated. Negotiations with our British allies quickly found agreement that seeking a new formulation—an International Access Authority (IAA)—was worth pursuing; French president DeGaulle initially was opposed to any negotiations over Western rights; Germany's chancellor Adenauer also opposed the idea initially. However, after intense exchanges, Kennedy won grudging assent to his IAA proposal.

The Berlin Talks

On January 2, 1961, the historic Berlin status talks began at the Soviet Ministry of Foreign Affairs. I accompanied Ambassador Thompson, as the embassy's Berlin specialist. Gromyko was joined by the former Soviet ambassador to Germany, Semyonov, and the ubiquitous translator Viktor Sukhodrov. Gromyko received us warmly in his outer office. He said, in his fluent English, "Tommy, I hope Jane is well," and inquired about my reaction to Moscow, patting me on the back after testing my Russian. We then adjourned to his inner office, where we sat on the couch with a coffee table in front. Gromyko and Semyonov sat in chairs across, with Viktor slightly behind Gromyko. Sukhodrov was an interesting fixture. The son of a Soviet diplomat, he had gone to prep school in both London and Washington. His English was truly fluent. For several years he was at the sides of Khrushchev, Brezhnev, and Andropov, at important conferences.

Ambassador Thompson opened the discussion, presenting the U.S. position according to his instructions from Washington, with his adjustments to emphasize to Gromyko that the first order of business must resolve the question of free Allied access to Berlin. He declared that his instructions were to determine whether there was a basis for negotiation. He concluded his opening remarks by restating that Western rights in Berlin could not unilaterally be abolished by the USSR and warned that threatening the West with physical interference with those rights would be strongly resisted. He then restated that the question confronting us was whether we could find a basis for negotiations so that the situation in Berlin could be handled "without war, which would be devastating to both sides."

Gromyko responded that the points we presented "require serious thought and consideration"; however, he said, he disagreed with our contention that "access" was the main problem. The main problem, he insisted, was a German peace treaty, recognizing the sovereignty of the GDR, in order to "write finish to World War II." It is not possible therefore, to discuss "access" in isolation. He said he had made it clear in his earlier discussion with President Kennedy and Secretary Rusk that if no agreement were possible between us about an inclusive peace treaty to end the state of war, the Soviet Union was prepared to sign a unilateral treaty "with all ensuing consequences for West Berlin and Allied access thereto." Allied power, he continued, would then bear responsibility to make agreements for access with the GDR.

Thompson then reviewed the series of incidents that recently occurred in Berlin that had increased tension and the danger of further incidents. He then introduced the possibility of establishing an international authority responsible for access to Berlin, which would include control over the autobahn route from Helmstedt in the Federal Republic of Germany to Berlin, and air traffic as well. He concluded that such an authority with control over access to all Berlin would be preferable.

Gromyko concluded this first session by restating the Soviet position that the essential element in any resolution would be accepting GDR sovereignty and that any suggestion that East Berlin be included in an access arrangement would be entirely incompatible with GDR sovereignty. He closed by restating that the unacceptability of isolating "access" from the entire West Berlin question and writing a finish to World War II. Gromyko expressed his readiness to continue our talks; "we have much to discuss."

Ambassador Thompson and I then departed. The first meeting had been pleasant in its beginning and business-like in its conclusion. It seemed clear that Gromyko expected to continue and therefore it seemed, in response to our instructions, that there *was* a basis for negotiations.

Beyond agreeing that we should continue the negotiations, Gromyko showed *no* flexibility on the basics of the Soviet campaign to force Western acceptance of GDR sovereignty over Berlin and thereby recognition of the final division of Germany. Their goal to erode and eventually terminate Allied rights in Berlin was unchanged; their continuation of dangerous incidents reflected Khrushchev's frustration and desperation to rid himself "of the bone in my throat," which was how he publicly described Western presence in the middle of the Soviet empire's Western outposts.

But, we felt that our focus on access and our blunt talk of remaining ready to defend it was acknowledged. And the introduction of the concept of an international access authority was not rejected.

In what turned out to be our standard procedure in these talks, we drove back to Spaso House (the ambassador's residence), and then I was driven back to the embassy. I took a secretary with me into our "secure plastic box" and dictated a virtually verbatim account of the meeting, which was made possible by the fact that after I wrote my translated version of Gromyko's comments in Russian Sukhodrov then translated them, which allowed me to refine and connect my own notes. Meanwhile, Tommy prepared his assessment of the meeting by hand at Spaso House. I then returned to

Spaso and he reviewed my verbatim report and asked for my views of his assessment (very flattering for me, especially when he accepted some of my suggested variations). Finally, I was driven back to the embassy with both messages and had them transmitted by "flash" ultra-high frequency immediate cable.

By then I was exhilarated by the drama of the moment, profoundly proud of Tommy, who was remarkably cool throughout the entire affair, and exhausted from the roughly five-hour procedure.

The historic importance of this first meeting was reflected by the intense interest of the Western press, which was waiting at the front entrance of the Soviet Ministry of Foreign Affairs as we exited. A photograph of our departure was front-paged in many U.S. papers (including the *New York Times*) the next morning. It is reproduced on the jacket of this book.

Our embassy colleagues and diplomatic allies were equally caught up in the moment. More than one stiff drink followed. "C" was as exhausted as I, having shared the pressure and exhilaration I experienced.

On January 12, 1962, Gromyko called us in to the Ministry to continue the Berlin negotiation. He opened by reading a lengthy declaration rebutting our insistence that Allied rights in Berlin, produced by quadripartite agreement following victory over Nazi Germany, could not be changed unilaterally by the USSR. He charged again that facts on the ground have changed, sovereign GDR was a reality and Western rights have in fact ended. Gromyko then said that in an effort to resolve this unsustainable problem of West Berlin, he presented a draft proposal to establish a "free city of West Berlin," which would include adding Soviet forces in West Berlin, and provide for a subsequent agreement between the Free City and the GDR, covering access questions.

Ambassador Thompson stated that the Free City concept was *not* acceptable, nor was the idea of adding Soviet troops to the three-power military garrison in West Berlin. "Allied access to Berlin is not and cannot be subject to GDR approval."

Gromyko responded that the Soviet Union did *not* agree that access could be negotiated in isolation from sovereignty of GDR, and that access was not the key question, only one of several issues in resolving the problem of West Berlin. "If you believe we will sign agreements perpetuating your occupation rights, you are wrong."

As the discussion continued in this confrontational tone, Thompson declared that the U.S. government considered the main point of the talks was not to draw a line under World War II, but to avoid World War III. Gromyko, set back by Tommy's blunt warning, concluded that he hoped that once we had studied the documents proposing a free city of Berlin, we would realize that we had been hasty in characterizing them as "a step backwards."

The next day, January 13, we were summoned back to the Foreign Ministry. In sharp contrast to the warm, friendly first meeting and the tense but business-like second meeting, Gromyko received us stony-faced, and immediately launched into a harsh diatribe, attacking the U.S. and its allies for having used West Berlin to incite unrest. He warned that unless the Allies could agree to a Free City of West Berlin, the USSR and others (Warsaw Pact members) would conclude a peace treaty reorganizing the GDR and Western access would then have to be controlled by the GDR. For almost forty minutes he restated the full menu of Soviet contentions that Western rights in Berlin were terminated. Referring to Ambassador Thompson's warning that the Allies were prepared to use force to defend their rights in Berlin, he warned that the USSR could not be threatened by the use of force and any such deterioration was very dangerous and could lead to such things as the incineration of New York City.

Thompson sat quietly, smoking, until Gromyko finally blurted out, "Well, Mr. Ambassador?" Thompson then in a very quiet voice rejected Gromyko's threatening language and added, "I deeply regret you have been required to present such a performance. You know as well as I that if there were to be a nuclear exchange between our two great nations, the Soviet Union would disappear from the face of the earth." We stood to depart.

On February 1, the next formal negotiations took place in the ministry. Ambassador Thompson delivered a memorandum presenting the agreed Western text of an all-Berlin proposal and the proposal for an international access authority. Gromyko replied that he would study our proposals, but that this did not imply any favorable attitudes to those documents.

Gromyko then continued, insisting the proposals to deal with access and create an international authority responsible for access are "not at all realistic." "The Soviet government is strongly opposed to the creation of any international policeman, fee collector, traffic regulator, or any other kind of servant of the Western powers to regulate traffic to West Berlin."

Increasing the threatening tone of his remarks, Gromyko again insisted that a new situation must be established in West Berlin; communications from and to West Berlin, "which are located in GDR territory" cannot ignore GDR sovereignty. He then flatly rejected the legitimacy of Western occupation rights in Berlin; the Western powers by their actions violated Allied agreements and occupation rights are completely divorced from "life today." "We shall never sign any document which backs these occupation rights, nor agree to sign any document supporting occupation rights in West Berlin.

Gromyko then reiterated the warning against threatening the Soviet Union with suggestions by certain American officials that the "West would stop short of nothing, including force." "If the West is seeking a test of strength or trying to get a war, they may very well succeed!"

Thompson again reiterated that the International Access Authority would pose no challenge to the Soviet Union or the GDR. He continued that the U.S. government was committed to maintain its rights in Berlin. "Certainly it cannot be considered a threat to state that if our forces were attacked, they would defend themselves." Gromyko concluded by stating that he would review our proposal.

The fourth session of the Berlin talks convened on February 9. Gromyko, again in a business-like mode, presented a fifteen-page declaration, repeating the full Soviet position, revealing no change. He repeated charges that the West wished to retain West Berlin as a military springboard, that the sovereignty of the GDR was now a fact, and that a treaty recognizing that fact was necessary.

Thompson expressed his disappointment with Gromyko's declaration. He said that our goal was to seek agreement to reduce tension and therefore we needed to resolve the Berlin access question first. He rejected the charge that the West wished to retain our Berlin garrisons as a military springboard, pointing out that Khrushchev himself had told President Kennedy that our troops in Berlin had no military significance, "And in case of conflict, he would prefer to have as many as possible since they would all be taken prisoner!" Our garrisons in Berlin, Tommy added, were important to the people of Berlin to demonstrate our commitment to our obligations.

Thompson then repeated that the creation of an International Access Authority would prevent tension over access. He added that he was perplexed by how the Soviets could believe that they could dispose of the sector of Berlin, and then pretend to have rights in the Western sector. "The U.S. does not accept any suggestion that a symbolic contingent of Soviet forces be allowed in West Berlin." He concluded by reiterating that Western rights in Berlin were threatened by Soviet suggestions that a "peace treaty" with the "GDR" could end other vital rights in Berlin.

Gromyko again responded with a full statement of their changes and added that the Soviet Union "categorically refused to agree to the maintenance of the existing situation in Germany," which was the source of possible conflict. He set deadlines for the presence of Western troops in West Berlin because indefinite retention of Western forces was "quite impossible."

Thompson again reiterated that Allied rights in Berlin would be monitored until there was a full resolution of the entire German question. He concluded that he would of course transmit Gromyko's fifteen-page declaration to "our government" immediately. *The Washington Post* of February 10 reported this meeting as "the Berlin stalemate."

On February 12, we met again for the fifth session. Ambassador Thompson presented a full fifteen-page proposal for an International Access Authority and read a two-page summary thereof. The summary stated:

Summary of a Proposal for an International Access Authority For Berlin

The main purpose of the access authority would be to establish an International authority to govern free access from West Germany to West Berlin on the autobahn and through air corridors which would supplement the existing access arrangements. The authority would be governed by a board of governors. The actual management of functions of the authority would rest with the General Manager named by a board of governors. To maintain free access in and out of West Berlin, the authority would be given control over the Helmstedt-Berlin autobahn, Berlin Air Safety Center, airport facilities in West Berlin and any other facilities in West Berlin whose operation is essential to free air traffic in the air corridors. In addition it would have the power to govern traffic to and from West Berlin in the air corridors and the Berlin air control cone. The areas covered by the air corridors, the air control zone and the autobahn right of way would be set forth on maps annexed to the main agreement! It was now being envisioned that the air corridors would have the present 20-mile width and control zone with a 20-mile radius.

In order to carry out its mandate to insure the free flow of traffic between West Berlin and West Germany the authority would be given certain rights, powers, and duties (the most important of which would be the use of appropriate means to insure the safe and unrestricted flow of traffic on the highway and in the air corridors), to appoint officers, traffic police, etc., to carry out its functions; to fix and collect fees and charges to cover costs of operation; to construct necessary or convenient facilities along the highway including a communication system between

203

West Berlin and West Germany; to operate the Berlin Air Safety Center; to construct navigation aids in the air corridors, and to deal with public or private bodies in carrying out its functions.

The authority would be given the power to promulgate rules and regulations governing traffic on the highway covering traffic speeds, permissible loads, etc., the document would give the sole right of arrest upon the highway to the authority. It is contemplated that this provision, along with the provision specifying that the rules of the authority will have precedence in case of conflict with any other legal requirements, would enable the authority to exercise physical jurisdiction over the traffic on the autobahn and would eliminate the need for establishing a basic legal system apart from that already existing.

The authority would also have the power to promulgate rules and regulations covering traffic in the air corridors, but there would be an up-to-date version of DAIR/P (16) 71 second revised which would permit the authority to begin with an agreed set of air traffic regulations. The sole right of arrest for violation of such regulations on the facilities operated by the authority in West Berlin again would be in the authority.

Provision would also be made that no law of West Berlin or East Germany shall have any force or effect on the highway or on facilities operated by the authority in West Berlin if in the judgment of the authority such a law would impede it in carrying out its functions or would impede the free flow of traffic on the highway or through the corridors. The authority would require other privileges such as tax exemptions, immunity for its officers and staff from suit and legal process relating to acts performed by them in their official capacity, and exemption of its property from search, requisition, attachment, or execution except in cases where suit is brought against the authority pursuant to its charter.

We would contemplate that the authority would be set up by an agreement between France, the U.S., the

U.K., and the USSR with the provision that the agreement will enter into force only upon proper certification by France, the U.S., and the U.K. on one hand, and the USSR on the other, and that steps have been taken to make the agreement legally effective and binding in West Germany and West Berlin, as well as in East Germany and East Berlin.

Our instructions from the Berlin task force in Washington (coordinated with the British and French), emphasized that the West wished to avoid pushing towards a breakdown. In short, it was our objective to keep talking.

Thompson then reviewed the Western position again, stressing that we should put our attention on finding common ground on practical matters, while putting to one side the broader issues on which we had found no agreement; it was the appropriate place to begin with an effort to assure free access to West Berlin. Thompson stated that the Soviet Union was overlooking basic facts:

- West Berlin and our access thereto was NOT subject to any Soviet occupation rights.

- There was no way by which the Soviet Union could confer on the GDR regime rights which it did not have.

- Any attempt therefore to confer "sovereignty" on the GDR was limited by the Western position in Berlin.

- We were prepared to discuss how Western rights would be exercised but not how to turn them over to GDR "authorities".

Thompson continued that Gromyko had said they cannot be expected to confirm Western occupation rights. He pointed out that we were not asking for confirmation of our occupation rights because they required no such confirmation. We expected acceptance of those rights. Therefore, because we assumed both sides had an overriding interest in avoiding a collision course in Berlin, we assumed we could agree to concentrate on finding a working arrangement to avoid such a course.

Thompson then suggested we meet again, after Gromyko had had a chance to review our proposal for an International Access Authority. He agreed, but warned that this did not mean any favorable attitude toward our proposal.

Gromyko then concluded with a full reiteration of the Soviet position and warned again that U.S. references to take any steps to protect its current status would constitute a threat and would not work with the Soviet Union. He insisted that such remarks suggested that "the U.S. was looking for a test of strength, as if they are trying to get war—if so they may succeed. Language such as '"test of strength' should not be spoken when negotiating with the USSR!"

Thompson again stated that it was the Soviet Union that threatened Western rights in West Berlin. He added that he wished only to make clear what we would have to do if "anyone tried to throw out Western garrisons in Berlin or block their access to Berlin."

Thus ended the fifth session, again with threats of force, and no discernible progress. Gromyko continued to insist that Moscow would conclude a treaty with its puppet-state GDR and thereby end Allied right in Berlin. Ambassador Thompson continued to press the idea of an International Access Authority to reconfirm Allied rights of unencumbered access to Berlin and to warn that we would forcefully resist any effort to terminate those rights.

Air Corridor Incidents Increase

While we had achieved Gromyko's agreement to keep talking, dangerous Soviet pressures continued to mount, particularly on the sensitive air corridor access issue. On February 15, pursuant to our instructions from the Washington Berlin task force, we prepared and delivered to the Soviet Ministry of Foreign Affairs (MFA) a sharp protest of Soviet actions. We confirmed this in the following urgent cable:

> Following to MFA at approximately 1:00 P.M. today after coordination with British and French colleagues. They will submit same with appropriate changes in paragraph 1 regarding their respective or Allied (instead of U.S.) aircraft, and with substitution of "Soviet statements of desirability" for "Gromyko's agreement" in paragraph 3. On February 14, 1962, Soviet aircraft on three occasions seriously threatened, by close approach, U.S. aircraft flying in the North Corridor to Berlin in accordance with quadripartitely agreed flight rules, under flight plans on which customary flight information had been made available to the Soviet element of BASC, the four-power council established to govern air corridor traffic. The necessary flight

information for the Soviet aircraft had not been submitted by the Soviet element in BASC.

Prior to that, On February 8th, 9th, and 12th, Soviet authorities in BASC sought to reserve the use of a number of flight levels in the Berlin air corridors for Soviet aircraft during a specified time. They were informed in BASC that Allied aircraft wanted to continue to fly in accordance with established procedures and that Soviet authorities would be held fully responsible for flight safety. The air corridors are for the use of the aircraft of the Four Powers in accordance with established procedures which also specify procedures for crossing the corridors (DAIR/P[45]71, paragraph 8). BASC has the role of ensuring flight safety in each case and for avoiding flight interference. It has carried out this role under these procedures for many years. Any effort by one of the Four Powers to arrogate to itself the exclusive use of flight levels for any period of time is entirely unacceptable. Such a practice would amount to an arbitrary limitation on the free use of air corridors by the aircraft of the Three Western powers as guaranteed by quadripartite agreements.

The attempt to force changes in established procedures in this manner is incompatible with Soviet Foreign Minister Gromyko's apparent agreement in talks with President Kennedy and Secretary Rusk that both sides should refrain from "actions which might aggravate international tensions" and with the explicit commitment to this effect in the join statement of September 20, 1961 on principles for disarmament negotiations.

Air access to Berlin along the three corridors from West Germany is and has been unrestricted since the end of World War II in 1945. Rights with respect to air access to Berlin derive from precisely the same source as do the rights of the USSR in East Germany and East Berlin, namely, the joint military defeat of the German Reich and the join assumption of supreme authority over Germany. These rights are confirmed by the circumstances under which the four powers entered Germany, by their subsequent discussions and agreements, and by open and established practice over a period of fifteen years. Reports of the Air Directorate of the Allied Control Council and the decision of the Council itself regarding flight in the corridors reveal both the nature of the rights of the respective parties and arrangements as to the exercise of these rights.

The U.S. government attaches the utmost importance to the maintenance of the free use of the air corridors as well as to the observance of established procedures. By their actions on February 14th the Soviet Union is running the gravest risks. The U.S. government expects the Soviet government to ensure that its authorities prohibit such aggressive and dangerous behavior by Soviet aircraft, and that they refrain from demands to reserve the use of flight levels in the air corridors. U.S. aircraft will continue to fly in the corridors as necessary and in accordance with established procedures. The U.S. government will take the necessary steps to insure the safety of such flights and will hold the Soviet government responsible for the consequences of any incidents which might occur.

Sixth Gromyko-Thompson Meeting in Berlin: March 6, 1962

At our request, Gromyko received us again on March 6. Thompson opened with a strong statement condemning Soviet attempts over the past few days to disrupt existing long-standing arrangements in the air corridors into Berlin, "just at the time we are discussing the possibility of new arrangements." He then presented a full memorandum restating the Western position in Berlin:

> Throughout the exchanges that have taken place between the Soviet and U.S. Governments on the question of Germany and Berlin, the U.S. Government has for its

part earnestly sought to find a basis for agreement which would meet the legitimate needs of all parties concerned. In this endeavor, the U.S. Government has had as its aim to promote peace and tranquility in central Europe without sacrificing such basis principles as the right of self-determination.

The U.S. government remains convinced that the best solution to the German and Berlin questions would be the signing of a peace treaty with a Germany reunified on the basis of self-determination and the restoration of Berlin as the capital of a free, peaceful, and democratic Germany. Because it believes that a lasting European settlement cannot be achieved on the basis of a divided Germany, the U.S. Government could never join in any move which would legalize the division of Germany.

Nevertheless the Western powers have made clear in actions and in words that they do not contemplate any use of force or any unilateral action to change the present situation. If the Soviet government would likewise make clear that it does not contemplate any use of force or any unilateral action to change the present situation, tension over the Berlin question would be relaxed. The Soviet Government must recognize that unilateral action such as the aggressive harassment of allied planes which took place in the Berlin air corridors after February 7 creates the danger of a serious incident or incidents which could rapidly develop into major proportions.

It is, and has been, the sincere desire of the U.S. Government to ascertain whether or not there exists a basis for negotiations in Berlin. It is equally true that the U.S. Government is convinced that the appropriate place to begin, since this is obviously the critical point at issue, is with the assurance of free access to and from Berlin. For this reason it proposed the international access authority, which would operate without prejudice to the divergent positions of the various parties in interest.

The U.S. Government would like to think that it is possible to solve more than simply the problem of access to West Berlin, and it was for this reason that it proposed an all-Berlin solution. It is not convinced by the Soviet argument that such a solution "is not in the nature of things." However, should it not be possible for whatever reason to solve larger questions at this time, the U.S. Government considers that the question of access, which is the only area of acute danger, is the sensible place to begin in the conviction that if some tentative understandings can be reached here, it would then be possible to move to agreement on other questions.

It is obvious that all questions in issue cannot be discussed and decided simultaneously, but this is no reason why discussions on one or two aspects should not take place to the point where the outline of a possible agreement begins to take shape. It might then prove easier to discuss the remaining questions, Far from attempting to exert pressure or impose preconditions, the U.S. Government was in this way—by choosing a logical starting point— attempting to avoid the vicious circle or marking of time which the Soviet Government indicates it seeks to avoid. Access was not intended to be the sole subject of all negotiations but, because of its over-riding importance to the maintenance of peace, it is clearly the key to what agreement might be possible. This importance has been underscored by Soviet actions in recent weeks which have created a dangerous situation of a type both sides presumably wish to avoid.

The goal of the United States in these discussions is the equitable and peaceful settlement of controversies existing between it and the Soviet Union, and it had hoped that the Soviet goal is the same.

The United State- Government is no less anxious than the Soviet government to tidy up the remnants of the Second World War But it would be a grave mistake to suppose that a line could be drawn under the second World War by unilateral Soviet actions which violated the right a of the western partners of the Soviet Union in the common victory over Nazi Germany. Such actions

211

would not tidy up the remnants of the Second World War but create a serious danger of a new war. It should be pointed out that it was not the Western powers which sought immediate changes and thereby endangered the peace. It was the Soviet Union which made changes and threatened other changes which would have this effect.

The Soviet Government is correct in saying that the Western powers cannot prevent the Soviet Union from concluding a so-called "peace treaty." What the Soviet Government cannot do is to affect thereby the legal rights of the Western powers.

The U.S. Government wishes to make it quite clear that by virtue of the defeat of the Third Reich, the U.S., U.K., and France are entitled to be present in Berlin and to have wholly unimpeded access thereto. The three powers do not exercise these rights on the sufferance of the Soviet Union or the East German authorities. No treaty between the Soviet Union and East Germany can terminate the occupation rights of the western powers.

It should be added that the presence of the Western powers has the wholehearted support of the Germans most directly affected, the people of West Berlin. This is a fact which could be demonstrated at any time by means of a properly supervised plebiscite. Contrary to the assertion of the Soviet Foreign Minister, it would be entirely possible to hold a plebiscite while Western troops remain la Berlin. The purpose of adequate international supervision is precisely to ensure that no possibility of pressure on the free expression of popular will can exist.

If, as the Soviet foreign Minister has stated, Berlin harbors a "threat of explosion" or has become "a dangerous knot of international tension," it is because the Soviet Government and its allies have chosen to make it so. It should not be forgotten that for the decade between the soviet-imposed blockade of Berlin and the Soviet ultimatum of November 1958, Berlin existed in a situation of relative peace and quiet and was not a threat to world peace.

The U.S. Government is persuaded that the Soviet proposal for Berlin would produce a city that was neither peaceful nor independent.

The Soviet Government has stated that it has examined the Berlin question in light of the city's situation within a "sovereign state" a situation, it should be pointed out, created by the Soviet Union—and concluded once again that there is no better basis for agreement than the transformation of West Berlin into a free, demilitarized city. In this Soviet proposal an effort has been made to weave beguiling words such as "free," "demilitarized," and "normalizing" into a document which would seem designed, in fact, to subvert the freedom of West Berlin. This proposal has been examined and found unacceptable many times since it was first put forward and rejected three years ago. It is still unacceptable in the form of the statute and protocol which the Soviet Foreign Minister handed to the American Ambassador in Moscow on January 13, 1962.

Among the many objections to the Soviet proposals are the following:

Above all else is the fact that these proposals are overwhelmingly opposed by the vast majority of the West Berliners, a fact which can he substantiated by a properly supervised plebiscite at say time. The West Berliners would be deprived of the essential security they now enjoy through the creation of uncertainty as to how long the protecting forces would remain.

The Soviet Government and the East German regime would be interfering constantly in the internal affairs of West Berlin. The Soviet proposals would permit the prescription of legitimate activities of individuals or organizations in West Berlin by labeling them "fascist and militaristic", or engaged in "revanchism and war propaganda"• It is well-known how these terms can be applied freely to any activity—however praiseworthy—of which the Soviet or East German regimes disapprove.

213

The Soviet proposals would require West Berlin to enter into "appropriate agreements" with the East German authorities in order to obtain access to the Federal Republic "based on generally accepted international norms regulating transit through foreign territory". The immediate effect would be to make traffic between West Berlin and the rest of the world subject to the whims of the East German regime. One has to take only a brief glance at the long list of wholly legitimate visitors whose presence in West Berlin the East German authorities have violently protested, including President and Mrs. Luebke, Chancellor Adenauer, The Reverend Billy Graham, parliamentarians from NATO countries, and most recently the Attorney General of the United States, to see how much free travel would be permitted under such an arrangement.

The proposals would prohibit "activity or propaganda hostile toward any state".

It has long been clear that the mere existence of a free press and radio in West Berlin are considered as "hostile" to its interests by the East German regime.

With regard to the proposed United Nations membership for West Berlin, this is merely a further confirmation of the Soviet thrust towards the permanent division of Germany.

The Soviet government proposes that the "freedom" which it seeks to confer upon West Berlin be guaranteed by various governments, including the Soviet Union. There would be a "joint guarantee" and in the event of a "threat" the parties would consult regarding measures to eliminate each threat. They would adopt "concerted Measures" to insure the neutrality of the free city.

Proposals for establishing joint controls with regard to Berlin bring vividly to mind the protracted and frustrating efforts of the American, British and French authorities to cooperate with Soviet authorities both in Germany, and in Berlin itself pursuant to quadripartite agreements. It became clear at that time that such an arrangement could not

be made to operate effectively in the face of differing national objectives. Thus the U.S., U.K., and France
originally acquired occupation rights in all of greater Berlin
along with the Soviet Government but through unilateral
and illegal actions the latter has persistently sought not
only to exclude the other three powers from East Berlin
but also to undermine their position in West Berlin.

The reasoning underlying the Soviet proposal that
West Berlin be "demilitarized" is obscure. West Berlin is a
relatively small area, populated by some two million
people. It is completely surrounded by a hostile East German regime, which has frequently boasted of its military
night and of its designs on West Berlin. The present security of West Berlin is guaranteed by the presence of an
allied garrison of about 12,000 which are surrounded by
more than twenty-six Soviet and East German divisions.
Under these circumstances, the U.S. government cannot
assume that the Soviet government seriously expects it to
agree to leaving the city defenseless. The Western powers
are firmly convinced- as are the West Berliners- that,
stripped down to essentials, the single element which con-
tributes most to the continued freedom of West Berlin is
the presence there of the troops of the three powers. Far
from contributing to tensions, these troops are an assurance against provocative actions against West Berlin and
thus contribute greatly to the preservation of world peace.

The withdrawal of these troops or the entry into West
Berlin of Soviet troops would accordingly be unacceptable
to the Western powers and to the West Berliners. It is
difficult to see how the Soviet government can maintain
that the U.S., U.K., and France have no role to play in East
Berlin and at the same time propose a large role for their
troops in West Berlin. As the American Ambassador has
previously stated, the western powers can scarcely be expected to give up their position while the Soviets maintain
and improve the essentials of their position.

The U.S. Government is mindful of the fact that the
Soviet Union had already, in 1944 and 1945, entered into

agreements with the U.S., U.K., and France regarding Berlin and Germany. The Soviet Government now takes the position that not only is it no longer bound by those agreements relating to Berlin, but that it also has the legal right to determine the present rights of the other states which participated in the war against Germany with respect to Berlin, faced with such assertions, the United States could envisage entering into new agreements only if they were framed as to ensure their effectiveness and permanence.

The Soviet Government contends that it is being requested to place its signature literally or figuratively under an agreement which would perpetuate the presence of troops of the Western powers in West Berlin. The U.S. Government has not requested that this be done because, among other reasons, it is unnecessary. As pointed out previously, Western rights in Berlin do not derive from the Soviet Government, and that Government is not being asked to sign any document containing terms which seem to have acquired unpleasant associations for it. What the Soviet Government is being asked to do is to accept the fact of the Western presence in Berlin and to draw the appropriate conclusion from that fact.

Finally, these discussions can achieve nothing if they should begin to revolve about threats to resort to force. The Western powers have no desire whatsoever to attempt to solve any questions by force, though they are prepared to take whatever steps may be necessary to fulfill their responsibilities. They remain convinced, however, that reasonable men and nations can resolve the issues which divide them without the use of force if good will is shown on both sides. It is in this spirit that the Western powers will continue to attempt to resolve their difficulties with the Soviet Government, with confidence that there are no inevitable obstacles to arriving at a peaceful and honorable solution given Soviet cooperation. In the memorandum handed to the Soviet Foreign Minister on February 1, 1962, the U.S. Government suggested a num-

ber of possibilities which might be explored. In his response, the Soviet Foreign Minister did not address him-
himself to a number of important points made in this
memorandum. It is hoped that the Soviet Foreign Minister will carefully re-examine this document with a view to
ascertaining whether, as it suggests, a useful discussion
cannot be conducted by concentrating on those areas of
activity where at least some working arrangement might
be possible. Meanwhile, the U.S. Government again draws
the attention of the Soviet Government to the necessity
that both sides refrain from unilateral action that aggra-
vates tensions and involves grave risks.
Embassy of the United States of America,
Moscow, March 6, 1962

Gromyko responded first on the air corridor situation. He
insisted that "tensions in the air corridors" that lie in the air
space of the GDR had been created not by the Soviet Union,
but by the Western side. We obviously disagreed on the
facts here, but we denied that the Western powers have "the
right to establish the truth." He warned again that if the
Western attempts were made to aggravate the situation,
Soviet force would reply to them. While Soviet threats of
forceful action were becoming almost routine in these
critical meetings, it did not diminish the somber reality that
we were exchanging threats of war!

ThenGromyko reiterated the Soviet position that the
occupation regime in Berlin and in Germany itself had
expired over time and needed to be resolved once and for all.
He warned, again, that if the Western powers continued to
block this resolution, the Soviet Union would sign a peace
treaty with the GDR that would end all occupation rights.

"This is absolutely inevitable." He called on the West to recognize that the Soviet Union had not *yet* signed the peace treaty, in order to facilitate agreement with us. He repeated that the Soviet government would never agree to any arrangement that would perpetuate maintenance of the occupation regime in West Berlin. He added that the peace treaty would resolve critical questions, i.e. Western rights in Berlin and access thereto.

Thompson responded first by rejecting Gromyko's interpretation of the air corridor tensions. He pointed out that the current spate of incidents did not result from Western actions, but rather from the fact that the Soviets had suddenly changed procedures that had existed, largely without problems, for sixteen years. He warned again that the U.S. government "takes a most serious view of such actions."

Gromyko then agreed that in his planned meeting with Secretary Rusk in Geneva on disarmament, he would discuss a German settlement further. I reiterated that he should expect Secretary Rusk to put access resolution as the necessary first step.

The March 6 meeting concluded that series of tense and dangerous meetings in the search for a basis for an understanding on access to Berlin. The continuing exchanges of threats to unilaterally end our rights in Berlin in spite of our virtually automatic response that we would take whatever action necessary to sustain those rights were sobering indeed. Soviet harassment of Western flights in the designated air corridor underlined the reality that Khrushchev was playing a very dangerous game!

However, we had noted at several junctions in this very tense process that our unyielding insistence on maintaining our rights in Berlin was having an effect. The original six-month ultimatum to terminate our rights had been twice postponed and then evolved into an insistence that the instrument to accomplish the basic Soviet objective of removing us from Berlin (110 miles within the Soviet zone, "The GDR") was inevitable, *without a deadline*. In fact, we seemed to have succeeded in stymieing Khrushchev's rash offensive. His frustration was dramatically confirmed as he shifted his focus in an even more dangerous roll of the dice; placing nuclear missiles in Cuba a few months later.

At Geneva, in mid-April, Rusk and Gromyko traded threats that again failed to show any progress. On returning to Washington, Rusk continued to meet with Soviet Ambassador Dobrynin without any positive developments. By this time, Khrushchev had abandoned the pretense of a treaty and the need to draw a line under World Was II; he let it be clear that he was demanding the withdrawal of Allied garrisons in West Berlin. On May 30, Rusk and Dobynin held their final meeting. The negotiations were over.

A month later I concluded my Moscow assignment. Departure was truly an emotional experience. Following a series of farewell parties, we packed up and returned to the infamous Sheremyetevo airport, immunized by now to the dreary, tacky aspects of Moscow and its airport; all of which added to the emotions we experienced as we stepped aboard the KLM jet that was to fly us to Amsterdam. With Tigger safely stowed in his crate, we entered a different world. Three very pretty hostesses met us at the door and whisked our boys to the back of the almost empty plane where they were served Cokes and started playing games. "C" and I sank into the plush first-class seats and started to work on the best martinis we had ever encountered. The sense of euphoria we both felt is impossible to describe; after two long, high-pressure years in a drab and hostile surrounding, we felt liberated. The clean, tasteful KLM interior, hospitable attractive hostesses, and the knowledge that we were returning to the freedom Americans take so for granted was overwhelming. The euphoria continued as we arrived at one of the world's most beautiful cities, Amsterdam. After a luxurious night in our hotel, we boarded a train, which took us to LeHavre to board the luxury-liner, the *United States*, in luxury again as we sailed to New York. Our trip was further enhanced when we discovered our old friend, CBS correspondent Dan Shor on board. Dan had served in Moscow before us and had dated my secretary in Berlin. We had a great time exchanging "war stories" as we returned to the U.S. with Dan.

CHAPTER VIII. BACK TO THE SOVIET DESK

In June of 1962, after two action-packed years in Moscow, we returned to Washington where the Berlin crisis boiled along and quickly morphed into the Cuban missile crisis. I was assigned to the Office of Soviet Affairs—"the Soviet Desk"—at the State Department. "C" and I experienced the joy of buying our first home, a small Colonial in Woodacres, a village in Bethesda. The first day we looked at the house, when we left we couldn't find Peter (now ten), Michael (eight), or Tim (seven). They had all climbed into a large tree—a boyhood pleasure unknown in treeless Moscow!

Ambassador Thompson had been recalled to Washington and he became President Kennedy's counselor on both Berlin and Cuba. The talks we had held in Moscow with Gromyko failed to produce agreement on Berlin, and specifically the critical element of Allied access to Berlin. However, they did demonstrate to Khrushchev Allied determination to remain in Berlin and defend our rights there. It was our sense, by June of 1962, that the crest of Khrushchev's threat to Berlin had passed. But, like all floods, pressures continued even as the direct threat gradually subsided. The Soviets continued to insist that a treaty with the Soviet controlled GDR was essential, but what had been standard threats that Allied rights in Berlin would be extinguished disappeared.

To maintain the pressure on the West in Berlin, the Soviets reinvigorated their "salami-slicing" activities in Berlin;

probing and leveraging wherever they could find what looked like a soft spt. On August 21, for example, a new confrontation occurred over the Soviet War Memorial in West Berlin. Built in 1945 when the occupation of Berlin was truly four-power in nature, the Soviets maintained a small honor guard at the Memorial. As the Berlin crisis mounted in 1958-62, the handful of Soviet troops found themselves exposed to the anger of the Berlin population and a small Allied presence was added to the monument to discourage incidents. However, in August of 1962, the bus carrying Soviet replacements to the memorial was stoned as it drove through West Berlin. On August 21, Soviet armored personnel carriers, with cannons, were employed to carry the soldiers to the monument. After consultation, the Allied commandants informed Soviet General Ivan Yakubovsky, their commandant counterpart, that no Soviet armor would be permitted and Yakubovsky backed down. Yakubovsky also announced that he had abolished the position of Soviet commandant and the Western allies would have to deal with GDR officials. That threat too, quickly faded as Yakubovsky continued to respond to his Western counterparts. This was an important channel. Even as late as September 25, Soviet MIGs buzzed Pan Am and Air France flights into Berlin via the designated air corridor.

Finally, on September 28, Defense Secretary McNamara issued a public declaration warning Moscow that the U.S. was prepared to use nuclear weapons to defend Berlin!

One wonders in retrospect whether Khrushchev's ardor for a power-play on Berlin might not have been more quickly doused had Dulles responded in 1958 with the same blunt warning McNamara made September 28, 1962.

John Ausland, a Foreign Service officer who served as deputy director of the State Department Berlin Task Force throughout the Berlin crisis has written a detailed account that is uniquely informative about the closing months of the Berlin confrontation, *Kennedy, Khrushchev, and the Berlin Crisis*. (See Bibliography.)

Khrushchev Switches to Cuba

Beginning in early summer of 1962, Senator Kenneth Keating (R-NY) began a campaign in the U.S. press, sounding an alarm that the Soviets were adding new troops to their small long-standing training force in Cuba. Obviously being fed a steady stream of military intelligence, Keating's charge became more and more demanding, and he was attracting more and more press attention. The arrival of some IL-28 light bombers triggered Republican demands that the administration "act" against the Soviet buildup. President Kennedy responded in a September 13 news conference, deploring "loose talk" about attacking Cuba. Recent declassification of White House records shows that the president believed that Khrushchev's actions in Cuba were meant to distract us, and the real threat would come against Berlin.

However, on September 15, the Soviet ship *Poltava* was observed arriving in Cuba with a shipment of nuclear capable missiles. Meanwhile, the construction of SAM anti-aircraft missile pads was confirmed by our intelligence. If Khrushchev meant to create a distraction from his pressure on Berlin, it was working. Ambassadors Thompson and Bohlen continued to advise that Cuba was a peripheral issue to Berlin, where, while Soviet pressure there had diminished, we remained in a much more exposed position. Berlin remained Moscow's principal objective.

The *Poltava*'s arrival led the President to set up a multi-agency task force on Cuba and issue a warning to Khrushchev against creating a new crisis in the Western hemisphere. Khrushchev responded that he had "put Berlin on ice" and Soviet arms in Cuba were strictly "defensive" weapons.

On October 15 the administration's posture toward Cuba was shocked into high-gear; the National Photographic Interagency Interpretation Center, housed in a nondescript office building in downtown Washington, received eight cans of film taken by a U-2 flight over Cuba. My close friend Colonel Thomas Cormack was the director of the film intelligence office at the Center. He confirmed that the film established beyond any doubt that construction was under-way on three medium-range launch sites and that missiles were "at site." This alarming information was immediately passed to Kennedy's security advisor, McGeorge Bundy. The President called his Joint Chiefs of Staff, Secretary Robert

McNamara, Secretary Dean Rusk, and Ambassadors Thompson and Bohlen into emergency session; thus ExCom came into being. (ExCom was the name given to this small special task force to deal with Khrushchev's latest gamble.)

In these daily emergency meetings, the military voices were increasingly aggressive in calling for a military strike as new photo intelligence flowed in. Rusk, Thompson, and Bohlen continued to call for direct communication with Khrushchev. Ambassador Foy Kohler, who had succeeded Thompson in Moscow, confronted Khrushchev in Moscow, who pooh-poohed reports of offensive missiles. He pointed out that his missiles were no different than the U.S. Thor missiles we had established on the Soviet border in Turkey.

ExCom and the President moved quickly. After an intense debate where Air Force chief General Curtis E. LeMay and Admiral Robert Anderson persisted in calling for an armed strike and invasion, the President decided on a blockade of Cuba to intercept any nuclear warhead shipments to Cuba. Ambassador Thompson pointed out that it was essential to leave an escape-hatch for Khrushchev to withdraw. The blockade, presented as "quarantine," worked. In a public statement Kennedy, following up on back-channel conversations between Attorney General Bobby Kennedy and Soviet journalist, Vladimir Bolshakov, known to be a senior KGB operative in the U.S., demanded that Khrushchev withdraw his missiles and declared that we would intercept the Soviet ships known to be carrying the nuclear warheads for the missiles. The Soviet ships approaching Cuba, and the submarines escorting them were intercepted and after a hair-raising 24 hours, turned around. Khrushchev gave up on this most desperate of his gambles.

By November, the Cuban crisis was over. The president had showed impressive restraint and determination. In the short period of a year, he had suffered a disastrous and embarrassing defeat at the Bay of Pigs, stood up to Khrushchev on Berlin, and stood him down in Cuba. His ability to pull together and absorb widely varying and often conflicting advice from the "best minds" of Ambassadors Thompson and Bohlen, his aggressive military advisors, and intelligence officials, deserves historic recognition. On November 20, President Kennedy lifted the quarantine. The dramatic deliberations by President Kennedy and his cabinet are described in fascinating detail in *High Noon in the Cold War* by *New York Times* correspondent Max Frankel.

Several noteworthy items:

- U.S. photo intelligence of Cuba was tremendously enhanced by a steady stream of information from the U.S. CIA and British controlled Colonel Oleg Penkovsky in Moscow. Colonel Cormack confirmed that Penkovsky's information on Soviet missilery enabled our intelligence interpreters to identify with certainty which missiles were en route and the capabilities of each.

- The President's uncanny ability to deflect and then harness Republican senators who were denouncing him as weak paid off. He joked that, "we had to prevail, or Ken Keating will be the next president."

- The President's cool rejection of the sometimes overheated demands of Admiral Anderson and General LeMay was critical to avoid a disastrous nuclear exchange. At one point, Anderson, in ExCom, actually called the President's decision "weak." Three weeks later he was transferred to Portugal as ambassador!

- Throughout the period, all "the action" had been pulled together at the White House by ExCom and was very tightly held; only sixteen people were meeting with the President, "Bobby," and Vice President Johnson. There were virtually no "leaks." The country noticed the mobilization of our military force, but until the President's quarantine speech, it was not appreciated how close we had come.

- On November 2, 2007, the *New York Times* carried an obituary that stated: "Colonel Alexander Feliksov (Alexander Fomin—cover name) had died at age 92." It added that in October 1962, Fomin had several meetings with Attorney General Robert Kennedy seeking an agreement to defuse the Cuban missile crisis. In his autobiography, Fomin recounted that, if the U.S. attacked Cuba, Moscow would retaliate on West Berlin. This was specific evidence that Soviet anxiety about Berlin's destabilizing effect on Moscow's deteriorating hold on Eastern Europe was really the motivation for Khrushchev's desperate and dangerous initiative, placing missiles in Cuba. From the beginning, Khrushchev believed he could persuade us to trade-off our presence in Berlin for Moscow's missiles in Cuba.

After the collapse of Khrushchev's nuclear gamble in Cuba, the temperature in our relations with Moscow settled down. Personally, I had watched from the sidelines as the cabinet-level ExCom team shaped and executed the U.S. response to Khrushchev's Cuban gamble. Khrushchev retreated into a labored effort to insist that his Cuban initiative had succeeded; "the U.S. invasion of Cuba was blocked." Of course there was no U.S. plan to invade Cuba until after Khrushchev's missile initiative provoked ExCom consideration of it. The Chinese openly condemned Khrushchev for backing down, and China's odd ally, Albania, which had remained more Stalinist than Stalin himself, openly spoke of Khrushchev's cowardice. From where we sat, the handwriting was on the wall; Khrushchev's days were numbered. His relations with Mao Tse Tung deteriorated and Khrushchev's military leaders, appalled by Khrushchev's nuclear gamble in Cuba and failure to oust the West from Berlin became more and more critical of his leadership.

The President, in a historic speech at American University on June 10, 1963, laid out a major proposal to end the military confrontation with Moscow, revive cooperation on arms control (SALT) and settle down into less explosive competition. In short, victorious, Kennedy reached out to Khrushchev to "reset" our relationship.

In Soviet Affairs at the State Department, we revived a number of initiatives to resolve bilateral issues that had persisted, to complement the president's actions to redefine our relationship with Moscow. The Defense Department quickly negotiated a hotline teletype connection to avoid the tortuous communication delays that occurred during the Cuban crisis. The Agriculture Department opened negotiations that were successful for the sale of subsidized surplus American wheat to the USSR. Crop shortfalls in the USSR persisted and they were forced to import massive wheat shipments—a revealing commentary on the historic failure of Soviet collectivization of agriculture and a source of continuing embarrassment for Khrushchev, who had proclaimed that the USSR would bury us economically. And arms control negotiators closed the agreement to end all nuclear tests in the atmosphere—completing the long, arduous talks between John J. McCloy and Soviet Deputy Foreign Minister Zorin, which had been initiated in Moscow the year before.

The Air Agreement

Flight connections between Moscow and the U.S. had long been a source of mutual frustration. Americans, especially the businessmen who were seeking to exploit the improved possibilities for sales of agricultural products and equipment, chafed at the absence of direct flights and the need for layovers in London, Paris, Frankfurt, or Vienna. For the Soviets, it was more a matter of pride to have their airline, Aeroflot, serve the U.S. directly. A detailed air agreement had been reached before the Berlin/Cuba crises, but was never implemented. Pan American was eager to add

Moscow to its destinations. The President gave his approval to reactivate the agreement and we moved ahead.

FAA director Najeeb Halaby, an accomplished World War II pilot and personal friend of the President's, was designated to meet with the Soviets to see if this agreement could be implemented. I was chosen to be "Jeeb's" political advisor, and we scheduled a flight to Moscow for Halaby to meet with the Soviet Minister of Transportation, General Loginov,also a World War II pilot. This was a particularly interesting change in my new assignment on the Soviet desk. The Soviet Desk consisted of a group of ten experts, most of whom had served in Moscow. We back-stopped the top State Department and White House officials dealing with the USSR.

In the State Department, I reported to Ambassador Thompson and the legendary Undersecretary Averill Harriman, on this issue. Thompson, at this point had been appointed as Counselor to the Secretary of State, and in reality was serving as the top Soviet affairs expert for both the President and Secretary Rusk.

Departing in the FAA jet—a ten-seat executive plane—Halaby and his four-man team and his wife Doris flew to Moscow via Greenland, Iceland, and Denmark. At Copenhagen we picked up two Soviet navigators, supposedly English-speaking, to assist us into Moscow. Halaby insisted on taking the controls and piloting the FAA plane himself.

He very much wanted to fly into Sheremetyevo and land the plane, and then go in to meet Loginov and say "I landed here." But about ten minutes into Soviet air space, Jeeb got on the loudspeaker (I was in the eighth seat back in this ten-seat plane) and he said, "Jenkins, get up here right away." So I went up into the cockpit where the two navigators were sitting behind the two pilots. I squatted down on my knees in between the four of them. Halaby said, "I can't understand what this guy is trying to tell me. He keeps pointing at things, but I don't get it." Of course, I spoke Russian—I was recently out of our Moscow embassy—but I didn't speak "aviation Russian." It's a different vocabulary. So it was a pretty nervous period. They would tell me and I would tell Jeeb what I thought they were trying to say, and he would say, "they must mean so-and-so." So then I'd go back to them and try to explain to them what Jeeb thought they meant, and get them to confirm it. And that's the way we flew into Sheremetyevo. It was pretty hairy. We arrived and, of course, we went into the negotiations with Loginov.

At the time, the Soviets had the largest plane in the world. It had eight engines; the TU-142—a very big plane. It wasn't wide-bodied, but it was huge. They wanted to be the biggest and the best always, and this was their aviation bid. They wanted to fly this damn plane to the United States and make a big publicity splash with it. Jeeb insisted that there wasn't any way in the world we were going to sign off on licensing this plane to land in the United States unless he flew it first. They weren't going to let him fly it because it was a brand new plane, and they weren't sure all the bugs were out, and he said, "Well, if I don't get to fly it, it doesn't go."

We went back and forth with Loginov in the negotiations. We made our presentation in English, it would be translated, and then the Russians would come back in Russian. As I heard the Russians, it was clear that Loginov was being urged by his advisor, "For Christs's sake, let him fly the plane. We want to get it in there." And Loginov was beginning to back off. All of a sudden it looked like Jeeb was going to give up. So I interceded with him and said, "Look, I can tell you they are about to give you what you want— don't back off, you'll get it." And, of course, he didn't back off, and we did get it and flew it. It was a terrible experience! The plane was very hard to fly, Jeeb said. "I damned near crashed the thing because I could barely turn it." It took two people; it was a huge flying boxcar. So we didn't license it even though Halaby flew it. Eventually it was allowed to fly in, but only after they installed a lot of hydraulic controls that they hadn't had before then. We eventually let it fly to Dulles Airport a couple of times, but it never became their principal carrier. Halaby recounted this experience in his autobiography, *Cross Winds*.

The agreement was implemented. Pan American established weekly, direct service to Moscow. Aeroflot had reciprocal flights to New York using their less grand Ilyushin. It was a big-money loser for Aeroflot, which suffered from poor service and comfort; but they relied on it for all

Soviet travel by its diplomats at the United Nations and their embassy in Washington. Pan Am benefited from the increased business activity.

Closed Area Battle

While the nuclear confrontation over Berlin and Cuba was disarmed, our relations with Moscow remained contentious and both sides relied on reciprocity as the basis for our activities.

You will recall that the U.S. Embassy travel program in Moscow was designed and coordinated to cover as many strategic areas of the USSR as possible (see Chapter VII). The KGB also expended tremendous "assets" to control our travel and that of all foreign embassies. Shortly after taking up my duties on the "Soviet Desk" in the Department of State, it was noted that Warsaw Pact country diplomats were traveling to areas where our new ICBM missile sites were being constructed, areas that were closed to travel by Soviet diplomats. On several occasions, Hungarian and Czech diplomats were observed with Geiger counters; obviously charged with trying to determine whether our launch pads were "armed."

Assistant Secretary of Defense Paul Nitze, a close friend of President Kennedy, and major actor among the collection of very special post-war statesmen (Harriman, Acheson, Forrestal, et. al.) who played such a major role in shaping the U.S. reaction to the Cold War, convened an interagency meeting to deal with this challenge. The Soviets, banned from visiting these "closed areas," had managed to deputize their "allies" who were not under travel restrictions. In this case our reliance on simple reciprocity betrayed our interests. I represented State at these sessions. We quickly realized that our policy of permitting Warsaw Pact diplomats to travel freely, because we were allowed to travel almost without limitations in Hungary, Poland, Bulgaria, etc., was jeopardizing our security interests. We overrode our embassy recommendations from Warsaw Pact capitols and placed all Pact diplomats under the same restrictions as the Soviets.

However, the sudden prominence of the travel control issue offered an opportunity to confront Moscow's paranoid travel restrictions, and perhaps open additional areas. I prepared a formal note to the Soviets proposing a joint review of travel limitations, with a view to permitting increased travel by both sides. Predictably, Moscow rejected the initiative. We issued public press reports regretting that the USSR reaction left us no alternative to, after review, sharply increase the limits on Soviet and Warsaw Pact travel. Under Nitze's direction, I pulled together—on a county-by-county basis—a master map identifying where the Defense Department had important installations, approximately ten percent of the continental U.S. By one excuse or another, up to seventy percent of the USSR was de facto closed to foreign and especially U.S. embassy travel. At the final Nitze meeting we presented our new formal "closed area" map to be presented to the Soviets and their allies; it covered all genuine militarily sensitive areas and another arbitrarily designed group of counties, designed to titillate Soviet suspicion, but with no real security issues. In presenting this to the Soviets on November 12, we reiterated our preference to expand freedom of travel on both sides, but insisted we would maintain strict reciprocity in dealing with Soviet (and their allies) travel in the U.S. We did sharpen our defense and applied some presence on Moscow to open up.

Protecting U.S. Citizens in the USSR- The Consular Convention

One result of the President's speech at American University in June 1962 was an increase in reciprocal visits by academics of both the U.S. and USSR. We greeted this action as a significant step forward, as called for by the President. However, before long, this small step toward more normal relations ran into the reality that Soviet paranoia about foreign contacts was too well established to vanish suddenly.

In late October, Yale professor of Russian history Fred Barghoorn visited Moscow to meet with Soviet historians. Barghoorn knew President Kennedy personally and was well known to all of us in Soviet Affairs. On October 31, he met with Foy Kohler's deputy chief of mission, Walter Stoessel, at his apartment for drinks. He then proceeded to the Metropole Hotel where he was scheduled to have dinner. As he was about to enter the hotel, he was accosted by a Soviet who thrust a roll of blueprint-like documents into his hands. Immediately two other husky Soviets grabbed him, arrested him for having military secrets, and pushed him into a car. He was driven off to the KGB prison at Lubyanka.

Several days went by with no word from Barghoorn. Stoessel's efforts to locate him were fruitless. Alarm bells went off in Washington. This was an unusually blatant violation of the understanding we had about academic exchanges. And it highlighted the fact that we had no treaty—consular convention—that would provide for embassy access to arrested U.S. citizens. President Kennedy had to personally write Khrushchev before Barghoorn was released. An excellent description of this affair is found in Nick Daniloff's *Of Spies and Spokesmen* (see Bibliography).

Walter Stoessel, Barghoorn's close friend, went on to become ambassador to Poland, Germany, and the USSR, as well as Deputy Secretary of State. Like Thompson, Bohlen, Kohler, and Matlock, he served in Moscow twice, and was a true "hall of fame" career diplomat.

The Barghoorn crisis led us to propose to the Soviets that we negotiate a consular convention to avoid crises like this. The Soviets had long had such a convention with Germany dating back to before World War II. Harriman and Thompson decided that we should move to achieve the same thing. I met with the German ambassador in Washington, Berndt von Staden, to review Germany's experience in protecting

German citizens visiting in the USSR, and the history of their consular convention negotiations over the years.

There was resistance among Congressional circles to negotiating a "treaty" with the USSR. Anti-Soviet feelings generated by the Cold War were running especially high after the Berlin/Cuban crisis and continued conflicts around the world in Vietnam, China, Korea, and Africa. It was difficult to persuade those who preferred a policy of isolating the USSR, that any treaty, even if it served our interests, would not be a "favor" to Moscow. However, Harriman and Thompson agreed, particularly if we could enshrine a concrete commitment for immediate notification and quick access to any arrested Americans it would be worth pursuing. I was given the green light and we opened negotiations.

By this time, Stoessel had been replaced as deputy chief of mission in Moscow by Malcolm Toon, and he launched the negotiations. Toon, another Russian-speaking career officer, had a well deserved reputation for being unusually tough— we called him our "drill sergeant" diplomat.

For eight months, the negotiations went on. The Soviets, eager to gain what they considered the seal of approval of having a formal treaty with the U.S., seemed determined to reach an agreement. But they also seemed unable to abandon their historic fixation on secrecy. Each paragraph became a struggle. Finally the treaty's prospects came down to the key questions of notification and access. The Soviets told Toon over and over that Soviet law did not permit what we sought. However, from von Staden I received copies of the series of consular conventions they had negotiated, which did deal with notification and access; usually in terms of "rapidly" and "as fast as possible."

Toon succeeded in winning Soviet agreement to "rapidly" and "as soon as possible," notwithstanding Soviet insistence that their laws did not permit this.

Close as it was, this issue was clearly critical; both to avoiding "Barghoorn incidents" and to sell the Senate on the advantages to the U.S. Harriman and Thompson wanted agreement, but agreed to my insistence that Soviet eagerness to get "the treaty" would carry the day and we could get language specifying one day notification and three day access.

Mac Toon was frustrated, and insisted that the Soviets would never agree to specific limits. "We have an agreement, let's agree on this." Taking a deep breath, I drafted a first-person telegram back to Toon from Secretary Rusk, which Harriman and Thompson agreed to: "I don't care if we have to wait until hell freezes over, there will be no consular convention unless it specifies one day notification and three day access, and you are instructed to inform the Soviets to this effect."

Toon held his ground. The Soviets gave in. We had a consular convention.

A few weeks later I accompanied Harriman to appear before the Senate Foreign Relations Committee. Chaired by

Senator William Fulbright, the Committee also included three Republicans who were very dubious about providing the Soviets with a treaty, including Senator Everitt Dirksen. As a former U.S. ambassador to Moscow during World War II, he had dealt regularly with Stalin. He was not awed by Senate concerns.

Harriman had approved the negotiation each step of the way. However, it was the first treaty between the Soviet Union and the United States, and all sorts of anti-Communist currents were in play. Why are we doing this, we're giving the Russians something. But Harriman spelled it out: "We are achieving something we've never had before, it gives us the ability to really protect American citizens." "How do you know they will adhere to it?" "If they don't adhere to it, they're breaking a treaty, and they'll pay a big price for that in terms of public image, etc., and I'm confident if they sign it, they'll do it." He said very little. They'd ask him questions, and he'd sit there and answer simply "yup" or "nope."

We left after an hour; I don't think he spent more than ten minutes talking. All the rest of it had been the senators trying to draw him out on things. He was very uncommunicative. I didn't say anything, obviously, except when he turned to me and asked me to say something. Going back in the car, I said, "Governor, that was the damndest performance I've ever seen, you didn't tell them anything." And he said, "That was deliberate. You wait and see, this thing will pass. This is one of those situations where if you give them anything they'll chew on it and turn it against you." He said, "I wasn't about to tell those bastards anything." Sure enough, it did pass.

The United States-Soviet Consular Convention

The United States-Soviet consular convention was signed in Moscow June 1 by Ambassador Kohler for the United States and Soviet Foreign Minister Gromyko for the USSR. The convention was submitted to the Senate for advice and consent to ratification on June 12, 1963.

The convention, concluded after eight months of laborious negotiations, is an important step forward in the field of consular protection and services. In view of the fact that between ten and fifteen thousand Americans visit the U.S.S.R. annually, the ability of United States consular officers to provide assistance to American citizens in the U.S.S.R. is clearly of increasing importance. This convention augments the usual consular conventions which the United States has with some 30 other countries in three significant areas:

First, it guarantees immediate notification by the receiving state to consular officers of the sending state in the event that one of the citizens of the sending state is arrested. The term "immediate" is defined in the convention to mean from one to three days depending upon the locale of the arrest. This leeway is necessary for both Governments, of course, to cover the possibility that the arrest might take place in some distant area such as Siberia where communications might be limited. An example of the importance of this provision is the arrest of the American student Marvin Makinen which came to the attention of the American Embassy in Moscow only after nine weeks had elapsed.

Secondly, the convention provides for access to any arrested citizens "without delay". The convention specifies that "without delay" is to be within two-to-four days. Furthermore, it is provided that this access shall be granted on a continuing basis. Prior to this convention, Soviet regulations prohibited access to a prisoner until the investigation had been completed; the investigative period could, under Soviet laws, take up to nine months.

Finally, the convention differs from earlier consular conventions in that it provides full immunity for consular officers and employees from the criminal jurisdiction of the receiving state. The United States sought this immunity provision for the protection of the American personnel who will serve as consular officers and staff members in any consulates which we may establish in the U.S.S.R.

As a matter of background, it may be useful to review the past record of consular activities with the Soviet Union. Following the establishment of diplomatic relations in 1933, the U.S.S.R. opened consulates in 1934 in New York and San Francisco, and in 1937 in Los Angeles. In 1946 there was one Soviet consular officer in Los Angeles, two in San Francisco and five in New York. In 1948 all three consulates were closed. In January of 1941 the United States opened a consulate in Vladivostok. It was closed in September of 1948 after the Soviet Government announced that it was closing its consulates in the United States. In May of 1947 our government requested and received permission to open a consulate in Leningrad.

Initial Soviet cooperation was followed by obstruction and delay as Soviet-American relations deteriorated in 1948. After the Soviet consulates in the United States closed in August and our post in Vladivostok closed in September, it became clear that a consular post in Leningrad would not be opened at that time.

The present convention does not itself authorize the opening of consulates. This will be the subject of separate negotiations between the United States and the Soviet Union. It merely provides the legal framework for their operation, when opened. We hope to open a consular establishment in Leningrad and we anticipate that negotiations for the reciprocal opening of consulates will take place in due course. The United States Government will be guided by reciprocity in these negotiations.

Soviet consulate employees in an American city would be subject to the same visa and customs requirements as officers and employees of the Soviet Embassy in Washington. They would also be subject to the same travel restrictions which now apply to Soviet citizens who travel to the United States. In addition, the convention also spells out the right of the receiving state to expel any consular official, and provides for practical methods of screening all nominees for consular assignments in advance.

The Department of State considers the consular convention a solid step forward in our ability to assist and protect American citizens abroad.

Office of Public Services
Bureau of Public Affairs
Department of State3/13b - 964BT
Washington, D. C. 20520.

Kennedy's reign had spanned almost a thousand days. Starting out with the Bay of Pigs disaster, he weathered Khrushchev's blusters at Vienna and then prudently but, ever more determined, stood up to Khrushchev's ultimatum on Berlin, and finally managed the nuclear confrontation over Cuba forcing Khrushchev to back down. Seizing on his victory, he moved quickly to convert it and put our relations with Moscow on a less dangerous path continued containment, but seeking areas of agreement that would diminish the chance of another nuclear crisis. His American University speech was almost Lincolnesque and laid the groundwork for a series of bilateral initiatives such as the "hotline," consular convention, and renewed cooperation on nonproliferation and extension of our cultural agreement. All this led to a sense of relief and of some hope in Washington—a mood of confidence about the future.

His dramatic assassination shattered all that. I was in my office in the "Soviet desk," working away on the consular convention, and went down to the Department's cafeteria for lunch. There I learned the news. The entire cafeteria, some 200 people, was in a state of shock. I returned home where my wife "C" and our boys watched television nonstop. On the day of the state funeral, we bundled the boys into the car and went down to stand on the curb along with all Washington to watch the grand procession.

The mood in Washington was thick with pathos. Perfect strangers would embrace. Everything slowed to a crawl. (Some 38 years later, on 9/11, the same sense of shattered dreams occurred again.) President Johnson assumed command, and Senator Hubert Humphrey was selected as Vice President. The unique American transition process again impressed the world. But the sense of triumph and hope for more placid waters was destroyed. Before long the seed of U.S. intervention in Vietnam that was planted by President Kennedy and his brother, the attorney general, grew to dominate our foreign policy. It was in Kennedy's administration that the fateful decision to escalate the U.S. presence from strictly training to allow participation in combat was made.

President Johnson enjoyed universal support at that time and was able to move ahead on several fronts. He continued on the path to sustain our basic containment policy towards the USSR, but was quickly consumed by Vietnam and civil rights. On the latter he was of course dramatically successful, relying on his legendary skills as a legislative genius, co-opting opponents and bending the agencies his way.

Vietnam was a different story. Relying on Kennedy's team, Mac Bundy at the National Security Council (NSC), his deputy Walt Rostow, and Secretary of State Dean Rusk, Johnson accepted their determination to "win" in Vietnam.

I believe that history will present our costly effort in Vietnam as a national catastrophe—who can argue with the cold fact of some 55,000 U.S. combat deaths? Vietnam did have one positive aspect to it; it demonstrated that the U.S. was prepared to shed blood to defend our interests—a point completely understood in Moscow. Containment was bolstered as a policy. The fundamental question of whether our national interest was served, or the military action was justified is another matter. There were no "WMDs" in Vietnam either—the Tonkin Gulf incident, which history shows Lyndon Johnson doubted and agonized over, was in fact a fraud as official Navy records have revealed.

It was difficult in Washington after Kennedy's assassination to regroup, but we did.

Opposition to any relaxation of our confrontation with Moscow was widespread. Conservatives continued to warn

244

that we must avoid any agreements with Moscow that might reduce their isolation or lead us to drop our guard. Democratic senator "Scoop" Jackson emerged as a leader of hard-line policies. He had collected an unusually bright and qualified team of staffers, who labored under his Committee Staff Director, Dorothy Fosdick (daughter of Harry Emerson Fosdick). "Dickie," as she was known, led this brilliant team including Richard Perle and Elliott Abrams who labored to build up Jackson as a conservative presidential candidate—he did not resist. Initially, as I returned from Moscow, Perle and "Dickie" sought me out at the Soviet desk. I found them very supportive as we cracked down on Soviet bloc travel in the U.S., and held out for the unprecedented specific access and notification procedures in the consular convention. We worked so amicably together that when I remarried some years later, the senator and his staff sent in a congratulatory telegram from "Scoop and his troops." Little did we know in the post-assassination period, Scoop's troops were already laying the groundwork for his campaign on Jewish emigration from the USSR and his historic Jackson-Vanik amendment.

Meanwhile the U.S. government soldiered on in our efforts to "contain" the Soviet Union while we simultaneously searched for areas to engage in a positive way. KGB efforts to exploit the relatively open nature of our society to collect intelligence information about our nuclear weapons programs and recruit Americans to serve their cause were unrelenting. I have described the massive KGB controls over

American diplomats in Moscow and alluded to parallel efforts on our part in Washington (radiating embassy window panes and controlling embassy travel, and foiling KGB recruiting efforts, among others).

It fell to me, on the Soviet desk, to be the point man with the FBI division of Soviet affairs, which was responsible for monitoring and blocking KGB activities in the U.S. As a result, I received a steady flow of FBI reports on Soviet embassy activities in the U.S. Occasionally, the Bureau would entrap a Soviet "diplomat" attempting to purchase secret defense information from a U.S. citizen working on defense projects and prepare a case to expel that Soviet. On the Soviet desk we had to review these cases, because, when the Soviet was expelled, the KGB immediately would retaliate and expel one of our officers in Moscow. This PNG (*persona non grata*) process had to be weighed carefully, because on balance we would often lose a key embassy official in Moscow (on whom two years of language and area training had been expended) in exchange for an insignificant Soviet embassy operator. While there was an obvious tension built into this process, we resolved most cases. On balance, notwithstanding the openness of our society, I believe we held our own. We did find J. Edgar Hoover's propensity to personally showboat every FBI success wearing, believing that this essential struggle was better waged behind the scenes.

Thus after these dramatic years in Washington, I worked to influence my next assignment in the hopes that I could continue to be involved in the "Cold War" and utilize my Soviet affairs experience. The established U.S. policy of in-depth training of four officers a year for Moscow assignments was producing a steady flow of four officers a year from Moscow that needed to be placed where the Moscow experience was important. Ambassador Thompson and I had a long conversation about this, and he agreed with my suggestion that we needed to establish a strategic practice to ensure that these uniquely valuable officers not simply be put back into the global assignment pool.

At his direction, and with Harriman's support, I put together a select list of U.S. embassies around the world where Soviet activities were important. In addition to the obvious London, Paris, and Berlin, we identified Tokyo, New Delhi, Montevideo (where you will recall, the Soviets had more than 100 accredited diplomats who ran their Latin American efforts), Mexico City, Caracas (a target for Castro's influence), Santiago (whose leftist President Salvador Allende was growing in influence), and Cairo. This proposal was adopted and we proceeded to assign Moscow returnees to each embassy—identified as Soviet specialist political offices.

CIA had long established a policy of having officers assigned to such countries, designated especially to promote defections among Soviet embassy personnel. The new State Department program was directed at monitoring and countering Soviet embassy activities with the host government. In both cases there were successes. The agency did harvest a small but significant flow of defectors. The State

Department political officers did uncover numerous Soviet initiatives around the world and with some success revealed these Soviet activities to the host governments, and when appropriate exposed them to the local media.

Thompson encouraged me to pick my own slot! I was immediately drawn to New Delhi, which was in fact a hotbed of Soviet activity—arms sales; a powerful Communist party; and extreme Communist influence in labor issues. However, taking into account the education needs of our three boys, my wife "C" and I decided to go for Caracas, Venezuela. Caracas had an excellent bilingual American school, whereas embassy children were suffering in New Delhi as the Anglo-American school situation there was in chaos.

CHAPTER IX. VENEZUELA: A CASTRO TARGET

Once assigned to Venezuela, I spent six months refocusing from direct involvement in Soviet affairs to the arena of "wars of liberation," Moscow's campaign to break out of our containment policy and establish beachheads in the third world. I had studied Spanish in high school and college, but had only a narrow command of the language. Three months at the Foreign Service Institute quickly remedied that. Utilizing the same immersion method that had given me German and Russian, the FSI native speakers had me up to a solid conversational level. We were then off to Caracas, where I was assigned as a political officer, and soon rose to head the Political Office as Political Counselor, the third-ranking position in the Embassy.

On a personal note, we had had to put our beloved Tigger down at thirteen—a traumatic affair for all of us. The three boys, who had grown up with Tigger, and "C" and I had always marveled at his noble adaptability as he traveled with us from Germany to Thailand to Berlin, on to Moscow, and then home to Washington. He had become very uncomfortable with the typical enlarged heart problems large dogs develop. We wept as we held his head and felt him relax as the shot took effect; at peace at last. We quickly acquired a new Airedale puppy, "Pooh," who of course accompanied us to Caracas on his first overseas experience.

As we left for Venezuela, a total redirection for us, terrorist insurgent activity in Caracas was erupting. The economic growth and successful democratic elections incited the extremists to take desperate measures to try and derail the increasing success of the pro-American government. "C" and I had chosen Venezuela, expecting our Moscow experience to be relevant; we were not disappointed.

My seven years in Berlin, Moscow, and the Soviet desk in Washington had put me in the center of the Cold War confrontation. The three Washington years from 1962 to 1965 had seen the Berlin crisis morph into Khrushchev's desperate gamble in Cuba. I'd been stunned by President Kennedy's assassination. Khrushchev, in turn, was overthrown in the fall of 1964 by his colleagues who had had enough of his "hare-brained schemes" (*Pravda*'s language). Moscow's probing for chances to promote "wars of liberation" continued. And the U.S. had stepped into the bottomless pit that was Vietnam.

Much as my colleagues and I admired Kennedy's cool courage in blocking Khrushchev in Berlin and forcing him to back out of Cuba, history has shown that his policies and judgment on Vietnam had put us on a path to calamitous defeat. Eisenhower, notwithstanding Dulles' constant pressure to intervene and take over the French burden in Vietnam, had held firm in prohibiting U.S. forces from participating in combat missions against the Communist Viet Minh. He continued providing military equipment to the South Vietnamese government, but limited U.S. officers to overseeing the equipment delivery and training.

Historians speculate about how Kennedy's policy would have evolved had he not been assassinated. The fact is that he, urged on by his brother Bobby Kennedy, Secretary McNamara, and Assistant Secretary John McNaughton , had made the fateful decision to allow our military advisors to engage in combat missions in Vietnam—a slippery slope.

In fact, virtually no one at a senior policy working level had spoken out against the fatal decision to authorize U.S. military advisors in Vietnam to join the combat missions of South Vietnamese troops. In later years, after the U.S. campaign faltered, Undersecretary of State George Ball and Senator Fulbright emerged as vocal leaders in opposition to our massive involvement in the battle against the Viet Minh insurgency. To my own knowledge, only two career diplomats, Paul Kattenburg, and Sterling Cottrell who had briefly chaired an interagency task force early on, as we took the fateful decision to participate in conflict missions, spoke out against U.S. intervention. Paul, who had served in Vietnam earlier, was following developments in Vietnam in the State Department's intelligence bureau. He was transferred to the dead-end post of Guyana for his efforts. Cottrell was shipped off to Venezuela as deputy chief of mission.

President Johnson, relying on the Kennedy team he inherited, has been shown in now public documents to have initially resisted this escalation. The infamous Tonkin Gulf incident in which a U.S. destroyed was allegedly fired on by North Vietnamese gunboats has been revealed to have been a false construct. President Johnson agonized over the Navy reports, which were conflicting. Pressed hard by the Joint Chiefs and even Senator Fulbright (who subsequently led the long effort to get us out of Vietnam), Johnson succumbed, and the massive buildup of U.S. forces began.

Johnson was also pressured by increasingly harsh criticism from the Republicans, as the presidential election drew near. Within the Republican Party a historic shift was unfolding which culminated in the nomination of ultra-conservative, nationalistic Barry Goldwater. Although LBJ overwhelmed Goldwater in the election, the torch had been passed within the Republican party from the moderate center—the Rockefeller wing—to the right wing of the party; a process that continued with little deviation through 2008.

The election campaign also saw tactics by both sides resort to a shocking level of smear tactics. Poor Goldwater was a popular, cautious, and decent man, and a really very good spokesman for the conservative cause. However, the Johnson campaign was successful in portraying Goldwater as an extremist who would lead us into a nuclear war. A truly unforgettable Johnson TV ad portrayed a young girl, plucking petals from a daisy, chanting "yes, it will, no, it won't," with a nuclear mushroom cloud behind her. Vicious campaign tactics in our country go all the way back to Thomas Jefferson vs. John Adams, but nothing was more devastating than this ad portraying Goldwater as a nuclear war-monger.

Republican strategists Lee Atwater, Karl Rove, and Democrat Bob Schrum had nothing on the Johnson campaign.

Caracas Arrival: Urban Terrorism Rampant

The day we arrived in Caracas more than a dozen traffic policemen were machine-gunned by terrorists determined to undermine the increasingly established democratic order in Venezuela. This terrorist action contrasted with the generally prosperous atmosphere in Caracas. The government of Venezuela seemed to be well on its way to becoming Latin America's greatest success story. Evolving out of the classic, almost comic opera, military dictatorship of Perez Jimenez, Venezuela had elected an effective dedicated moderate, Romulo Betancourt, as president, and embarked on a solid reform course. A genuine two-party system unfolded with the moderate secular socialist Accion Democratica of Betancourt and the Catholic COPEI party dominating the parliament. Betancourt, considered the father of democratic Venezuela, was succeeded by his party's candidate Leone, who in turn was replaced by the COPEI leader, Rafael Caldera, who in turn was followed by AD leader Carlos Andres Perez. With this steady pattern of peaceful change of administration, a two-party system emerged, unique in Latin America.

However, while the political system was developing admirably, the macro-economy prospering due to Venezuela's massive oil production, and a solid (often U.S. educated) middle class was developing, the bottom of the economic class structure was mired in deep poverty. Caracas, the beautiful capital city, was ringed by slums (*barrios*) with no running water and electric wires everywhere from which the *barrio* dwellers stole power. Secondary cities had the same slum blight pattern—in fact, this was a feature of most Latin American cities at the time. Close geographically to Cuba, with a massive poverty class and the challenge that the success of the Betancourt revolt against Perez Jimenez posed, it is not surprising that Venezuela was at the top of Castro's target list.

The urban insurgency supported by Castro was small in number, but strategically well-located in the university in Caracas (university campuses in Latin America were historically and constitutionally "no-go zones" for police) and inspired by "Che" Guevara's high-profile efforts to promote "revolution" throughout Latin America. The U.S. presence in Venezuela was prominent due to the dominance of Venezuela's oil production. U.S. major oil companies ran the production facilities and had set up prominent virtual American colonies for their American employees. Originally granted very liberal conditions by the military dictator Perez Jimenez, many U.S. oil company executives (and the British-Dutch Shell executives) made no bones about their preference for the "stability" that Perez Jimenez had provided them and their gated colonies. This reality, of course, contributed to the social confrontation between Venezuela's legitimate democratic government and the *barrio* poverty. It was stimulated by Che, who inspired left-wing students.

Large caches of weapons were maintained on the inviolate campus, and student rebels mentored by Cuban professionals regularly ventured forth to create chaos.

The week before we arrived, the home of my predecessor, Political Counselor Ted Long, was invaded by a group of machine-gun wielding student terrorists. Ted and his wife were tied up and the terrorists proceeded to spray paint the living room with Communist slogans. Our Moscow-sensitized assumptions, however, were deeply impressed that the terrorists carefully removed the paintings from the walls before spraying, to ensure they were not damaged. For us, this was a revelation of the Latin nature of extremism!

In another high-profile terrorist action, a month before we arrived, a car full of Castro-supporter students drove by the embassy and machine-gunned the façade. No serious damage, but by the time we arrived in Caracas, an armored van with machine gun turrets was permanently manned, in front of the embassy.

As a precaution in the face of these threats, the ambassador was provided with an armored Cadillac and an armed guard who rode shotgun with him. We became accustomed to the sight of shoulder holsters. For the rest of the embassy, we established controlled patterns of travel; I never took the same route to the office and all official parties were graced by obviously armed guards.

It became routine to us, but we did take it seriously. One bizarre event: we had a dinner party at out house for the

Minister of Education, and his brother, a Venezuelan army general. They arrived late, as is the custom, accompanied by two machine-gun bearing guards. I escorted them into our library where they were served dinner also!

Our embassy staffing reflected the unusual priority of the Cuban threat and the energy importance of Venezuela. Our ambassador, Maurice Bernbaum, like Tommy Thompson in Moscow, was a distinguished career officer with more than three decades of experience in Latin America. He had been ambassador in Ecuador, number two in Buenos Aires, and was one of the top U.S. specialists in international petroleum politics in our government. Venezuela was the number-one foreign supplier of oil to the U.S. at the time. Bernbaum was especially effective with President Leone and his cabinet, while at the same time a powerful force in educating the U.S. oil company officials to the reality that "PJ's stability" was a thing of the past. He led his unusual embassy mission with the easy confidence found in experienced professionals.

Bernbaum was backed up by another senior career officer, Sterling Cottrell, as deputy chief of mission. "Cott" had been the director of the interagency task force on Vietnam, but found himself cross-wise with the zealous attorney general Bobby Kennedy who was impatiently promoting a full-scale commitment to Vietnam. He was "banished" to Venezuela, to our benefit, as I noted earlier.

The embassy had a strong economic section with a twen-
ty-year veteran of petroleum affairs, and a veteran Labor
Department specialist, along with three other fluent Spanish
speakers. The political section included three more experienced Latin American hands. I was the "fish out of water."
Thanks especially to the ambassador, I was welcomed by all
and quickly plugged in. The labor specialist, the late Jack
Ohman, was a superb officer with close personal relations
with the AD leaders, including President Leone, who had all
come out of Venezuela's labor movement, and had known
Jack for years. Whenever we needed "inside" information
about the political machinations within the AD government, Jack was able to produce it for us.

Taking the traditional embassy political, economic, and
labor functions as one leg, the U.S. mission, dedicated to
blocking Soviet-Castro efforts to destabilize the emerging
democratic pro-American government, had two other
principal legs: a large well-funded CIA station committed to
developing Venezuela's police and secret service capabilities;
and a large, growing Defense Department "milgroup" to
deliver and train the Venezuelan military on U.S. equipment.

As in my experience at other embassies, the working relationship with the large CIA station was an especially critical
issue. Led by an experienced European specialist, Henry
Hecksher, the agency team concentrated on the Castro-
supported Marxist movement. With the exception of
Hecksher, who had also served in Berlin when I was there,

most of the CIA "station" were Latin American specialists, some with Hispanic backgrounds, and usually fluent in Spanish. Hecksher's deputy was especially problematic for the ambassador and me. An arch-conservative, he was convinced "leftist" military officers were always about to overthrow the government and establish a Castro base in Venezuela.

The most effective anti-Castro program mounted by this station was the establishment of a secret service intelligence group within the Ministry of Interior called the Digepol. Major financial and technical training support were provided by the "station," and the Digepol became a feared instrument under the direction of one of Leone's cabinet members, Carlos Andres Perez. "CAP," as he was known, became the "station's" chosen instrument. And though he came from the same labor union movement as the other AD leaders, he quickly became a force unto himself. Let there be no question, CAP's Digepol did identify and expose many terrorist plots. They also, however, failed to capture several Communist leaders who survived, often underground; two of whom under today's left-wing Chavez regime, have reemerged as Vice President Jose Vicente Rangel and Minister of Interior, Luis Miquilena.

Assessing the importance of these leftist forces was a major challenge for us. Predictably the State Department political section, including me, and the ambassador were inclined to downplay the influence of the terrorists; serious threats to order, but marginal to the stability of the government. CIA's team was much more alarmist about the urgency of the threat. It is worth noting that, for more than thirty years, we were proven correct. It is also worth noting that today, with the election of Chavez, the "station's" predictions finally came to pass!

With the ambassador's full support, we worked out an arrangement with Hecksher that enabled the embassy and all its components to report to Washington with a degree of consistency. Prior to our "arrangement," the political section would cable its assessments, which were often at odds with the "station's" reports on the same issues. CIA reporting went directly to Agency headquarters, where it was massaged and then distributed throughout the intelligence/foreign policy community: State, NSC, Department of Defense, and the FBI. From where we sat, the ambassador and his political section often found the station's reporting to be somewhat alarmist and lacking context. Thus, Ambassador Bernbaum, exercising impressive leadership, brought Hecksher, myself, and the defense attaché together and established a new process: all "station" political reporting and political section reporting would be passed through him, allowing me to add a political section comment on the "station" report, should I feel it necessary. This was very well received by CIA and the other agencies in Washington as well as providing a valuably consistent picture of events in Venezuela. The same process did not cover so-called operational intelligence reports, which were available only to the ambassador (reflecting the fact that all

U.S. government activities in Venezuela were under his control), and involved such things as recruiting agents or financing the Digepol, e.g. Hecksher was proud of his new arrangement as providing value-added, but his deputy chafed at the "intervention" by our political section.

An important distinction in the differing perspectives of the Agency's activities and its reporting from the State Department's political section was in the acquisition method. In the traditional diplomatic practice, we, the political and labor officers, cultivated targeted officials on a personal and social basis to build a sense of mutual interest. In my own case, my Moscow experience generated a lot of interest among Venezuelan diplomats, senior military officials, journalists, and members of the parliament. I worked diligently to provide the "latest news" from my former embassy in Moscow and assessments of the Moscow-NATO confrontation. I set up a regular channel to my replacement in Moscow, Bill Luers (who subsequently replaced me in Caracas, and then later became ambassador to Venezuela), who would pick up articles in the Soviet media and political journals about Venezuela that invariably attacked or ridiculed the Venezuelan government and society in general in insulting language, bragging to its own agitprop audience in the USSR. Luers cabled them to me in Caracas where I would translate them into Spanish and feed them to Venezuelan officials and newspaper editors. As you can imagine, they were outraged by Moscow's insulting reports about Venezuela. The effectiveness of this scheme was confirmed when Radio Moscow attacked me by name, for my "nefarious Cold-War activities in Caracas"!

Agency political reporting, on the other hand, reflected the fact that they were focused on recruiting allies, often with financial rewards that produced a more speculative product. On a balance, a complimentary harvest, enhanced by Ambassador Bernbaum's systematic mutual commitments by the two embassy elements.

However, for all of its complexity and tensions, the relationship between the state and CIA was less central to U.S. objectives than the Defense Department program in Venezuela.

Counter-Insurgency: The Main Focus

From the very beginning of the new Kennedy administration in 1961, the President's brother, Attorney General Robert Kennedy, was the President's closest advisor and became the administration's point man on confronting Soviet expansionism. This was, perhaps, a product of the devastating embarrassment that the Bay of Pigs fiasco created. It seemed clear to most observers and those of us in the Cold War trenches that the new President, goaded on by his brother, was thereafter absolutely determined not to be caught again in a defeat that brought his manhood into question. The reaction spread across the broad range of crises that Kennedy found in his short presidency: first in Berlin, where after a painful search for a peaceful resolution, Kennedy finally faced Khrushchev down; in the Cuban missile crisis, where Kennedy prudently but very firmly defeated Khrushchev's desperate gamble; and in Vietnam where his less-than-prudent decision to abandon Eisenhower's determined rejection of a combat role for U.S. military advisors contributed to the failure of the U.S. effort.

It is clear that Bobby Kennedy was a powerful voice for "tough guy policies," especially in dealing with Communist sponsored insurgencies, beyond our increasing involvement in Vietnam. Deputy Chief of Mission Cottrell recounted to me Bobby's role in directing the administration's slide into conflicts in Vietnam. The attorney general took to convening daily meetings in his office with four-star generals, intelligence leaders, and Cottrell to plot the next steps. Cottrell described Bobby tongue-lashing senior Defense Department general officers as wishy-washy and insisting that the U.S. would never be embarrassed again, as it was in the Bay of Pigs affair.

White House directives began to flow out, at Robert Kennedy's direction, for a government-wide training program in "counter-insurgency" to cover all USG employees assigned to countries like Venezuela, whose Communist insurgencies threatened friendly governments. As is often the case, the program produced serious overkill in setting up tough training, by roping in thousands of unlikely candidates including secretaries, finance clerks, and other civilians who would be completely insulated from insurgent events. However, the attorney general's instinct and vision were certainly prescient, as today's (2009) challenge to U.S. interests by Al Qaeda terrorists confirms.

A more substantive product of the Kennedys' policy focus on counter-insurgency was the sharp increase in equipment and training for Venezuela's military. The goal was to produce a mobile military force with updated communication capability that could move quickly to interrupt insurgent activities.

The U.S. priority for military modernization equipment was rapidly elevated when, early in my assignment to Caracas, a thirty-man terrorist team from Cuba landed on the Venezuelan coast. They were quickly intercepted by Venezuelan military units, twenty-six killed and four captured. The attempt created an uproar in Venezuela, and among the Latin American governments in the Organization of American States (OAS). A high-profile OAS delegation arrived in Venezuela within days, including U.S. ambassador to the OAS, Sol Linowitz. I was assigned to work with Sol. We visited the landing site, observed the captured Cubans, and led the OAS team, in producing a strong report condemning the Cuban intervention in an OAS state. Cuba was expelled from the OAS. More importantly, any Venezuelan reluctance to accept U.S. assistance for its military-police force evaporated. And, critically, the U.S. government increased and accelerated its training programs and equipment delivery.

For the record, Sol Linowitz was a brilliant, dedicated, and very effective leader of the OAS team. He and Maury Bernbaum led the Venezuelan government team in producing an unusually effective report, and then led the OAS to act against Castro's regime. Linowitz had been a successful corporate lawyer who helped to launch Xerox, and an active supporter of Lyndon Johnson. I have always opposed the appointment of non-career political figures and financial contributors as ambassadors—a decidedly third-world type of practice. But every now and then such an appointment makes a significant contribution to our national interest: Linowitz ranks with Averill Harriman, Douglas Dillon, and Paul Nitze in my estimation.

Following the Cuban "invasion," the U.S. milgroup program took off. A major counterinsurgency training camp was established by the Venezuelan army, enhanced by an outstanding team of U.S. Spanish-speaking officers who helped design the program. President Leone was personally active in establishing a strong priority for the program, ensuring that the most promising officers were selected for it. With the Attorney General's personal commitment in Washington, U.S. shipments increased, in spite of competing demands for this equipment as our commitment in Vietnam ballooned.

A small dramatic illustration of this "competition for resources" occurred, following President Johnson's attendance at the OAS meeting in Punta del Este, Uruguay. President Leone cornered Johnson there and asked for six more "Huey" helicopters to provide mobility for his rangers dedicated to blocking insurgency attacks. Johnson, influenced by Linowitz and the dramatic Cuba attempt to invade Venezuela, readily agreed and pledged that the "Hueys" would be sent on a priority basis. Of course, the helicopters had also become the workhorses of our forces in Vietnam, and the Pentagon bureaucracy was reluctant to divert six of them to Venezuela. Leone called in Ambassador Bernbaum after three months had passed with no sign of any helicopters. The ambassador was frustrated and his milgroup team lacked the clout necessary to move the project. Bernbaum had me dictate a first-person cable to President Johnson for him, stating that his personal commitment to President Leone "was in jeopardy" and requested him to instruct the Pentagon to act on the Venezuelan request. Johnson did. The helicopters arrived soon after and the Venezuelans quickly became adept at deploying them, under the tutelage of the U.S. milgroup trainers.

Earlier in my assignments, America's astronaut hero, Neil Armstrong, visited Caracas as part of a triumphal tour of Latin America. I drew "the duty" and "C" and I had a terrific three days with Neil, a wonderful gentleman. He was given a hero's reception by all Venezuelans who treated him as though he were their own! Arranging the Armstrong visit provided me with excellent contacts with the top Venezuelan military who were in charge of his visit. Armstrong made us proud and did the U.S. very proud. My new Venezuelan military contacts proved invaluable in our counterinsurgency programs.

Not long after the helicopter issue, the President's special envoy for "counterinsurgency," Ambassador Clare Timberlake visited to inspect the U.S. efforts to bolster Venezuela's programs. "Tim" had been consul general in Hamburg a decade earlier when I was assigned in Hamburg. I enthusiastically joined him in a week-long review of the U.S. milgroup program and the CIA parallel effort in strengthening the Venezuelan police and its "secret service" Digepol program. Tim provided a key stimulus to our efforts to have the Venezuelans establish a multi-agency insurgency control center. The center included army, navy, air force (helicopters), and police and multi-agency intelligence officers at one central location. It also set up a successful interagency communication network. It quickly became very effective and led to a series of successful actions against insurgent bands across the country.

Under longstanding presidential directives, the U.S. Ambassador as the President's personal representative in a country was clearly designated as the director of all U.S. government activity in that country. The effective coordination of all U.S. activity in Venezuela, under Ambassador Maury Bernbaum was a textbook illustration of how this should operate. The record of our ambassadors around the world is, too often, spotty. Non-career political appointees are all too often infatuated and intimidated by either the "secret" missions of the CIA station, or the powerful U.S. military assistance programs. Career ambassadors are more likely to manage the key role of stringent oversight and effective coordination. But even with career ambassadors, personality and executive skill varies. In Venezuela, under Bernbaum, it was done as it should be.

Tennis, Again

While I had found tennis clubs an excellent means of establishing ties with the local citizens in Munich, Hannover, Hamburg, and Berlin, it was in Venezuela where it became, for me, a truly effective instrument of diplomacy. Before leaving Washington for Venezuela, I had our club pro, who happened to be Pauline Betz, the number-one woman player in the world, write a letter introducing us to Venezuela's best club, Altamira Tennis Club. We chose a house in Caracas, a few blocks from Altamira, and quickly joined. Each day after returning from school, my three boys would don their tennis whites and walk down to Altamira. We were in Venezuela for three years, which meant that the boys had three years of daily coaching and play. It was here that they became fluent in Spanish. The had had a good grounding under Pauline Betz and developed rapidly into talented players. The Altamira pro was the Davis Cup coach and very effective. By the end of the second year, all three boys were winning tournaments at ten, twelve, and fourteen years old. In the third year, my second son Michael defeated his younger brother Tim in the national finals. *El Nacional*, the top newspaper featured them on the first page of the sports section!

I write this not only out of oversized parental pride, but also because their success added greatly to my influence in Venezuela's political and military circles. In fact, one of Venezuela's top generals was also an avid tennis enthusiast and chaired the Venezuela tennis association. Needless to say, he became a close friend and an excellent "source."

When the annual big international tournament was held in Caracas with all the top international players, we co-hosted a big, successful cocktail for the players. I played at Altamira also, but only socially. A beautiful setting with the mountains as a backdrop produced a rich harvest of happy memories for us.

This most happy time for our family was suddenly shattered when "C" developed breast cancer. We flew up to the U.S. military hospital in Panama to verify the finding and then she proceeded to have major surgery in Caracas. The surgeon was, in fact, my tennis partner at Altamira, a Massachusetts General trained surgeon. Subsequent tests confirmed that the cancer had spread and we faced our last six months in Caracas with deepening concern.

It was ironic that on "C"'s first night out after recovery from the operation, a historic earthquake hit Caracas. Reaching 6.8 on the Richter scale, buildings all over Caracas collapsed, killing more than 600 people. We in fact were at a penthouse cocktail party talking with the Israeli ambassador about the war with Egypt when the floor started to rock and our drinks spilled. The building next to us collapsed and our building tilted sharply and settled down, crushing two lower floors. Earthquakes are truly humbling, and this one was a dilly. We rushed home, after crawling down the stairs, to find our boys and the dog Pooh out in front of our house, which had major cracks but survived, together with our Colombian-Indian maid/cook, who was never the same again—convinced that God had forsaken her to the devil. The Venezuelan government's response was impressive, thousands were saved, and reconstruction began quickly. By the time we left Caracas, things were getting back to normal, although the haunting sight of collapsed apartment buildings reminded us, daily, of the catastrophe. The embassy was not damaged seriously, but two embassy clerks perished in an adjacent apartment.

Due to "C"'s cancer we made the decision to return to Washington in 1968 after the third year in Caracas, but not before we had another fascinating political experience.

Bobby Kennedy had made a private decision to run for president and seek the nomination against President Johnson. Kennedy immediately captured the imagination of the media in the U.S.—and throughout Latin America where his brother had been universally revered. He dispatched a four-man advance team to the countries in Latin America he chose to visit, to dramatize his campaign. He anticipated that he would receive a tremendous welcome, and he was correct. The advance team spent a week selecting places to visit that would provide the best backdrops. After three days in Venezuela, they picked our depressed *barrios* where

Kennedy could demonstrate his concern for the poor, a poverty-stricken village, as well as glamorous evening events with President Leone. I was put in charge of the visit. When Kennedy and his entourage arrived, we were shocked. He had invited fourteen U.S. journalists, four TV crews, a dozen political advisors, and Mrs. Kennedy (Ethel), who had five of her best women friends along, complete with their hairdresser.

It was a spectacle. In spite of airily changing the schedule (the farm village, which had worked hard to repaint their homes and line the dusty street with white washed stones, was unceremoniously dropped), it did produce a lot of pro-American sentiment. Kennedy plunged into crowds repeatedly, gave two rousing speeches, and came across as very presidential. His traveling media entourage produced colorful daily stories throughout his tour and his presidential campaign was on a roll. I was exhausted by the disorganized, hectic nature of it all, and very disappointed by Ethel's pack of friends who treated the ambassador's wife very rudely throughout the visits. The conclusion, a gala poolside dinner at the posh Tamanoco Hotel, was instructive. Bobby was eloquent, and his media team exuberant. Much alcohol was consumed, a huge bill run up (which was left for the embassy to pay). I have to add that Kennedy had my wife "C" seated next to him while I "handled" Ethel. "C"'s comment was, "for all his arrogance, when he turned those blue eyes on me, it was effective." That's charisma!

Farewell Caracas

We had made detailed arrangements for "C" to go into the Naval Hospital in Bethesda to review her cancer case before leaving. Departure was especially poignant. We had made dozens of friends and truly loved our assignment. The ambassador held a large departure reception for us, which was attended by virtually the entire Venezuelan cabinet, including the President, as well as our tennis world, the press, and our Venezuelan neighbors. "C" was in some discomfort, and the Bernbaums had a special stool for her in the receiving line. It was long, but she would not have missed it for the world, an outpouring of solidarity from all who knew why we had to curtail our "tour."

CHAPTER X. A COLD WAR INSTRUMENT: CULTURE AND INFORMATION AT USIA, 1968-1973

Washington was having a turbulent summer in 1968. Martin Luther King Jr. had been assassinated, race riots had produced widespread looting and burning in downtown Washington. Demonstrations throughout the United States against the war in Vietnam intensified as our casualties in Vietnam spiked. Bobby Kennedy's campaign for the presidency picked up momentum, but was suddenly ended by his assassination. To the world and to Americans there was a deep sense of despair about our fate. President Johnson had surprised us all with his sudden declaration that he would not run again for President. Richard Nixon quickly revived his political career—after losing to Jack Kennedy in 1960, he had returned to California to run for governor and was again defeated. It was universally believed that Nixon's political career was over. But Nixon confirmed the adage that you can't keep a determined politician down!

By the late summer of 1968, Nixon and Johnson's vice president Hubert Humphrey were locked in a bitter campaign to replace Johnson. Humphrey was disadvantaged by his association with Johnson's Vietnam policies, and Nixon gained traction as a wise, experienced political leader who would lead us out of the Vietnam quagmire.

As we struggled with this dangerous crisis in our history, the Soviet Union under Brezhnev's uninspiring leadership, ploughed ahead. Soviet nuclear forces grew until they achieved an equality of sorts—numbers of warheads, even though U.S. forces remained far ahead in terms of delivery systems and sophistication. And Brezhnev seemed to be presiding over greater political stability within the Soviet empire—that is, until Czechoslovakia boiled over.

Prague had become the latest center of dissent and political unrest in 1968. As in the earlier eruptions within Moscow's enforced hegemonistic empire, cultural and intellectual ferment was never far below the surface. The first of these challenges to Moscow's occupation had come in 1947 in East Germany when Berlin workers had rioted against Soviet controls, and the Red Army had to resort to force to put down the outbreak. In 1956, a much more serious outbreak occurred in Budapest. The Hungarian revolution provoked a full scale Soviet tank-led invasion, which was required to put down the revolt. Beginning in the early 1960s, stimulated by the Soviet confrontations with NATO and the U.S. over Berlin and Cuba, intellectuals, trade union leaders, and the Roman Catholic and Episcopal churches throughout Eastern Europe began to slowly build resistance to Moscow's domination. In 1968 resistance boiled over in Prague. Under the new young Communist leadership of Alexander Dubcek, Prague had begun to blossom with enthusiastic cultural, labor, and academic activities. Open discussion of withdrawing from Moscow's Warsaw Pact finally triggered a violent Soviet reaction. Brezhnev, in desperation, forced his Warsaw Pact "allies" to join in the bloody Soviet occupation of Prague.

It is interesting that Romania, under the thumb of Stalinist Nicolai Ceauşescurefused to join in. Ceauşescu was gradually constructing an image of independence from Moscow, which was popular within Romania and intriguing to the U.S. and other Western countries. At the same time his regime was growing more brutal internally as he tightened the screws on what he claimed was Soviet plotting to replace him. In fact, Ambassador Dobrynin, in his memoir (see Bibliography), confirmed that Brezhnev had been irritated by Ceauşescu's "independent posturing" and was outraged by his refusal to support the invasion of Prague. Dobrynin refers to Brezhnev's order to conduct military exercises on Romania's border as designed to warn Ceauşescu that he was risking a Soviet invasion of Romania, too.

Both the Czech crisis and the Romanian confrontation underlined the basic vulnerability of the Soviet empire; the Warsaw Pact nations were involuntary prisoners of Soviet military forces. Ruled by life-long Communists, usually loyal to Moscow's *diktats*, the populations of the Warsaw Pact countries were to one degree or another longing to become part of free Europe. Moscow's control was fully dependent on Soviet military forces stationed throughout the Pact countries, and the puppet local forces which were under

KGB control and were often more Stalinist than the KGB in Russia itself.

In short, the countries in Eastern Europe were prime targets for our programs—cultural, media, and academic. We officially and individually (any U.S. diplomats with first-hand familiarity in the area) were convinced that Soviet control over Eastern Europe was fragile. The subsequent final collapse of Soviet control over the area in 1989 bore out this assessment.

USIA

The United States Information Agency was the principal agent for U.S. efforts to that end. Originally a product of the World War II Office of War Information, it was integrated into the State Department immediately after the War, as the U.S. Information Service. It designed, reformed, and refined what had been our war-time propaganda agency. It had played decisive roles in occupied Germany (as I described in my second chapter) and Japan in building pro-Western democratic societies after the war, and demonstrated the value of media and cultural programs in the Cold War. The Eisenhower administration determined that these programs, including the Voice of America, cultural exchanges, media programs, and international exhibit programs, would be more effective in a stand-alone agency that would facilitate the recruitment of officers with backgrounds in journalism, graphic arts, broadcasting, and cultural efforts. Thus was born the USIA. It did indeed benefit from its autonomy, with larger, easier to defend budgets and specialized personnel. It was a key instrument in our Cold War campaign. (Subsequently in an ill-advised decision by then Secretary of State Albright, responding to neo-isolationist Senator Jesse Helms, it was folded back into the State Department, with reduced resources, in 2000.)

I assumed my new responsibilities at USIA in Washington in August 1968, as the Prague invasion unfolded. USIA was then run by Director Leonard Marks, a savvy communications lawyer from Texas who was a close personal friend of President Johnson. Marks was an enthusiastic leader who had developed an impressive appreciation of the importance of projecting a strong image of the U.S. around the world and exploiting the opportunities extant in the powerful but fragile Soviet empire.

Marks' deputy, Henry Loomis, directed the largest USIA asset, the Voice of America. Loomis was a brilliant engineer and strategist whose father, Alan Loomis, had dedicated his fortune (made on Wall Street by anticipating the Great Depression) to one of the world's most advanced laboratories, on his personal estate, Tuxedo Park. It was at Tuxedo Park that the U.S. radar program was developed, and in cooperation with the British government, the radar defense network that arguably won the Battle of Britain. Loomis, suffice it to say, had electronics and communications wizardry in his genes.

Marks and Loomis were a powerful team. Both had developed impressive knowledge about our Cold War targets and the potential of the USIA instruments to achieve U.S. goals: continue the basic containment policy while exploiting every crevice in the Soviet empire to erode its control over its territory. And both were superb "inside the government" players in winning budgetary support for USIA. The impact of the Vietnam War made this a daunting challenge indeed for Marks and Loomis.

The Soviet invasion of Czechoslovakia in mid-1968 was a true watershed. Brezhnev had been increasingly confident as stability in the Berlin confrontation was established and the Soviet nuclear weapon inventory grew. Brezhnev had purged his potential adversaries within Moscow's political leadership and, "more comfortable in his saddle," reached out to the U.S. on arms control programs and a possible summit with President Johnson. President Johnson had been eager to advance improving relations with Moscow. He had met Andrei Kosygin, Brezhnev's deputy and top economic planner in Glassboro, New Jersey, and had hopes for a summit meeting with Brezhnev. The Prague invasion shattered those plans.

Soviet ambassador Dobrynin, in his memoir *In Confidence*, lamented that the invasion turned our gradually improving relations "sour." Dobrynin's description of the events that led up to the invasion are revealing. He admitted that Moscow's control over the Warsaw Pact allies was severely strained. They had, under intense pressure from

Moscow, contributed token forces to join in the bloody repression of Czech dissidents, but were humiliated by the naked revelation of their subservience to Moscow. Their embarrassment was heightened by the fact that one of their number, Romania, had successfully flatly refused to participate—all the more remarkable since Romanian president Ceauşescu ran the most Stalinist of the East European regimes. His *Securitate* secret police were the most brutal and the arbitrary arrest and execution of internal dissidents was infamous. Ceauşescu thus demonstrated that a "strong" leader could thumb his nose at Moscow.

When Dobrynin informed President Johnson of the invasion of Czechoslovakia, as it was occurring, President Johnson obviously did not appreciate the significance of the invasion. He stated his hope that "our relations" could continue to improve, and that the planned summit meeting could take place. However, within forty-eight hours, the President had absorbed the momentous importance of the invasion, and talk of improving relations and a summit ended. Johnson's national security team recognized that the strategic statement the Soviets were making: once falling under a Communist regime, no one would be allowed to leave! Thus was the Brezhnev Doctrine established. Dobrynin insists that the formulation of the "Brezhnev Doctrine" was an invention of the Western press. But he continued on to define it as "the determination never to permit a 'socialist' country to slip back into the orbit of the West" and admitted that it was an "accurate reflection of the sentiments of those who ran the Soviet Union."

Alarm bells began to ring as intelligence flowed into Washington reporting that Soviet troops were massing on Romania's borders. Dobrynin, in his memoir, insists that the Soviet government had no intention of going beyond Czechoslovakia and invading Romania. His protestations of innocence were ignored by U.S. officials who remembered that Gromyko and Dobrynin had baldly insisted that there were no Soviet nuclear warheads in Cuba as the Cuban missile crisis unfolded in 1962.

Dobrynin writes that there were sharp disagreements within the ruling Politburo, but that Soviet military leaders carried the day when they insisted on the invasion. Proponents argued that if Dubcek's reforms were allowed to continue, they would infect other East European regimes, and the Warsaw Pact could collapse.

It was also noteworthy that President Johnson had given Dobrynin his private phone number, "in case of emergencies." Dobrynin used that number at 11:00 p.m. on August 20 to arrange to meet with the President and inform him of the invasion. Johnson's gesture had reflected his genuine hope that U.S.-Soviet relations were on the mend, prior to the Czech event.

Thus, as I entered on my new responsibilities, the Czech invasion and Brezhnev Doctrine were dominating our attention. While President Johnson initially did not grasp the strategic significance of Moscow's brutal intervention and the suppression of the promising reform programs which Dubcek had initiated, this had quickly changed.

Two days after the August 20 invasion, the national security team, at President Johnson's direction, ruled out any direct U.S. or NATO military move to contest Moscow's invasion as unrealistic, risking a full-scale war, and short of that, doomed to fail. Yet, it was clear that the U.S. and NATO must react with vigor.

Career Soviet specialist Malcolm Toon was appointed chairman of an interagency task force that included Defense, CIA, Treasury, State, and USIA, charged with proposing actions that would exact the maximum price on the Soviets; discourage Soviet consideration of further military actions in Eastern Europe; reinforce NATO forces in Central Europe; suspend economic and trade initiatives with Moscow; and beef up U.S. (and NATO countries') cultural and informational activities to assure the Warsaw Pact member countries of Western determination to support their efforts to expand ties with the U.S. Toon's task force also recognized that the Brezhnev invasion exposed for all to see that the Eastern European members of the Warsaw Pact constituted a vulnerable "soft underbelly" of the Soviet Empire.

The limitations that reality imposed on the Western response meant that military steps in the area would be limited. It quickly became apparent that the greatest psychological impact would have to rely on our USIA programs.

We agreed to look for every opportunity to expand our presence—plant the U.S. flag—as widely as possible. We acted quickly to seek agreement from Moscow's "allies" to open U.S. cultural and information centers in Krakow, Poland; Bratislava, Czechoslovakia; Plovdiv, Bulgaria; and in the five regional capitols of Yugoslavia. We increased VOA broadcast hours in the languages of the area, and Radio Free Europe did the same.

I selected candidates and initiated language training for eight new USIA officers to staff these centers. They were trained and in place within nine months. While a press/cultural response to a military intrusion into Prague may seem a pale reaction, in the Eastern European cities the appearance of a U.S. installation staffed by young, enthusiastic language officers under the U.S. flag had a significant positive impact. And when the Warsaw Pact forces largely withdrew from Prague, leaving a loyal team of Moscow's people in charge, our installations remained and grew steadily more active and popular until the end of the Cold War in 1989.

The staffing, funding the budget, negotiating with the host governments, and buying or renting the properties for these America centers fell to my office. I first visited each Warsaw Pact ambassador in Washington to explain our effort to expand our cultural program in each country, and seek their support and facilitation of meetings with the appropriate ministers in the capitol. Without exception, they were each flattered by my proposal. They had been embarrassed by the forced participation in the invasion of Prague and assumed that they would be "put in the freezer" by Washington. This was the beginning of a long-term initiative on my part as assistant director of USIA, which I continued after shifting back to the State Department in 1973; to build personal relations with the Warsaw Pact ambassadors, in the expectation that they would, to one degree or another, respond to our courtship effort. They did, and became valuable sources of information for us.

I launched a programmed effort to build on these new ties with the Warsaw Pact ambassadors. Polish ambassador Wittold Trampczynski was particularly responsive. My wife "C" had the wives for tea, and we had a series of small dinners at our house.

The sudden emergence of Romanian tennis star Illie Nastase and Ian Tiriac provided a special entré to the Romanian ambassador Corneliu Bogdan. After Nastase won at Wimbledon, he suddenly became a sports icon. The Romanian government, very short of popular figures, to say the least, went to work planning a tour in the U.S. and a special tennis event and reception for him in Washington. Once again tennis was a valuable asset for me professionally. I had met Ambassador Bogdan on my rounds of the Warsaw Pact envoys following the Czech invasion. I contacted him and offered USIA's assistance in arranging for Nastase's visit to Washington. He accepted with alacrity, and I went to work in contacting the sports editors and columnists interested in Eastern Europe and the USSR to help Bogdan build a reception invitation list. The party was a big success, Nastase was a most colorful personality as well as being the top tennis player in the world. Bogdan became a true and remarkably candid friend. As a Jew he was always under suspicion by Ceauşescu's brutal *Securitate* secret police. When in 1989, Ceauşescu was overthrown and executed with his wife, Bogdan emerged as spokesman for the reform-ist government led by his old friend and protector, Ian Iliescu, who became Romania's first post-Ceauşescu presi-dent.

Subsequently, Nastase and Tiriac led Romania's Davis Cup team into the finals against the United States. The matches were assigned to the Quail Hollow Country Club in Charlotte, North Carolina. I was elected to attend as the official U.S. government representative. Quail Hollow is a beautiful, lush setting. The center tennis court is set in a bowl. It was packed by tennis fans from all over the country. I joined Ambassador Corneliu Bogdan in the center box, along with General William Westmoreland, who was home on a brief leave from his command in Vietnam, and tennis officials. Nastase and Tiriac were to play U.S. stars Stan Smith and Bob Lutz; Nastase was favored. A few hours prior to opening time, a thunderstorm soaked the arena and a crisis arose. Westmoreland, in a suitably dramatic gesture, "called up" an army helicopter from a nearby military base and it settled just above the court and proceeded to dry the court with its mighty blades! At this point the warm-up began, and the small Army band (presumably provided by

Westmoreland) struck up the *Star Spangled Banner* and what was presumed to be the Romanian national anthem. All of a sudden, Bogdan grabbed my arm and said with some desperation, "they are playing the old, pre-Communist royal anthem." Since the entire event was being broadcast live by VOA back to tennis-crazy Romania, Ambassador Bogdan had a reason to panic (Ceauşescu had people executed for less). I pulled Westmoreland into our conversation and he had his aid stop the Army band and we "strategized." Westmoreland found that the Army band leader had the correct current anthem and had simply chosen the wrong one. I called the VOA broadcast team over and we staged a series of interviews with the ambassador, me, and Westmoreland, about U.S.-Romanian relations while the band, from behind the amphitheater, tootled away practicing the Communist Romanian anthem. They then reappeared, the players resumed warm-ups, and the entire ceremony was done over again! My friend, Ambassador Bogdan, was visibly shaken but relieved. Nastase, rattled by the crisis, proceeded to lose to Smith!

In my project to develop a more visible American presence throughout the Warsaw pact countries, I traveled to Warsaw and met with Deputy Foreign Minister Romauld Spassowski (a subsequent high-profile defector to the U.S. in Washington; more later) who agreed to have the historic Polish capitol city, Krakow, provide us with a centrally located building in exchange for authority to open a Polish cultural center in Chicago.

In Prague itself, I was surprised that, in spite of the fresh wound from the invasion, Czech authorities agreed to allow us to reopen the old U.S. consulate in Bratislava, the capitol of Slovakia. Prague's obvious reluctance to accept my proposal gave ground to ethnic Slovak pride in this instance. I visited the old consulate, to which the U.S. still had title, located in the heart of Bratislava. A very ancient groundskeeper opened the creaky door and I entered a real time-warp; in the main office of the dusty building was a large picture of President Harry Truman behind the "consul's desk." It was here that Senator Claiborne Pell had served as a new U.S. vice consul. Pell never failed to recollect his foreign service experience in Bratislava when I testified before him, as chairman of the Senate Foreign Relations Committee.

However, Yugoslavia was our top priority. The Brezhnev Doctrine had created the scenario that Moscow might follow up the invasion of Prague with a similar move on Yugoslavia. Marshall Tito, in 1948, had in fact withdrawn Yugoslavia from Moscow's international Communist party control organ, the Comintern, and refused to join the Warsaw Pact. Dobrynin confirms in his memoir that Yugoslavia was in fact a "bone in the throat" to many Politburo officials and that hard-line military officials were constantly pressuring to teach Tito a lesson. While our task force doubted that Moscow, encouraged by their successful repression of Czechoslovakia's effort to back away from Moscow's hegemony, would take on Marshall Tito and his large, well-trained armed forces defending in mountainous terrain, we also had assumed that they would not use naked military force to overthrow Dubcek in Prague. In 1948, Tito had been able to back out of Stalin's embrace because his partisan forces had defeated the German invasion with only limited support from the Red Army and important material support from British and American liaison officers. Khrushchev had attempted to woo Tito back into the fold in the sixties, but had failed and been criticized by his Politburo colleagues for acknowledging Tito's autonomy and "kowtowing to this renegade."

A U.S. military assistance team quickly met with Yugoslav army officials and stepped up supplies of armor and aircraft. Tito was treated with renewed respect by the U.S. and NATO.

I travelled to Belgrade with a proposal to significantly expand our presence throughout Yugoslavia. In a brief meeting with Tito, he blessed the idea, then he and I held a series of negotiations with his minster of information, Budomovski. The minister was a large, gruff Macedonian. Notwithstanding Tito's approval, he only gradually warmed to my proposal that we establish America Centers in each of four autonomous republics of Yugoslavia: Croatia, Slovenia, Macedonia, and Bosnia-Hersogovina. After three long sessions, enhanced by thick black coffee and numerous shots of Slivovitz (Yugoslavia's national drink, plum brandy) we became more enthusiastic. At the final meeting, where we signed the agreement, I asked Budomovski whether he personally was anxious about the possibility of a Soviet invasion. He turned, opened his closet, and revealed a full combat uniform with boots and a machine-gun. He turned back and said, "There is your answer, we will fight them to the bitter end, as the Nazis discovered!"

I followed on to Bucharest, which had from the beginning seemed a likely next target for Brezhnev who was outraged by Ceauşescu's refusal to join in the Warsaw Pact invasion of its neighbor, Czechoslovakia. Soviet troop mobilization on Romania's borders added to the apprehension that the Brezhnev Doctrine would lead to more Soviet initiatives to squelch any moves by Warsaw Pact members to loosen Moscow's control. I met with Ceauşescu's foreign minister and information minister to propose that we be allowed to open an America center to provide American cultural and educational activities for Romanians. They did not show any signs of having been intimidated by Soviet troop exercises on their border, and quickly agreed to provide us with a facility. I proposed they sell or lease us a particular lovely old decrepit residence, directly next door to the Soviet House of Culture. They enthusiastically rose to the bait and agreed, savoring the image of a U.S.-Soviet competition, which they were confident Moscow would lose. Within six months we had renovated the old mansion, replete with bright modern colors, a theater, and an excellent library. USIA had sent out our top decorator and she (Andrea Schmertz) converted the creaky old house into a vibrant modern institution. I dispatched one of USIA's most creative active young officers,

Jim Rentschler, after four months of Romanian language training, as the new Public Affairs Officer. Jim had been cultural affairs officer in Paris and was fluent in French. Romanian (unique among the languages spoken in the Warsaw Pact countries as Latin-based) was a short hop from French. Within a few months, the America Center was jammed with young and old attending our programs, while the Soviet Center next door remained virtually empty. Ceauşescu, obviously enjoying the embarrassing contest with Moscow's programs, told the U.S. ambassador in Bucharest that he greatly valued this American presence in Romania.

Our efforts in Hungary and Bulgaria were less successful. The U.S. embassy had become the refuge for Cardinal Mindszenty during the brutal Soviet invasion of Budapest in 1956, and his presence remained a major issue between the U.S. and Hungarian governments. The Hungarians were embarrassed by his "house-arrest status" as well as their participation in the crackdown on Czechoslovakia, but the hard-line regime imposed by the Soviets in 1956 was thoroughly under Moscow's thumb. In spite of the best efforts of our brilliant PAO in Bucharest, Ed Alexander, we were unable to accomplish much. Bulgaria, always the most loyal of Moscow's colonies, also refused to respond to my efforts at that time.

With President Johnson's retirement and Nixon's victory in the November election, Marks was replaced by Nixon campaign media advisor Frank Shakespeare. An arch-conservative, Shakespeare had been a senior executive at Westinghouse Broadcasting. He reportedly designed the campaign technique of positing a dignified still-life of Nixon against an action backdrop of crime wars (to underline Nixon's campaign theme that he would crack down on crime), and military parades. This was designed and did succeed in overcoming the image of eye-darting deviousness that Nixon, live, projected on TV.

Shakespeare wisely kept the apartisan Loomis on as deputy director, which softened somewhat his own ultra-conservative outlook.. Restless, very energetic and ideological in his approach to Communism, Shakespeare was a challenge for me, as I was in charge of programs directed against the Soviet Union and the Warsaw Pact. However, he also provided great opportunities. Like Marks, he had excellent access to the President, which translated into strong budget support for our programs. He was absolutely convinced that the battle against Communism must override all other policies, and he made it clear that I could select the best and brightest for the public affairs positions in Moscow and the other Warsaw Pact capitols. It would be fair to say that while his rationale was sometimes questionable, he did an excellent job of beefing up our programs in the Cold War battlegrounds.

Perhaps my most important challenge was to seize on Shakespeare's simple anti-Communism and expand his appreciation and support for the sophisticated objectives of stoking East European nationalism, basic unhappiness with

Soviet domination, and presenting a forceful picture of the magnetic qualities of Western societies. In the beginning, Director Shakespeare perceived the Communist members of the Warsaw Pact as indistinguishable from the Soviet regime in Moscow. As he and his new Republican team of political appointees, all drawn from the arch-conservative wing of the party, became personally involved in our programs throughout the Warsaw Pact countries, they quickly became receptive to the proposition that the peoples of Eastern Europe were potentially invaluable allies in our policy to contain and erode Soviet power.

In addition to scheduling Shakespeare's team to visit our operations in the USSR and Eastern Europe, we worked aggressively to bring them into contact with leading academics and press people experienced in Soviet affairs. A successful example of this was a seminar-luncheon at USIA that I arranged for my former Harvard professor, Zbignew Brzezinski. "Zbig," who is one of the most articulate men in my experience, "wowed" Shakespeare and his six Republican associates. Gradually this new team absorbed the reality that the people of Eastern Europe were a priority target and that Soviet hegemony in the area was, in fact, vulnerable.

VOA Broadcasting: A Vital Weapon

The most public of our "propaganda efforts," broadcasting was a critical instrument to rally Eastern European populations and to break through Moscow's massive efforts to insulate the people of the Soviet Union itself. Not long after its birth in 1917, the Soviet regime had always promoted radio as a means to communicate the party line throughout Russia and all of the so-called autonomous regions and republics. That same communication network effectively created the shortwave capacity for reception of Western broadcasts—a dilemma for the regime that attempted to maintain the isolation of its many peoples with a system of "jammers." Over the years, Soviet authorities surrounded first Moscow, and then other major cities across the vast reaches of the USSR, with huge jamming towers, which resembled tall palm trees. They were prominent in the skylines of all major cities. The "palm trees" were essentially individual broadcast towers set to the frequencies of West-ern broadcast channels. They were adjustable and allowed the cat-and-mouse game that was a fact of life between our shifting broadcasts and Soviet palm tree jammers. They were obnoxious to many thinking Soviet citizens, but they were successful in the cities. However, Voice of America and other Western broadcasts were freely picked up in the countryside. A major source of outside information for Soviet citizens developed as country-folk would come into market in the cities and cautiously repeat the news from VOA!

Western broadcasters were led by the VOA. However the British voice, BBC, was also very widely heard and respected as a reliable source throughout the USSR. The German counterpart, *Deutschewelle*, was less effective at penetrating and carried the obvious baggage of WWII hostilities.

A unique and very effective broadcast force was *Kol Israel*, the official voice of Israel. It was, of course, targeted to Jews in the Soviet Union, and heavily jammed.

VOA broadcast in all the major minority languages in the USSR, but due to "budgetary restraints," usually only one or two hours a day, even though Soviet jamming was much less effective on the widespread areas of Ukraine, Kazakhstan, Uzbekistan, and the Baltic states of Lithuania, Estonia, and Latvia. This was a clear example of Shakespeare's value as director of USIA. He lobbied the White House and won major increases in VOA's funding, which allowed me to double the hours of our broadcasts to these "minority areas." A valuable, effective, and long-lasting response to the Brezhnev Doctrine and Prague in 1968.

In addition to battling to increase our VOA broadcasts into the USSR (and Eastern Europe where efforts to block VOA were ineffective), I regularly visited BBC and Deutschwelle in London and Bonn to exchange technical advances to counter Soviet jamming and the evidence, which was hard to accumulate, about actual listenership throughout the USSR. The evidence, while limited (tourists, official travelers, and individual Soviets) was universally positive: VOA was listened to and had good credibility. VOA broadcasts, a subject of skeptical Congressional criticism, reported official U.S. government activities, feature articles on life in the United States, world news, and jazz. The latter, produced on a daily one-hour show by the legendary Willis Conover, was perhaps the most popular U.S. propaganda effort of all.

VOA broadcasting was the object of intensive Congressional oversight and controversy. Conservatives criticized the "Voice" for not being sufficiently aggressive and confrontational. Liberals chafed at the idea of "propaganda" in general. World news coverage of our difficulties in Vietnam was particularly controversial. It was constantly a struggle for the Voice to report negative developments in order to retain credibility.

More difficult for VOA and me to deal with was the unending battle with the American diaspora community. The United States had a great Cold War advantage in our diversity. At the same time that diversity produced several strains. The Ukrainian-American community, for example, which provided many of VOA's Ukrainian-service people, never was satisfied with the number of hours dedicated to "their" service.

Yiddish Broadcasts?

In a fascinating side-effort in the VOA-U.S. diaspora issue, I suddenly found myself face to face with a politically contentious crisis: should VOA broadcast in Yiddish to Jews in the Soviet Union? The question first arose when Congressman Ben Rosenthal, a Democrat from Long Island, called me to meet with a collection of Jewish congressmen in his office to discuss the USSR and our campaign to penetrate the essentially closed Soviet society. When I arrived at his office, I found twelve other congressmen—not their staffers but the members themselves. This was most unusual, and I quickly grasped that I was "on the grill." Ben opened by lamenting that while VOA broadcast programs in Russian and English reporting on Jewish life in the U.S., developments in Israel, and a great deal about religious freedom in general, there were no VOA broadcasts in Yiddish. Each member then added to Ben's arguments, concluding with a demand that VOA establish a "Yiddish service" directed at Soviet Jews.

I was, admittedly, caught by surprise. I immediately agreed to call together my colleagues from the State Department to consider the issue and promised to get back to them within three weeks. I concluded by putting down some "markers," pointing out the only elderly Soviet Jews still spoke Yiddish, Hebrew was the language of choice for Soviet Jewry, and that all Soviet Jews spoke and largely lived in Russian. The congressmen then argued that precisely because Yiddish was dying out, it was essential that VOA act to help preserve Yiddish among Soviet Jews. Obviously, preserving Yiddish did not seem to me to be an effective contribution to eroding Soviet hegemony. However, the diaspora political priority reflected in the turnout in Ben's office meant that I was dealing with a serious political issue, not to be dismissed lightly! I resolved to find a resolution. At home, I told my wife "C" about Ben's meeting, and the sense that he had blindsided me. She counseled that the issue was obviously "bread and butter" with his constituents, and obviously was not going to evaporate. The next day, I met with my deputy, Ed Alexander, a seasoned public affairs officer with long experience in Budapest (and an Armenia-nAmerican, who belonged to one of the most powerful diaspora communities in the U.S.) and General Alex Barmine, a sixty-five-year-old former Soviet officer who had defected to the U.S. in the forties. Because he was especially wise about Russian attitudes, Barmine brought unique insight into dealing with the powerful diaspora lobbies in Washington. We agreed that this was a major challenge, and in a stroke of creativity, we agreed I should seek advice and support from the government of Israel. Shakespeare quickly assented, and I flew off to Tel Aviv, hopeful that I would find support there against initiating Yiddish broadcasts.

Israel's *Kol Israel* broadcasts were heavily jammed in the USSR. Therefore, I took along with me VOA's top jamming engineer. We had two intense days of meetings with the foreign ministers, the special advisor to the president of Israel for Jewish questions in the Soviet Union and Warsaw Pact countries, and finally with *Kol Israel* officials. My VOA engineer was immensely helpful to my talks and aided *Kol Israel*'s anti-jamming efforts. As I anticipated, the Israelis were strongly opposed to VOA establishing a "Yiddish service" and urged that VOA concentrate its efforts in

Russian and English, leaving Hebrew broadcasts to *Kol Israel.*

I returned to Washington, reinforced, and met again with Ben Rosenthal's "gang of twelve." They were completely chagrined by my report and the push for Yiddish broadcasts was over!

*

While I was thoroughly enjoying the exciting and fast-moving interagency role I had in USIA, my life was increasingly overwhelmed by my wife's declining health. Not long after my trip to Israel, we lost "C." Those who have lost a spouse appreciate the pain, grief, and panic that engulf you. It had been a four-year struggle in which her courage, humor, and confidence buoyed us all. Now, in the cold reality and totality of her loss, I redirected my life to raising our three sons and tried to refocus on my role in the Cold War.

*

Diaspora pressures were a permanent political issue in the politics of international broadcasting, especially VOA. At the same time, there was general recognition within the post-Prague invasion task force of the fact that VOA and other Western broadcasts were the most effective single method of reaching over the barriers set up by the brutal Soviet-controlled regimes to insulate their populations from the magnetic force of free societies.

Each budget year, we would again be pressured by the various ethnic communities in the U.S., and their Congressional representatives to increase or redirect our resources to target the ethnic group of choice. After "Prague," I had worked diligently with my colleagues at VOA to increase broadcast hours, and sharpen the content directed at the Russians, the Soviet minorities, and the audiences in Eastern Europe. We received strong support from Shakespeare, the interagency task force, and the White House. And we did enhance the broadcasting effort.

However, the Congressional oversight of this political activity was constant. The Yiddish incident was unusually intense, but at each budget hearing we would be buffeted by Congressional invitation (both parties!) to add, increase, or redirect our broadcasting programs. There was general support for our buildup of broadcasts to Soviet minority audiences—especially Ukrainian, Uzbek, and Kazakh. But when I attempted to shut down marginally important language broadcasts to Slovenia, for example, to create more resources for Uzbek broadcasts, I was called into Congressman John Blatnik's (D-MN) office and "instructed" to continue the Slovene service. In spite of the clear evidence that Slovenes were not listening to VOA (they bordered Austria and Bavaria and relied on *Deutschwelle* broadcasts), Blatnik insisted. Blatnik's congressional district had a large Slovene-American population and they considered VOA's Slovene service emblematic of U.S. support for the aspirations of the Slovene people. I was able to overcome Blatnik's insistence, when I briefed him and his chief-of-staff Jim Oberstar on our fast unfolding plan to open an America center in Ljubjana, the capitol of Slovenia, and staff it with a new Slovene-speaking public affairs officer. Oberstar eventually succeeded Blatnik and in 2009 is one of the most powerful House members—still a friend and strong supporter of American cultural and information programs.

Similar American diaspora pressures blocked our efforts to redirect resources in the Baltic languages. Latvia, Lithuania, and Estonia had become vibrant independent nations between World War I and World War II, before being brutally absorbed into the USSR after the infamous 1940 Ribbentrop-Molotov pact, when Stalin joined with Hitler to divide up Central Europe. The flood of Baltic refugees created an instant diaspora in the U.S. The Soviet takeover produced widespread support for these heroic little countries. Each of the three countries, subsidized by the U.S. government and their diaspora populations, established embassies in Washington, and the U.S. government announced a formal policy of refusing to recognize Moscow's hegemony over the three nations. This policy was maintained until the collapse of the Soviet Union in 1989. Thus, VOA's Baltic language services were virtually sacred. We, in fact, increased Baltic language broadcasts following the Prague invasion.

While diaspora oversight was intense and reflected in Congressional reviews, it provided solid support for this

298

most important element in our offensive against Moscow's hegemony.

Radio Liberty and Radio Free Europe

A second major piece in U.S. broadcasting activity directed to erode Soviet control of the Warsaw Pact countries and erode Soviet power within the USSR was the two-pronged "covert" program embodied in Radio Liberty and Radio Free Europe. Created shortly after the beginning of the Cold War, RL and RFE were funded and directed by the CIA, in close cooperation with the State Department and USIA. For its public face, this pair of broadcast programs was partially funded by public subscriptions raised at high-profile fundraisers. It was generally recognized that official funding was a major component. CIA officials actually directed the two stations, located in Munich where large concentrations of disaffected refugees from the USSR and Central Europeans had settled. The two stations took on distinct responsibilities and a very effective division of labor with VOA was established. VOA was responsible for broadcasting world news, official U.S. policy, and news about developments in the United States. RL-RFE were (and still are) responsible for broadcasting on developments within the USSR (RL) and the Warsaw Pact countries (RFE). RL-RFE, operated by recent anti-Communist refugees with excellent sources within the USSR, provided a steady stream of news, often embarrassing to Moscow, about local KGB acts of oppression, food riots (which were frequent throughout the USSR), student unrest, among other issues.

I regularly visited RL-RFE offices and we worked seamlessly to chase information and divide up our efforts. Listenership research confirmed that both programs were effective. RL-RFE attracted massive jamming efforts, but still succeeded penetrating the "palm tree forests of the USSR," and reached the captive nation populations of the Warsaw Pact. Palm trees were too expensive to blanket the entire area. And, the characterization of RL-RFE activities as "non-governmental" provided a useful fig leaf.

Later, in the anti-Vietnam atmosphere that pervaded, a headstrong staffer in Senator Clifford Case's (R-NJ) officer, John Marx, orchestrated a dramatic "exposure" of CIA's direction of the allegedly non-governmental RL-RFE programs. Case by then had joined with his Democratic chairman, William Fulbright, to declare that the Cold War was over and we should retreat from these efforts to contain and erode Soviet power. I testified before Fulbright and Case in the Foreign Relations Committee, repeatedly, in support of the important and clearly effective bi-level broadcasting programs of VOA and RL-RFE. It is worth noting that this concept prevails as I write this in 2009, under a new overt-funding program, the Board for International Broadcasting, and an additional set of new program services directed at Iran, North Korea, and Cuba.

It is also worth noting that the Soviet leadership acknowledged the effectiveness of broadcasting by expending double our effort with their multiple-hour programs into Latin America, Africa, and the Middle East.

The Cultural Agreement with Moscow: Exhibits, Publications, Cultural and Academic Exchanges

Soviet leaders were torn by the inevitable clash between their paranoid determination to insulate their population from the magnetic pull of the West and their appetite for international respect, and even fear, of their accomplishments. As mentioned above, they outspent us by far on international broadcasting. The founding of Lumumba University in Moscow to attract, train, and recruit third-world students was part of their historic effort to expand their authority and promote Moscow's interests and Communism around the world. The second of these objectives, creating respect and expanding the influence of the Soviet Union led Moscow to agree to a multi-year cultural agreement between our two governments. The negotiation for these biannual agreements was tough but successful. I was the USIA representative on the inter-agency team that took on these negotiations. The Soviet side consistently sought agreement from the United States to receive major Soviet performing groups such as the Kirov Ballet, the Bolshoi Ballet, and top Soviet musicians such as David Oistrakh, the violinist. On our side, happy to arrange tours for such premiere Soviet events in the U.S., we sought reciprocal tours in the USSR for the Philadelphia Symphony Orchestra, Benny Goodman's band, and the University of Michigan's marching band. The Soviet negotiators agreed, but then attempted to limit the itinerary for the U.S. programs to Moscow and Leningrad. We insisted, and occasionally won agreement that our performers could venture more broadly to Kiev, Alma Ata, and Irkutsk in Siberia. The Soviets resisted, acknowledging that their facilities (including, in reality, KGB local capacity to control and monitor contacts) were inadequate. Our experiences confirmed that visits beyond the relatively jaded (and carefully controlled by ticket distribution) audiences in Moscow and Leningrad, had a truly electric effect on more distant cities, starved for contact with the West.

Both the Goodman concerts and the Michigan band were huge successes as I reported earlier. In both cases, Soviet officials had managed the tickets to ensure that only "trusted" party members would be exposed to these American influences. The Michigan band performed in the huge outdoor sports arena that was packed, largely with uniformed soldiers. The Michigan fight song, familiar to all who have seen Michigan football games on TV, had a tremendous impact on the young uniformed audience. We joked that the band could have led the entire audience out of the arena in a victory march around Moscow. I repeat these accounts to demonstrate the value of these cultural exchanges. Soviet propaganda, which had been unrelenting in portraying the United Stated in the worst possible light, had to some extent numbed the Soviet public. Cynicism was perhaps the most accurate description of Soviet audiences to the regime's claims of revolutionary economic progress and portrayal of the "evil West." However, with the exception of VOA broadcasts, there was little accurate positive portrayal of the U.S. High-profile cultural events like Goodman and the Michigan band put flesh on our image. They were surprisingly effective, precisely because of the barren landscape in which they appeared.

Reciprocity, which was the rule in all our relationships with the USSR, meant that we hosted Soviet cultural events in the U.S. Exactly the same number of performances in exactly the same number of cities. Soviet ballet troupes, symphony orchestras, and opera companies were very well received by U.S. audiences, but the political and psychological impact was infinitely less in the free audiences of the U.S., which expected top quality from foreign performers.

The second major section in the cultural agreement negotiation provided for mutual distribution of publications. Paranoid as they were about foreign influence penetrating their closed society, the Soviets were confident that they could effectively limit distribution of any American publication because the KGB, in fact, controlled the distribution systems. For our part, we believed, and were proven correct in practice, that we could evade much of the control system. We agreed on mutual distribution of 70,000 copies of *Amerika* in the USSR and *Soviet Life* in the U.S., monthly.

Amerika was produced by the first-rate publications division of USIA. It was a beautiful, glossy production with carefully tailored material to emphasize the quality of life in the United States in terms that would be meaningful to Soviet citizens. There was constant emphasis on freedom to travel and freedom of worship, which were fiercely controlled in the USSR. Articles, each month, about the productivity of our agriculture struck at the decades-long decay of agriculture in the USSR. And each month *Amerika* featured an article about the success of our minorities, in the academic world, for example. This contrasted, of course, with the permanent under-class status of minority populations in the USSR.

Each month I chaired an *Amerika* meeting in which we selected the themes that would be struck in the next issues. We then launched a series of VOA stories promoting that issue, and discussing the chosen theme. The photography was selected and always of top quality. The most challenging part of producing *Amerika* each month was how to deal with race problems, Indian tribe life, and poverty. We did cover these issues, but in a positive context, always centered on progress being made.

Soviet Life, on the other hand, was a dreary publication, full of transparently propagandistic material, printed on typically low-quality paper, with occasional good photography of such places as beautiful Lake Baikal (the world's largest fresh-water lake).

Distribution, as noted above, became the critical question. *Soviet Life* was not popular in the U.S. because it was of such low quality. But, if we were unable to distribute 70,000 copies, the Soviet side would contend that they too had been unable to move virtually the same number of copies of *Amerika* and the Soviet (government owned) distributor would return the "unsold" copies to the U.S. embassy in Moscow. Our embassy cultural office would then work to ensure that all embassy officers traveling in the USSR would leave multiple copies of *Amerika* in airplane seats, trains, and generally distribute by hand whatever they could. On its publication date, embassy officers would visit the kiosks around Moscow to try and confirm that *Amerika* had been put on sale. Often we were told that *Amerika* was sold out, even if we could spot copies under the counter. We did easily confirm that there was a lively black-market in *Amerika,* which priced at one ruble, was fetching up to ten rubles.

On balance, the publications exchange was a small but important victory for our campaign to penetrate the closed society of the USSR.

The most surprising of our cultural agreement programs was the agreement to exchange national exhibits each two years of the agreement. In the agreement negotiations we battled Soviet efforts to limit the travel of our exhibits to Moscow and Leningrad, where the KGB was most effectively staffed to control access to our exhibits, and we insisted on reaching out to the minority Republics to play to the restive populations there. We had some success in this regard, because we could freely bargain to provide authorization for Soviet exhibits to go to any city in the U.S. Thus, in the early 1970s, we scheduled each exhibit into six cities for a total of a year in the USSR, including such sensitive areas as Tbilisi, Georgia, Kiev, Ukraine, and Irkutsk in Siberia.

As in the case of *Amerika*'s publication, I chaired a multi-agency team that selected the subject matter of the exhibit. We deliberately selected subjects such as "kitchens," camping, medical instruments, and education. You will recall that the early exhibit on kitchens was the site of a spirited debate between then Vice President Nixon and Soviet leader Khrushchev. It also hit a very vulnerable spot in Soviet society since kitchens in the USSR were so dismal and dysfunctional. The topic of camping turned out to be a great success since Soviets were enthusiastic campers and so limited in the ability to move anywhere outside their home; internal passports were an odious fact of the Soviet control system.

Perhaps the most valuable element in the U.S. exhibits were the American guides in the exhibit. Our interagency committee placed top priority on the selection process. We chose fifteen bilingual (Russian and some who also had Georgian or Kazakh, e.g.) young Americans who spent a year traveling with this exhibit. They would stand each day in front of an exhibit section and engage the Soviet visitors in free and open conversation about any and all subjects. The popularity of the exhibits was truly magnetic and huge crowds overcame all police efforts to limit attendances.

VOA, of course, would report on the exhibit schedule and promote stories on the subject matter. Picture a young black American woman with good control of Russian (Harvard), standing in front of a new Chevrolet pick-up arguing with an obvious KGB provocateur about U.S. actions in Vietnam and Brezhnev's invasion of Prague! KGB officers labored hard to entrap the adventurous guides and local police, under KGB direction, tried to dampen attendance. Occasionally the KGB would succeed and we would have to quickly ship a guide home. But, with few exceptions, these U.S. exhibits had an amazing success record. Dozens of "former guides," like former Peace Corps volunteers, have become respected specialists and historians on Soviet and now Russian affairs. It is also worth noting that we had a seemingly unlimited flow of volunteers for the guide program. Many with Russian ethnic backgrounds and many graduates of Russian studies programs at our best universities. Another example of the unique strengths of the United States by dint of our diverse ethnic background.

One of Director Shakespeare's most successful innovations was the move to beef up the USIA advisory board. He added two superstars who brought great cache and proved to be very valuable in supporting USIA before congressional committees.

Bill Buckley

William Buckley, the conservative editor of *National Review*, agreed to join the board when President Nixon assured him he would be able to travel widely and critique USIA programs without limit. One of his first "assignments" was to visit the USSR in November and observe our travelling exhibit. Shakespeare had me accompany him; in fact it turned out to be a great experience. It was my first trip out after losing "C" in June, and I was distracted and depressed. Buckley had a national reputation as arrogant, self-centered, and violently anti-Communist.

However, perhaps because of his fascination with the USSR (he had never been to the USSR) and an innate sense of compassion, he was "just what the doctor ordered" for me. At departure, we met at the VIP lounge; a "breathless young thing" from *Time* approached and told Buckley that she had the "contract" for him calling for a quick story on the Olympics. It was an odd Olympics in which the Soviets had beaten us in basketball and short-dash races, while the U.S. had beaten Russian teams in long-distance races and wrestling, a complete upside-down result from expectations. The young *Time* woman had him sign the contract and promised he would be met with $5,000 in exchange for his story when he arrived in Paris. As we settled in our seats on the PanAm plane, Buckley, with a huge grin, said to me, "I don't know a damn thing about basketball or wrestling, do you?" By now, we had our first martinis, and I laughed and said, "You're in luck—I played varsity basketball in college at Bowling Green and I follow it closely." Within two hours, having great fun, I talked and he typed on his little portable type-writer. On arrival in Paris, true to form, another breathless young woman approached, accepted his story, and handed him a check for $5,000. We then boarded an Aeroflot flight to Moscow. By the time we arrived, he had grilled me about "C" and our great marriage and became very supportive. We remained great friends over the years; he sent me inscribed copies of each of his new books as they were published.

We had several very active days together in Moscow when Buckley came face to face with Soviet reality—completely replacing his black and white comprehension of the USSR with a sophisticated appreciation of the real danger that the Soviets would underestimate U.S. strength and the glaring vulnerabilities of the Soviet structure. He worked hard, absorbed several hours of intense briefings about the USSR, the various U.S. programs operating out of the embassy (USIA, Defense attaches, economic, agricultural, and political sections).). Our Moscow PAO, McKinney Russell, was another in our solid line of outstanding officers, and he and Buckley hit it off immediately. Buckley was amazed at how Russell's mission was able to penetrate Moscow's closed society.

We then departed to observe the operation of our major USIA exhibit and our guides in Tbilisi, Georgia. Our exhibit was a smashing success. Jammed by fascinated Georgians who largely overwhelmed the KGB-police efforts to control access and reaction, the exhibit scene was vibrant and full of discussion and individual debates between our young articulate guides and the huge Georgian audience. More than 200,000 turned out in Tbilisi before it was over (each one received a free copy of the latest *Amerika* magazine), and almost without exception full of praise for "this chance to learn the truth about the U.S." We observed two very confrontational efforts by the KGB provocateurs to embarrass our guides in front of their audience; on both occasions, the public turned against the provocateurs and supported the guides. Needless-to-remark, Buckley was deeply impressed, and became a strong supporter of our young guides and the exhibit program.

We departed our hotel for the Tbilisi airport in a snowfall. On arrival, we were told that our Aeroflot plane was too iced-up to depart. However, we were quickly reassured that another flight that had just arrived would be made available to us. Buckley was astounded to watch as Aeroflot officials brushed aside the poor Soviets who were supposed to fly on that plane and we were ushered aboard to return to Moscow, ice forming on the wings as we boarded. We took off in a nervous state, to say the least.

En route back to Moscow, I briefed Buckley on the incredible success of the exhibit, numbers of visitors, and some of the anecdotal experiences of the guides, living in Tbilisi for several weeks. He was taken aback to learn that two of the guides had been drugged at dinner and expelled by the KGB overseers in an effort to frighten the guides.

Bottom-line: Bill Buckley became a great asset for USIA among conservative critics who opposed wasting taxpayer money on "cultural activities abroad." He also followed up his visit with major VOA interviews, one in world-wide English and several translated into Russian and Georgian and directed into the USSR.

James Michener

Shakespeare's second advisory board decision was to persuade world-renowned author James Michener to join with Buckley. Michener's recruitment was all the more remarkable because he was an established Democrat. He had actually just run as a Democrat candidate for Congress from the Philadelphia suburbs.

Michener, too, was eager to observe USIA Cold War activities first hand. Following my trip to the USSR with Buckley, we scheduled Michener for a "renowned author's" visit to Romania. Like Buckley, Michener's celebrity produced large enthusiastic turn-outs at Bucharest universities, meetings with the literary society, TV interviews and a meeting with Romania's Stalinist president, Ceauşescu. Michener was captivating as he described his works on Poland, and the Chesapeake, among other topics. The highlight of his visit was the gala reception at the stunning new America Center. Academics, journalists, students, and government officials paraded through to see the acclaimed international author. Our public affairs chief in Bucharest, Jim Rentschler, had procured hundreds of Michener's books, which he distributed free to one and all.

Michener left an indelible impression on Romanians. He, too, followed up with several VOA and Radio Free Europe interviews directed back into Romania.

A year later, Shakespeare resigned from USIA and was replaced by former *Time* editor and Nixon speech writer, James Keogh. Jim was a completely different personality and much easier to work with. Insightful, well-informed, and balanced, he was quickly embraced by USIA's brilliant career specialists who had dealt with Shakespeare's energy and prejudices uneasily. Keogh remained a close friend until he passed away in 2005. He, too, had excellent close ties to the President and USIA continued to benefit with good budgetary support from the White House.

The Congressional budget hearing provides an illustration of how the Congress exercises oversight of our foreign affairs budget. On June 4, 1973, I testified (as I did each year) before the House of Representatives Committee on State Department operations, chaired by the formidable Wayne Hays. Hays, a combative Democrat was always looking for targets in the Republican administration and was especially tough on Directors Shakespeare and Keogh. In my statement I described that we had quickly expanded our presence throughout the Warsaw Pact countries and opened America Centers in four Yugoslav regional capitols. We had held two very successful U.S. exhibits in the USSR that had each been visited by two million Soviet visitors.

Chairman Hays expressed cynicism about our claims for VOA listenership during Director Keogh's testimony. I took the opportunity during my subsequent testimony to contest Hays' skepticism. Our exchange was typical of the annual oversight confrontation with Hays, whose chairmanship gave him control of the USIA budget appropriation:

I would like to add two points in response to some of the points you touched upon with the Director this morning. First is listenership to VOA in the Soviet Union. I am not an expert on most parts of the world but I do know something about listenership in the Soviet Union.

As you know, we have on each one of these exhibits I mentioned to you 22 to 25 young American boys and girls who are bilingual in Russian and who had a dialogue with those two million Soviets. That is a large sample. The guides have found the VOA is very widely listened to.

Many of the people who come to the Exhibit heard about it on VOA. We had had members of VOA as guides in these exhibits so that they could update their knowledge of the Soviet Union. They have been recognized. Their voices have been recognized. People say, "I have heard you for 20 years."

When Madame Furtseva was here, the Soviet Minister of Culture, she was introduced to the staff at VOA. Even Madame Furtseva, who was a renowned sour-puss, had to break into a smile and say, "I have been listening to you for years."

I travelled throughout the Soviet Union extensively. I have found time and time again in discussions with Soviet citizens that people do listen to the Voice of America and in this closed society the injection of information about the United States and about our policies and what people are saying in this country is, in my judgment extremely valuable.

The other point I would like to mention is the question of language capability of our service. I cannot speak for other areas served by USIA and the State Department but I assure you, in Eastern Europe and the Soviet Union, there is not one substantive officer who is not fluent in the language to the country where he is assigned. I think it is a valuable principle. I know you support this.

Mr. Hays: You are saying there is not a single officer in the --

Mr. Jenkins: Single substantive officer in the Soviet Union or --

Mr. Hays: What do you mean by substantive?

Mr. Jenkins: There may be an administrative fellow who is in charge of getting shipments back and forth. I am talking about political and economic officers who are career foreign service officers in those posts.

Mr. Hays: Mr. Jenkins, I don't want to get into an argument with you but I have been to the Soviet Union many times and I have had trouble finding anybody in our embassies, except two or three officers, who are very fluent in Russian.

The best one that they had is not there anymore. The last I heard he is in Canada. He has a great use for Russian up there. He could speak it and he was my interpreter and I appreciated his fluency in the language. (FSO Vladimir Toumanoff.)

I know Mr. McCarthy just about destroyed him because he happened to have a Russian name, but I appreciate him. I hope what you say is more true than it has been. I have tried to insist on that but it was common practice in the Department and in your Agency to send a fellow to language school for a year and train him in Arabic and post him off to China.

I cannot understand and never have been able to understand how the rotation system works downtown. But it seems to be sort of an adverse proceeding so that you try to send a fellow to an area he knows the least about and where he cannot understand the language.

Mr. Jenkins: Since I have been in charge of the area in USIA, we have not sent a single officer to the field that did not have the language as a result of his attendance at the language school or through his ethnic background.

Mr. Hays: Do you think a fellow who comes from the language school can be fluent in Russian?

Mr. Jenkins: I went through the language school and I came out with a useful knowledge of the language. I can attend public lectures in the Soviet Union and converse with people on trains. I am not one who speaks Russian as well as English, but I can do my job in Russian.

Mr. Hays: I am glad to hear you say that, because I have long been a supporter of the language school.

Hays and other committee members also argued that we should abandon VOA broadcasts to Albania. I disagreed.

Mr. Hays: Why do you broadcast to Albania?

Mr. Jenkins: I think it is important to broadcast in Albanian. There is no other western broadcaster going into Albania. I counseled with the Yugoslavs and Italians. They are all agreed that what is happening in Albania now is a pretty interesting fermenting situation and that it is very important to have a Western voice going in there.

It is a small operation. We could save more money if we closed it down, but in the absence of any other Western influence in what had to be a very interesting cockpit between the Chinese and the Soviets, with ourselves being interested also, this is a worthwhile thing. Albania sits on the coast, across from Italy, smack in the middle of the Mediterranean. We have strong national security interest and I think it is to our advantage to have a voice.

These exchanges with the Congressional oversight committees were rich in flavor, larded with partisan sniping and decisive in establishing the funding for U.S. foreign affairs activity.

As I concluded my fifth year in charge of USIA's activities in the Soviet Union and Eastern Europe, Keogh agreed it was time for me to return to the State Department. I felt that we had seized on the Soviet suppression of Czech independence to significantly expand the U.S. presence in the Soviet empire—renew hope among the peoples of East Europe that the United States had a deep abiding interest in them, and that hope for eventual freedom from the Soviet yoke was not futile.

CHAPTER XI. CONGRESS, KISSINGER, AND THE COLD WAR: 1973-1978

With USIA Director Keogh's blessing, in mid-1973, I met with Dr. Fred Ikle, the brilliant Swiss-American director of the Arms Control and Disarmament Agency (ACDA). ACDA had been established by Congress as a semi-autonomous agency to coordinate U.S. policies and help negotiate the complex substance of the SALT pieces designed to contain the deadly nuclear arms race between the U.S. and the USSR. While NSC director and subsequently Secretary of State Kissinger was in total control of the SALT process, Ikle and his small, specialized staff provided the technical backstop support in the increasingly arcane arena where missile capabilities, "throw-weight," multi-warhead capacity, accuracy, fuel reliability, and mobility all became critical issues involving the Defense Department, CIA, and State. Ikle was seeking a deputy. The substance of the issue was obviously central to U.S. security and the Cold War. I left our meeting deeply impressed by Ikle's mastery of the subject, but convinced that his vision of ACDA's role and his dour scientist personality meant Ikle's ACDA was not the right fit for me.

That same day, I ran into Marshall Wright in front of the Department of State. Wright, an Arabic language FSO, had risen to become Assistant Secretary of State for Congressional Affairs—the position once held by Dean Acheson immediately after World War II. I had known Wright for

more than twenty years; he and I did Arabic and Russian
language training in 1957 at the Foreign Service Institute, at
the same time.

We had a quick conversation about my move back to the
Department of State from USIA. Marshall, on the spot,
asked me back to his office to discuss becoming Principal
Deputy Assistant Secretary (DAS) for Congressional
Relations (the bureau known as "H"). After an hour of
discussion, he turned and phoned Secretary Rogers' office.
We then marched down the seventh-floor hall to the
secretary's office where he introduced me to Bill Rogers,
former Attorney General in Eisenhower's administration,
and Nixon's first Secretary of State. Rogers, after a half-hour
discussion, assented. The next day Marshall had removed my
predecessor, a former Congressional staffer, and I moved into
my new paneled, seventh-floor office, in the Bureau, "H."

I had always, as noted throughout this book, been intrigued by the Congressional role in foreign policy, and its
often-decisive effect on our Cold War activities. Whether
handling Congressional visitors (CODELS) abroad, or
testifying on behalf of USIA activities, I found the experience exhilarating. Thus, when Marshall Wright offered the
"Principal DAS" position in "H," it seemed meant to be. I
never regretted the choice.

1973 was another watershed year in the thirty-five-year-
long Cold War. It ended badly: the U.S. was well on the
way to defeat in Vietnam; President Nixon had started

down the path to impeachment for his role in the Watergate scandal; Kissinger's sophisticated effort to draw the Soviet Union into a "helpful role" in enabling us to withdraw from Vietnam with some modicum of honor was falling victim to hard-line Congressional resistance to any cooperation with Moscow; the overthrow of pro-Communist President Allende in Chile produced a powerful liberal outcry against "Kissinger's meddling" in Chile; conservative attacks against what they called the sellout of America's control of the Panama Canal were mounting. A very rough patch with Congress.

The Nixon-Kissinger Grand Design

President Nixon and NSC director Kissinger had come to office only six months after the Soviet invasion of Czechoslovakia, determined to establish a policy of "triangular diplomacy." Exploiting the new leverage that Nixon's opening of Communist China provided, the U.S. would activate our ties with Beijing; thereby seducing Moscow into seeking initiatives with Washington to divert the apparent Washington-Beijing rapprochement, enlisting both Moscow and Beijing in a maneuver that would allow us to withdraw from Vietnam. Lest there be any doubt about the principal priority in the triangle policy, one need only note that there were more than 500,000 U.S. troops engaged in Vietnam, in a war that was going badly on the ground, producing thousands of casualties, and tearing apart the social fabric in the U.S.

319

In the early years of Nixon's presidency, the policy was, in fact, working—up to a point. It was especially promising in its effect on Moscow. Under the fabric of "détente," Kissinger with the enthusiastic collaboration of Commerce Secretary "Pete" Peterson launched a major effort to increase trade and U.S. investment in the USSR. Subsequent to becoming a prime target for Senator Jackson and other conservative senators opposed to any engagement with Moscow, détente was successful initially, especially in adding substance to Kissinger's concept of building mutual interests with Moscow, all designed to exploit Moscow's concern about improving U.S.-China ties. A major agreement between Moscow and the U.S. was concluded in 1973, to this end.

Kissinger wrote in his *Years of Upheaval*, "We did not believe that trade itself could moderate Soviet conduct. Our basic reliance was on resisting Soviet adventures and maintaining the global balance of power; economic incentives could not substitute for equilibrium. We believed however that Soviet restraint would be more solidly based if reinforced by positive inducements including East-West trade."

Kissinger's principal NSC aide on Soviet affairs, Bill Hyland, described this stage of the triangular policy as placing the U.S. in "the cat-bird seat." (See *Mortal Enemies* in Bibliography.) While our influence grew with both Moscow and Beijing, Brezhnev grew increasingly concerned that the new balance of power was moving against Moscow's interests. In two consecutive meetings with Kissinger,

Brezhnev, in fact, proposed that the U.S. and the USSR should move toward an alliance directed against the People's Republic of China. Moscow hardly raised its voice against our aggressive bombing of North Vietnam in the expectation it would force Hanoi to a settlement. In fact, U.S. planes bombed Hanoi harbor as Soviet Prime Minister Kosygin arrived in Hanoi and no Soviet reaction followed. In fact Brezhnev proclaimed that the Soviet Union sought to make détente with the U.S. irreversible.

It was this point in history when an amateurish burglary of the Democratic Party headquarters in Watergate occurred; a harbinger of the collapse of the Nixon presidency and détente as well.

It was also a moment of dramatic change in the Middle East; danger that threatened the essence of détente and produced a historic confrontation between U.S. and Soviet military power. The October 1973 Arab-Israeli War erupted. Israeli tank forces, led by "Arik" Sharon, broke through Egyptian lines, quickly crossed the Suez, and were on the way to Cairo. Moscow panicked. Brezhnev warned Nixon that Soviet troops were preparing to move into Egypt, to prevent Israel's capture of Cairo. It was at this moment that NSC director Kissinger, presumably on instructions from President Nixon (this became a little-noticed, but very important subject of Congressional concern), ordered a U.S. military alert. Kissinger also called Tel Aviv and insisted that Sharon return behind the Suez Canal, or all U.S. assistance to Israel would be suspended. Sharon stopped and returned behind the Suez. Kissinger informed Moscow of this action and warned that the Soviets must *not* send forces into Egypt. They stopped their mobilization.

In this treacherous, fluid international setting, given the U.S. domestic political eruption over Vietnam and the deterioration of Nixon's political position, the balance between the executive branch and Congress shifted dramatically in favor of Congress. And congressional involvement or intrusion into foreign relations also changed dramatically. Assistant Secretary Marshall Wright and I were deeply concerned about this erosion of executive power in foreign affairs, and we carried out the first steps to beef up our activities with Congress. After a few months, Wright was tapped for an embassy and I became Acting Assistant Secretary—a role I found myself in for more than three of the next five years.

I launched a full reform of "H" by replacing former congressional staffers with career foreign service officers, experienced in the areas they were assigned to cover. And I persuaded my fellow assistant secretaries to appoint officers in their bureaus as their liaison with "H" and Congress. Quickly it became apparent that, as I anticipated, congressmen and senators were much more respectful of policy discussion by the career area experts that we dispatched to the Hill. I personally revived the numerous friendships I had accumulated with members from CODEL visits and my experience testifying before the House and Senate members in my USIA days.

On August 22, 1973, President Nixon, in a surprise action, announced that he had appointed Henry Kissinger as Secretary of State to replace William Rogers.

Nixon, at the same time, confirmed that Kissinger could continue on as the Director of the National Security Council. This was unprecedented. It empowered Kissinger to continue his dominant role over the interagency processes affecting all foreign affairs, while at the same time bolstering the prestige of the Secretary of State by placing the Nixon administration's one figure who was recognized as the controlling figure in all foreign policy issues in charge. No longer behind the scenes, Kissinger now publicly forced coordination of all cabinet level policies affecting the United States' "national interest." This included not only the obvious diplomatic activities of the Department of State, but included trade policy, international financial activities, as well as defense and intelligence programs.

The role of the National Security Advisor to the President over the years has varied widely, reflecting the perceived needs of each President. Beginning with President Truman, all during the Cold War, this key role has had as its primary goal coordinating the policy inputs of the cabinet members, refining them for the President's consideration, and following up on the President's decisions to ensure their implementation. How this has been carried out has changed with each President and reflected the personalities of all those involved.

Kissinger was now, publicly, in charge. Certainly Nixon's decision to concentrate authority in Kissinger was motivated in part by the descending Watergate crisis that drove Nixon to "circle the wagons" and simplify his control of international policies.

This historic change highlighted the complex role of the National Security Council within the government. No NSC advisor has refined this elusive power more effectively than General Brent Scowcroft, Kissinger's deputy at the NSC, and subsequently advisor after Kissinger gave up his dual role. Scowcroft returned to the NSC function for President George H. W. Bush. In retrospect, in 2009, Scowcroft's mastery of the function stands as an example for all NSC advisors.

Assuming his new position as Secretary of State, Kissinger quickly reshaped the Department's tier of senior officials; unprecedented in history, he placed a career Foreign Service officer (FSO) in every Assistant Secretary position (except one, John Richardson, the respected long-time director of the Bureau for Cultural Affairs, was retained). In my judgment, his decision to staff the Department's sub-cabinet positions with career officers was critical to his remarkable success (and my effectiveness with Congress) in what was perhaps the nadir of America's international position in the world. He moved several FSOs from the NSC staff and elevated others from abroad. He was ruthless in insisting on demonstrated competence, and quickly shifted out those who failed to measure up. A brief review of these critical appointments illustrates his agenda. Larry Eagleburger (a future Secretary of State in the Reagan administration) and European expert Hal Sonnenfeldt were brought over as Undersecretary and Counselor, de facto "right hands" to Kissinger. The legendary Joe Sisco became Undersecretary for Political Affairs and chief director of Kissinger's Middle East shuttle diplomacy effort. Winston Lord took over the China portfolio, and the brilliant Tom Enders became Undersecretary for Economic Affairs. Kissinger added top Western European expert Arthur Hartman, outspoken superb negotiator Phillip Habib, Chinese expert Arthur Hummell, long-time Latin American specialist Pete Vaky, and the brilliant Sam Lewis as Assistant Secretary for Africa. Lewis subsequently became Kissinger's ambassador to Israel where he confronted Sharon's aggressive policies. This may not exhaust the list; the one constant was performance. For my "sins," I was retained.

While Congress was "riding high" in this era of a wounded executive branch, some were also uneasy about the disproportionate responsibility they had assumed. They tended to eagerly latch onto the solid expertise the new "H" team represented, and the heightened effort we made to make the entire department and its top officials readily available to consult and cooperate. Kissinger was an ideal figure for this new high-profile role. He grasped and enjoyed the Byzantine nature of Congressional activity and responded quickly to "H" and our initiatives. And he made it clear to all hands in the Department that they were to do the same.

With the notable exception of Senator "Scoop" Jackson and a handful of conservative colleagues, in the uncertainty of Watergate and Vietnam, Kissinger was viewed with respect and even gratitude for his clear, steady promotion of the U.S. national interest in the many crises we faced.

I worked with my "H" team to delineate the foreign policy issues (in the broadest sense to include trade policy, for example) of urgent importance. We identified the key members of Congress who had particular influence and interests in these issues. Often it involved members who were not members of the foreign relations committees, but who had personal knowledge from CODEL visits, or strong constituent interests from the various diasporas in their districts. We were able to refine this effort and successfully match-up interested members with our critical foreign policy issues.

We also concentrated on determining which Congressional staff members were particularly influential with the Congressional committee members on given subjects. They received our active attention, including meetings with Secretary Kissinger—unprecedented, but very effective.

Kissinger was a tremendous asset for our efforts. I put particular emphasis on analyzing which influential members of Congress would be receptive to his personal attention, with considerable success. In addition to the obvious focus on the senators on the Senate Foreign Relations Committee, for example, I introduced the Secretary to the powerful chairman of the Senate Finance Committee, Senator Russell Long. I was able to establish once-a-month private breakfasts for Kissinger with Long that paid great dividends on a whole range of issues. Long was very influential among his colleagues, and flattered by Kissinger's attention. In addition to his leadership on contentious trade issues, he was very helpful on issues that had no Finance Committee jurisdiction. He absorbed and supported Kissinger's sophisticated balancing act with Moscow and Beijing—especially valuable in the face of unending, occasionally vicious attacks against Kissinger's détente policies by Jackson and his allies.

Congress: U.S. Troops Out of Korea!

In the general state of anti-military spirit prevalent after our collapse in Vietnam, a sudden Congressional initiative to force withdrawal of our forces from overseas zeroed in on our position in divided Korea. Our monitoring of this initiative indicated that the administration would lose on this issue, and our troops would have to be withdrawn from Korea.

This perilous situation demonstrated the value of the effective Congressional relations I had worked to cultivate with Wayne Hays. Hays was the infamous chairman of the House Committee dealing with the State Department budget, and chaired the full House Committee on administration which controlled all perks for members of the House, including office space and parking. He was truly feared by his colleagues.

327

One morning, his personal staff aide called me to "request a favor for Chairman Hays." As indicated in the previous chapter, I had come to know Hays when I testified before him on USIA; I had a healthy respect for his influence over the House of Representatives and the State Department. His aide explained to me that the House was holding a birthday party for Hays in the Rayburn House Office building hearing room. The chairman realized that it would be unusual, but "would be thrilled" if Kissinger could drop in on that party. She then admitted that it was also a Democratic Party fundraiser for Hays.

Seizing on this opportunity, I sent a short action memo to the Secretary outlining the potential value that might flow from extending the favor to Hays. Action memos to Kissinger always provided him with at least two options with blanks for him to check-off. To my delight, he checked "approve" and I alerted Hays' office. On the date of the "birthday party," I accompanied the Secretary up to Congress in his limo. On the way he told me that he had received criticism from White House political advisors who found it inconceivable that a Republican cabinet member would attend a political fundraiser for a Democrat. He chuckled about it and stated he recognized how valuable this could be for his relations with Congress. On arriving at the Rayburn House Office Building we were met and led into the hearing room, which was packed with some 200 members of Congress, including Republican Senator Javits and a dozen other senators. Kissinger strode to the center of the room, stood up on a small platform to heavy applause, and stated, "I know it is unusual for a Republican cabinet officer to be here, but I wanted to wish the Chairman happy birthday. He is one of the great parliamentary diplomats in our history!"

The next morning, at 9:30 a.m., Hays called me and said, "Jenkins, I don't know how you managed that, but you tell the Secretary that anything he needs up here, I will deliver!"

Anti-military sentiment dominated the mood in Congress, as our position in Vietnam deteriorated. More than "anti-military," it was actually a return of fundamental isolationism. Senator Fulbright, who had turned with a vengeance against our involvement in Vietnam, led this movement, which began to question maintaining our troops in Europe (NATO), our support for radio broadcasts into the USSR (RFE and RL), and our major troop deployments in Japan and Korea. Weakened by the unfolding Watergate scandal as well as the losses in Vietnam, President Nixon was fighting a losing battle. Thus, when a bill introduced into the House of Representatives proposed withdrawing our forces from Korea, it suddenly picked up steam and was, in my judgment, going to pass. Kissinger and Nixon recognized the strategic ramifications that would follow; forced out of Vietnam, and we would now voluntarily withdraw from Korea—a strategic retreat from Asia. In 2009, as this is written, it is hard to imagine our position in Asia today if that had occurred. In terms of the Cold War, it would have been a most serious breach of the containment wall, which had been the basis of our thirty-year confrontation with Moscow.

When I suggested to Kissinger that I call Chairman Hays to seek his advice and help, he said, "you might as well, but I fear the worst." Our monitoring of the vote on this unexpected challenge showed us losing by fourteen votes in the House. Hays received me warmly, had his chief-of-staff double check and confirm our head count. He listened as I outlined Kissinger's concerns about the historic, strategic nature of the moment. He then said, "Let me see your list of the key votes you need." After checking them off one by one, he stated, "You tell the Secretary not to worry, those fourteen sons-of-bitches will vote with you on this historic issue, or they won't park within a mile of the Capitol!" We got all fourteen! A dramatic tribute to Kissinger's sophisticated appreciation of how to deal with Congress.

My most painful failure in the campaign to build support for the administration's foreign policy goals had to do with the crisis in Cyprus. Long a bone of contention between our NATO allies, Greece and Turkey, a major crisis erupted in Cyprus when the Greek military dictator suddenly decided to annex the mixed Greek-Turkish populated island. Stimulated by the nationalistic ranting of Bishop Makarios in Cyprus, the Greek army moved to take over. This triggered a Turkish military countermove into the Northern half of the island, and created a major crisis in NATO, which persists as a neuralgic focus even as this is written in 2009. The Greek-American community in the U.S. is well-organized in

a diaspora movement named AHEPA. There is no significant Turkish American counterpart. Like the Armenian-
American community and Jewish American supporters in
AIPAC, AHEPA plays a very effective Congressional relations lobbying game. They also put their money into the
game with strategically directed contributions to key members of Congress.

I struggled to cope with aggressive Congressional intrusion into this sensitive arena, which threatened to do serious
damage to NATO, our critical Cold-War alliance. I had
known the most senior House Greek-American member,
John Brademas, who visited Moscow while I was there. A
Harvard graduate, Brademas was very influential and
sophisticated. And, while I knew him only slightly, Senator
Paul Sarbanes, an academically inclined Princeton graduate,
struck me as another possible supporter in our efforts to
defuse this NATO crisis. Sarbanes was the principal
spokesman for Greece in the Senate. Confident that the
personal chemistry between these two usually moderate ivy
leaguers and Secretary Kissinger, who shared academic
backgrounds, would be fruitful, I arranged a breakfast for
them in Kissinger's private dining room to discuss Cyprus. I
was wrong—neither Brademas nor Sarbanes were the least
bit helpful. Kissinger, in an attempt to get them on the team,
showed them the latest sensitive classified cables from our
mission and the CIA station on Cyprus, outlining the
difficulties and the reckless behavior of the Greek junta.
However, Brademas and Sarbanes immediately met with

journalists as they left the State Department and revealed some of the sensitive information Kissinger had shared with them. Kissinger was outraged, and I was in the dog-house! Fortunately, this didn't happen often and the Secretary continued to actively support our campaign to build support with Congress, notwithstanding institutional hostility and skepticism between Congress and the White House in the Vietnam War and Watergate era.

A success story followed involving the sale of Hawk missiles to King Hussein in Jordan. Long the most reliable ally we had in the Arabic world, Jordan felt threatened by Syria and Nasser's Egypt and growing Soviet influence in the Middle East. Viewed with suspicion by their Arab neighbors, Jordan had reason to be nervous. Earlier in the Nixon administration, it had been determined that the U.S. needed to reassure the Jordanians and their neighbors that the U.S. was in fact a reliable supporter. It was decided that a significant sale of Hawk missile batteries would make the point. However, to my consternation, New Jersey Republican (usually moderate) Senator Case, who was a powerful member of the Senate Foreign Relations Committee, reacted violently against the sale. Obviously stirred by Israeli concerns that the Hawk might limit the effectiveness of the Israeli air force in a conflict with its Arab neighbors, Case declared that he would block any such sale.

I reached out to Case's principal foreign policy aide, Steve Bryen, who had become a good friend and helpful on some issues, but was a dedicated Zionist and supporter of Israel.

He agreed that Case did not want to embarrass King Hussein, but insisted that Hawk missiles were a serious threat to Israeli air power. We wrestled over the subject and came up with a solution that Case, Bryen, and the Israelis accepted: the Hawks would be sold, embedded in concrete bunkers, pointing north at Syria! Sale completed.

As part of our campaign to preserve Congressional understanding of our foreign policy, I negotiated a program with Congressman Dante Fascell, an influential Democrat from Florida who played a major role in the House Foreign Affairs Committee. He and his chairman, Clement Zablocki, both lamented the damage being done to our foreign policy by the intense hostility among House members toward the Nixon White House. Fascell agreed to host (with Zablocki's blessing) a monthly coffee and donuts breakfast briefing, open to all, on a members of Congress-only basis for which I would supply an appropriate senior State Department official for an off-the-record, candid, no-holds-barred session on a topical subject. The first meeting, I provided Undersecretary Joe Sisco, a close confidant of Kissinger who participated in all Middle East shuttle diplomacy. Only fourteen members appeared, but it was a lively, sometimes heated session and all fourteen were enthusiastic. The following month I "presented" top Soviet specialist Helmut Sonnenfeldt; forty-two members appeared. It was a great success. Thereafter we averaged more than fifty members and built a growing cadre of Congressional members who were cooperative and increasingly convinced that, notwithstanding Vietnam and Watergate, our foreign policy was in good hands.

I set up a parallel program in the Senate where conservative Republican Senator Bill Roth, from Delaware hosted bi-weekly coffee sessions with a half-dozen conservative senators. I had approached him on the basis of his personal experience as a student in Japan. I arranged to have the Japanese ambassador, a graduate of Harvard, meet with Roth and six of his Senate colleagues so that he could assume an appropriate leadership role on U.S.-Japan relations, even though he was not on Fulbright's Foreign Relations Committee. As the struggle with Senator Jackson and his conservative hard-line Senate allies grew, it was invaluable to have the chance to win the confidence of Roth and six of his very conservative allies. I ran a steady stream of Kissinger's top aides such as Ambassador Ellsworth Bunker (to discuss the Panama Canal treaty) and friendly ambassadors from Germany and the U.K. into these coffees and built a core group of supporters of NATO. détente; arms control efforts; and the Panama Canal treaty, with Roth's help.

The Major Crisis with Congress: The "Jackson-Vanik" Amendment

The fundamental Nixon-Kissinger triangular diplomatic initiative had, as mentioned earlier, shown great promise. Nixon's China trip electrified the world and produced panic in Moscow. Chinese-Soviet relations had become genuinely hostile. Mao Tse Tung openly attacked Khrushchev for his campaign to disinherit Stalin and Stalin's hard-line policies. Actual armed battles were fought over contested islands in the river separating Russia from China in Siberia. Beijing, using tiny Albania, a Stalinist holdout, as a megaphone, constantly attacked Moscow for abandoning Stalin's heritage. When Brezhnev succeeded Khrushchev, Mao's attacks continued. The brutal Soviet invasion of Czechoslovakia in 1968 earned Moscow a respite from Beijing, but not for long. The Chinese were seemingly unimpressed with Brezhnev's continuing nuclear missile build-up and his initiatives to promote "third world wars of liberation" that could pierce Western containment. Brezhnev had, on more than one occasion, raised the possibility of a U.S.-USSR alliance of sorts to neutralize China. Thus, when Nixon and Kissinger suddenly opened relations with Mao's China, Moscow was thrown off-balance. As noted above, President Nixon was determined to exploit this strategic advantage to win Soviet assistance to enable us to withdraw our massive forces from Vietnam, achieve genuine cooperation in containing and reducing the nuclear confrontation between the U.S. and USSR—at its peak, featuring more than 10,000 warheads on each side, each of which was many times more powerful than the bombs we dropped on Nagasaki and Hiroshima. Kissinger, with the active support of the President and his Secretary of Commerce Peter Peterson, had launched a determined effort to prove that cooperation with the U.S. on Vietnam and arms control would produce important benefits for Moscow in the form of trade and U.S. Export-

Import Bank credits to promote U.S. investment in the USSR.

It is worth noting that the Export-Import Bank was, in fact, created by President Roosevelt in the early 1930s, specifically to promote trade with the USSR.

However, while the administration was focused on using increased trade and investment to lubricate cooperation between the U.S. and the USSR on Vietnam, and other key issues, a new movement among Congressional staffers, inspired by Israel and active members of the American Jewish community, seized on this critical moment to link trade and Jewish emigration from the USSR. Initially promoted by a small but brilliant core group of staffers, the emigration lobby recruited Senator Scoop Jackson, Democrat of Washington, who admittedly had presidential aspirations. While undoubtedly sincere, Jackson was obviously encouraged by his staff to recognize the value of becoming a champion of free emigration for Soviet Jews in his political aspirations. Jackson's team was centered on Fosdick, who had built a powerful young team of advocates, including Richard Perle and Elliot Abrams. I had come to know "Dickie" Fosdick and Perle when I was fresh back from Moscow on the Soviet desk in 1963. They were among the most knowledgeable of Congressional staff on the USSR and we worked together on several Cold War issues. Dickie was the daughter of famed philosopher Henry Emerson Fosdick and very impressive, as was Richard. We were friends by that point. Even today, in 2009, Perle and Abrams remain active and influential as leaders of the "neo-con movement" which promoted the ill-fated invasion of Iraq.

From the beginning, the Nixon White House underestimated the political power of the Jewish emigration issue and the commitment of the American Jewish community to the cause. Before long, Jackson had built a cohesive Senate coalition including Senator Adlai Stevenson of Illinois, and stimulated a parallel movement in the House of Representatives where respected Congressman Charlie Vanik of Cleveland emerged as the leader. As in the case of Jackson's staff, Vanik's chief of staff was a brilliant young man named Mark Talisman. When Perle and Talisman, working very closely together, got rolling, it soon became apparent that this issue had a life of its own.

The Soviet Union, and Russia before it, had long been a source of anti-Semitism. The phrase "beyond the pale," in fact, referred to that area around Moscow (the Pale) from which Jews were banned in early Czarist Russia—except for those favored few who provided critical financial support to the Czar. Even though many leading Marxist revolutionaries were Jewish, including Trotsky and Kaganovich, after World War II, Stalin turned on his own Soviet Jewish citizenry, including his personal doctors, and added them to the target list for assassination. This in turn produced initiatives among Soviet Jews and within Israel and the American Jewish community to assist the emigration of Jews in the USSR.

There was an interesting battle in the American community between those who wanted to assist Soviet Jews to move to Israel to invigorate the Zionist vision and those, Micah Naftalin being a key figure, who wished to assist Soviet Jews to come to the U.S. They both supported what came to be known as the Jackson-Vanik amendment.

Thus, while Nixon and Kissinger looked upon trade and investment as a carrot to win Soviet assistance for our crisis in Vietnam, the Jackson-Vanik movement (and it quickly became a movement!) successfully created a link between trade and freedom of emigration.

Brezhnev, as part of the Nixon-Kissinger initiative, visited the United States in June of 1972 for the conclusion of a bilateral trade agreement with the U.S. In meetings with U.S. congressional leaders, apparently caught off-guard, Brezhnev promised that barriers to Jewish emigration would be relaxed. However, the Soviets proceeded to impose an "education tax" on those who wished to emigrate, and by the end of 1973 repression of those who sought to emigrate, increased. These actions played right into the hands of Jackson-Vanik supporters, and the pressures grew to pass a congressional law linking trade and investment to freedom of emigration.

Kissinger, and Nixon personally, pressed Moscow hard to remove this problem. In meeting after meeting with Dobrynin, Kissinger and his Counselor, Hal Sonnenfeldt, warned that this issue was becoming a serious threat to cooperation between the two nations, across the board. The Soviets gradually did allow expanded Jewish emigration, reaching an increased level of 45,000 in 1974.

Increasingly this issue dominated my efforts, with Sonnenfeldt's help, with Congress. It became eminently clear to me that freedom of emigration (in reality the focus was on Jewish emigration) was not going to be avoided. The White House entered a zone of denial, stoked by reassuring statements from prominent Jewish leader Max Fisher of Detroit.

Jackson introduced his legislative proposal, and it promptly attracted dozens of co-sponsors and almost unusual support among American Jews. Temples across the country sported banners urging supports for Jackson-Vanik, and Congressional members in the House flocked to endorse the bill.

At this point in 1974, Kissinger began to see the writing on the wall and deployed me to the Senate and House to try and limit the damage. My reports back were consistently pessimistic. And then, Jackson persuaded Adlai Stevenson to add an amendment that limited Export-Import Bank credits for the USSR to $50 million unless Congress specifically authorized it, thus putting Congress in charge of any major U.S. investments in the USSR. I met with Stevenson repeatedly to emphasize that trade and investment were the critical carrot we could use to enlist Soviet support on Vietnam. Stevenson was a charming and bright man, but felt under immense dramatic political pressure; "I understand your point, and would accept it, but I simply cannot," he said.

The White House in mid-1974, frustrated by Kissinger's lack of success to head-off defeat on Jackson-Vanik, charged Treasury Secretary William Simon to lead a cabinet-level task force to block Jackson-Vanik. Simon, brilliant but abrasive and cock-sure, relished the opportunity. He called a "principals only" cabinet-level meeting to organize the counterattack. Kissinger was, predictably, outraged by this invasion of "his territory" (which included in his mind all relations with Moscow). He refused to attend Simon's meeting and sent me! (I pointed out that Simon would be furious. His answer was, "Precisely!") I approached this meeting with considerable apprehension, confident that I would not be admitted into Simon's board room. And, more importantly, dismayed that these senior officials still believed Jackson-Vanik could be stopped. On arrival, I met Gerry Parsky, Simon's Undersecretary, at the door. He stated forcefully that the meeting was for "principals only." He was nonplussed when I told him that Kissinger knew that and sent me anyhow. Parsky was well-informed; perhaps the only other man in the room who was up on the state-of-play. When I went into the small boardroom, Simon said to Parsky, "Who is that?" Parsky explained that "Henry sent him, he is an expert in Soviet affairs and on Jackson-Vanik." Simon bristled, but acquiesced. So, I found myself between then Labor Secretary George Schultz and Agriculture Secretary Earl Butz. Simon opened with a rather superficial discussion of the bill and the outlook for the vote. He was optimistic that a counterproposal bill could carry the day. And he cited Max Fisher's encouraging statements. I "crossed my fingers" as the discussion went around the table. It was obvious that no one really appreciated the reality that Jackson-Vanik would pass overwhelmingly. Finally, I spoke up, outlining the prospective vote count in each house. There was a clear look of dismay on their faces. Spurred on by questions from Schultz especially, I corrected several misperceptions about the bill, and provided a brief but very specific account of Soviet behavior on emigration, the division among U.S. Jews about emigration to Israel and to the U.S., and detailed the economic and trade impact of the Stevenson amendment. I finished by stating that Max Fisher was wrong, the alternative bill had no support, and Jackson-Vanik would pass with overwhelming support, thanks in part to heavy-handed and untimely Soviet repression. Schultz and the others thanked me. Simon was clearly angry at "Henry," and my message.

On returning to the Department, Kissinger was waiting for my report. He was clearly enjoying Simon's discomfort, but depressed by the outlook for Jackson-Vanik. I truly believe that that was the first time the administration absorbed the reality that Jackson-Vanik (with Stevenson) would pass. Indeed it did. On December 31, 1974, at 11:00 p.m., the Trade Bill of 1974 passed with Jackson-Vanik and Stevenson intact. A major Nixon-Kissinger initiative to use trade and investment as bait to lure Soviet assistance for our embattled position in Vietnam was dead.

Kissinger continued to press Brezhnev through Dobrynin on the emigration issue and trade possibilities to no avail. As we predicted, Jewish emigration from the USSR plummeted to a few hundred from more than 45,000 in 1974. Brezhnev cancelled the Trade Agreement on January 10, 1975, that we had signed in 1972. And we received no assistance from Moscow in trying to win an agreement on Vietnam with Vietminh leaders (now under pressure from Moscow).

For a brief moment after passage of the bill, Brezhnev indicated a possibility of improving emigration to meet the spirit of Jackson-Vanik, but that opening vanished when Senator Jackson (and Perle) publicly exalted over "his victory."

Kissinger, in his memoirs, wrote:

> Our policy toward the Soviets was based on a balance between the carrot and the stick. But we failed to produce MFN; we seemed to be unable to organize the financial mechanisms for even such trade as there was- and all this despite Soviet commitments on Jewish emigration that would have been considered inconceivable a few years earlier. By summer of 1974 the carrot for all practical purposes had ceased to exist.

I returned to my seventh-floor office to reflect on the outcome of our battle over Jackson-Vanik, and the historic importance of the "defeat" that it represented. White House blood was in the water and the outlook for administration Cold War goals was not bright. The Congress had engaged

342

in a flagrant example of "rain-dance politics" and won—
what Mark Twain once described as "a vigorous activity
which has no effect on the weather, but leaves the members
of the tribe feeling better!" I stood at my office window
looking down at the Lincoln Memorial and took solace from
the beauty of the daily light show that nature provided. As
dusk fell, the lighted stately memorial turned from rose to
gold to bright white. And I grieved that I could not share
this beautiful manifestation of nature with "C."

Arms Control/SALT Negotiations: Détente

Jackson-Vanik had in two short years become the dominant and distracting factor in the contest between the Nixon
administration and Congress. However, in reality the arms-
control negotiations between the two nuclear superpowers
were of historic importance and should have dwarfed the
emigration issue in terms of the national interest of the
United States. Arms control talks were initiated in the early
60s, in recognition by both the U.S. (and its allies) and the
Soviets that the potential for a nuclear exchange threatened
the planet itself. A major early step occurred in 1961 when
U.S. Special Emissary John J. McCloy came to Moscow with
a large delegation of experts to meet with the Soviet Deputy
Foreign Minister Zorin (as described in the earlier Chapter
on Moscow). However, McCloy-Zorin was but one of
dozens of negotiating sessions in what had become the
central battleground in the Cold War.

The Soviets, deeply embarrassed by Khrushchev's failed nuclear weapons lunge at Cuba in 1962, vowed never again to be caught so far behind in nuclear warheads. By 1968 and the invasion of Czechoslovakia, Brezhnev had presided over a massive nuclear missile buildup. The Soviets had, in fact, reached a sort of equivalency and felt themselves in a position to negotiate arms-control issues on a level playing field. The balance or equivalency, however, was misleading. There were important asymmetries in our two nuclear inventories that confused the issues of balance and provided ample opportunities for opponents of arms control negotiations within the U.S. The U.S. inventory was replete with smaller, more accurate weapons while the USSR had achieved superiority in "throw-weight"—i.e. had bigger missiles. Initially the U.S. had the lead in multi-warheads (MIRVs) on the new MX missiles, but in 1973 the Soviets launched new programs to reach equality in that category. MIRVs had from six to ten individually targeted warheads on a single missile—with Nagasaki-strength destructive capacity in each one. The U.S., with its nuclear missile capable Trident submarine force and B-52 intercontinental bomber forces, had a triad advantage over the Soviets, who were well behind in submarine capability and were just developing a long-range aircraft. The stark and terrifying reality was that both sides had more than 10,000 warheads, each more powerful than the bombs we dropped on Japan! This fact, in any objective analysis, put arguments over "equivalency" in a bizarre light. Nonetheless, that was the focus of the long, drawn-out arms control efforts through SALT I, SALT II, and subsequently START negotiations. As this is written in 2009, Russia and the U.S. are again engaging on this playing field, thankfully, this time to reduce our inventories to fewer than 1,500 warheads!

President Nixon established an executive branch "verification panel" with the Defense Department led by hard-line Secretary of Defense Schlesinger and Kissinger as representatives. The battle over SALT negotiations was centered in this panel. And the conservative Congressional forces, led be Jackson, having pocketed the victory on emigration for Soviet Jews, turned to the SALT negotiations. As chairman of the Senate Armed Services subcommittee on arms control, Jackson launched a series of hearings designed to block what he called concessions to Moscow. He, with the assistance of Richard Perle again, insisted that the U.S. must achieve equality in each category of weapons, even though our triad forces were clearly superior. Much attention was devoted to "throw-weight," notwithstanding the fact that U.S. missiles with superior accuracy did not need the heavy throw weight that Soviet SS-18 super missiles were achieving. Jackson charged that Nixon had made secret agreements with Brezhnev in Moscow in 1972; the charges, as Hyland writes, were absurd and soon fizzled. But they did illustrate the poisonous atmosphere in Washington. Nixon's wounded White House was in a weakened position to defend against them. Kissinger, placed in charge of the interagency verification panel, struggled to build an agreement within the U.S.

government, but failed. He writes in his *Years of Upheaval* that the Pentagon was quite satisfied to have a deadlock. And, when the Soviet and American delegations met in Germany, February 19, 1974, they did deadlock. Kissinger then proceeded to Moscow in March where he won some minor adjustment from Brezhnev. However, when he subsequently chaired an April 27, 1974, meeting of the verification panel, Schlesinger's opposition hardened into insistence upon absolute equivalence in all categories— identical with the public position created and actively espoused by Senator Jackson.

My role in the critical and byzantine struggle within the U.S. government and in negotiation with the Soviets was limited to dealing with Senator Jackson and his conservative supporters in the Senate. To illustrate, Senator Jackson called a classified hearing on the negotiation with Secretary Kissinger as the principal witness. I had prepared a detailed brief on Jackson's and Perle's activities prior to the hearing and accompanied the Secretary to the hearing. Kissinger was in no mood to compromise with Jackson, who, as I reported, had been working behind the scenes with Secretary Schlesinger and conservative media to torpedo any SALT agreement with the Soviet Union. En route to the hearing, I reminded Kissinger of two particularly egregious attacks by Jackson and read from a recent telegram exchange he had had with Eagleburger while returning from a Middle East trip. Kissinger looked at the cable I handed him and exploded. "That is a 'Cherokee message'," he said, "What are you doing with it?" Cherokee messages were designed to be solely between the secretary and Larry Eagleburger. I smiled, and pointed out that I had drafted it and sent it Cherokee via Larry. He subsided but this did illustrate the intense pressure he was under. He was quite paranoid as he confronted the Jackson-Schlesinger alliance in Washington and Brezhnev in Moscow, as Nixon's position was collapsing in the ashes of Watergate.

When we arrived at the Senate, we went immediately into "secret session" and Kissinger gave a detailed update on his meeting with Brezhnev. Jackson, with Perle seated behind, was confrontational and the meeting went poorly. At this point I noted that Perle had quietly stepped out of the classified hearing. Knowing Richard's penchant for playing to the media, I indicated to the secretary that I suspected foul play and followed Perle out to the corridor outside the hearing room. True to form, he was providing his version of Kissinger's testimony to three journalists, notwithstanding that this was a top-secret hearing. I confronted Richard and accused him of violating the classified status of the hearing. I then returned and reported Perle's actions to Kissinger. He was outraged, stood up and stated to Jackson and the other Senators present that the hearing was over and why. Jackson, visibly embarrassed, protested, but we left.

This incident also reveals the bitter division between the embattled Nixon administration and its conservative critics who were determined to undermine arms control negotiation on the spurious ground that Nixon and Kissinger were, allegedly, making too many concession on the one hand, and liberal critics who were leading a campaign to undermine U.S. military diplomats around the world, especially Vietnam. There was no booster club for détente. Kissinger wrote with melancholy of this tragic situation, "For our security and well-being in the nuclear age, and to give hope to the world, our foreign policy must have a sense of position, purpose, and design. That, in turn, requires a united people and a sense of continuity...foreign policy cannot be segmented into a series of domestic skirmishes. A divided America deprives the world of all hope..."

President Gerald Ford: An Admirable Substitution at a Critical Time in the Great Game

On the day President Nixon resigned, August 9, 1974, Secretary Kissinger called his assistant secretaries together and in somber tones reported that he had just received the letter of resignation from the President. The Constitution directs that a Presidential resignation is to be made to the Secretary of State. Kissinger, clearly moved, called on all of us to recognize the historic nature of this section, and with considerable emotion, pointed out the President of the United States had submitted his resignation to a Secretary of State born in Germany who had had to flee Hitler's Holocaust with his parents. He announced that President Ford was being inaugurated as we spoke. He concluded with an appeal to us. "I know," he said, "that you as well as I have frequently been critical of President Nixon's admitted frailties and you may have a sense of relief. But I would urge you to reflect above all on the majesty of our government as we proceed, without missing a beat, under President Ford." He suggested to us that we consider reminding "our friends in the media" and our friends in the diplomatic corps of this overriding reality. We all felt that this was Kissinger at his best and were especially proud to be part of his team at this historic moment.

As anticipated, the press projected a strong sense of *schadenfreude* about the unpopular, paranoid Nixon's demise, and proclaimed the resignation as an epitaph for détente. Liberals in Congress rejoiced at Nixon's departure and conservatives too rejoiced at what they saw as the end of arms control "concessions" to the Communists. Thus Ford faced an almost impossible challenge to find the means to blunt Soviet international initiatives and engage them effectively on arms control.

Ford, in his address to the nation, spoke eloquently of an end to a long dark chapter and his determination to start a new national direction of unity, a course he was admirably suited to pursue. He reactivated personal discussions with Brezhnev, attending a late fall summit meeting in Vladivostok (the Pacific coastal city) still hoping to continue arms control negotiation and deflect Jackson's amendment on Soviet Jewry. However, with passage of Jackson-Vanik in that tumultuous New Year's Eve Congressional session, these early Ford/Kissinger efforts to revive détente withered.

*

President Ford's stirring reference to the end of "our long, dark period" in his speech to the nation had a particularly poignant significance for me personally. After my "C"'s death in 1970, I had maintained my determination to focus on my boys and my official duties, eschewing any involvement with another woman, for more than four years. But it was a long, dark period for me. Some four and a half years later, the day after Jackson-Vanik passed, I happened to see, "across a crowded room" at a cocktail party, someone who was remarkably similar in appearance to my late wife. I was drawn to speak to her. She was the same size, same coloring, speaking in the same low voice with which she informed me that she was a widow. We both sensed that lightning had struck. A few weeks later we met again, and she accepted my presumptuous proposal that I stop by for a nightcap! After three days of long and intense sharing of our lives and tastes, I queried her as to how "Lucy Jenkins" sounded to her. She replied, "Beautiful!" Three months later, our combined five children held forth at our small private wedding, celebrating, and greatly relieved that they no longer had to take care of us! And I now had someone to share with me the beauty of the Lincoln Memorial as the sunset played its symphony in front of my office window. That was many years ago.

*

Ford's ascention to the presidency, rather than dramatic and unsettling, ushered in a much calmer era. The Cold War continued, but the poison in our relations with Congress gave in to Ford's sincere and effective effort to restore civility and start to rebuild bipartisanship in the continuing debate over foreign policy.

The Soviets, for their part, had sensed our diminished capacity to act decisively during Nixon's final months. However, they could not imagine the change in the White House, and did not know what to expect. Temptation was there, and they moved to take advantage of our problems, but with considerable caution. Kissinger's continued presence "at the tiller" and the enhanced role of Kissinger's brilliant deputy at the NSC, General Brent Scowcroft, made it clear that our overall commitment to containment was unchanged. It also confined that we would continue to pursue engagement with Moscow on arms control, the central issue in our relations.

Kissinger's Power Reaches an Apex

In fact, Kissinger emerged as more powerful than ever in leading U.S. foreign policy. Ford relied completely on the Secretary, whereas Nixon had had his own vision that Kissinger had to manage. Often characterized as arrogant (a picture he deliberately, often with humor, played to), Kissinger in fact was an incredibly effective manager and inspired strong, creative debate by his sub-cabinet team. I attended most of his daily 7:30 a.m. staff meetings and regularly observed (and sometimes engaged in) vigorous argument among his team and often with him personally.

Rather than arrogant and close-minded, he in fact regularly shuffled out of his team any who appeared to be yes-men. One of the most significant examples of this was the much argued, eventually successful conversion of Kissinger to accept the strategic importance of third-world powers who were gradually coming together and threatening a North-South confrontation over economic resources. Tom Enders, the tough and brilliant assistant secretary for economic affairs fought tenaciously with Kissinger until he finally came around. Before long, Kissinger's "new best friend" had become Algerian leader Bouteflika, who had become a lead player in the emerging third-world coalition. Originally, "Henry," as we all called him behind his back, had treated economic issues as secondary, even in the case of the Soviet union where commerce secretary Peterson had to persuade him that trade was a critical leverage issue in winning Moscow's collaboration on Vietnam. Enders, confident of his view, was relentless. "Henry" finally "got it," acknowledging the strategic importance of the issue, and particularly the potential it offered Moscow as they sought to break out of our "containment."

I had several similar experiences in which the Secretary increasingly recognized the threat and opportunity in the byzantine world of the Congress. He, in fact, became a historic powerhouse in dealing with the fractious collections of Congressional interest groups. He was intimidating, but most effective, once convinced.

An amazing anecdote from one of his 7:30 a.m. meetings illustrates this point, as well as his remarkable sense of humor. This particular morning we had a very lively argument about Korea in which the assistant secretary for Asia, Phil Habib, was disagreeing with Henry about the issue. Finally, in frustration, Habib, who was always outspoken and fearless, blurted out, "Goddammit, Henry, I explained to you last week that we were *not* going down that path!" The rest of us (there were usually six to eight assistant secretaries in these daily meetings) were thunderstruck. Kissinger looked up, turned to his right-hand man, Undersecretary Larry Eagleburger, and said, "Eagleburger, I want a memo out immediately to all Assistant Secretaries, no more obsequiousness in our staff meetings!" It is worth noting that Habib's view prevailed.

Kissinger had by this point placed his own selections in each bureau as assistant secretaries; all career foreign service officers and from my point of view outstanding experts in their areas. His inner-inner group was led by Eagleburger and included Hal Sonnenfeldt, Win Lord, Joe Sisco, Habib, and department spokesman Bob McCloskey, most of whom had been with him at the NSC. Added to that were Arthur Hartman, Hal Saunders, Roy Athenton, Sam Lewis, and Pete Vaky. All these men went on to prime ambassadorships and deservedly so, with the exception of Sonnenfeldt, who became Counselor of the Department.

The Cold War Plods Along

Arms control negotiations had become a permanent "cottage industry" by the time Ford replaced Nixon. Jackson (Perle) and his allies (often individual sources within the Defense Department) were unrelenting in their opposition to any and all negotiation that did not provide for a solid advantage for the U.S. in each separate category, even though in several of the categories the Defense Department admitted there was no need for U.S. superiority, such as "throw weight." The Defense Department positions became more disciplined when Ford replaced Schlesinger with his close friend Melvin Laird as secretary.

The Soviets, relatively comfortable with their overall equilibrium in the terrifying missile balance with more than 10,000-plus warheads on each side, continued to meet with U.S. negotiators, but no agreement was going to occur in this time frame.

In the extended global confrontation, however, the Soviets were making significant progress. Portugal, long a "reliable" military dictatorship under General Salazar, had finally elected a friendly civilian government under Marcello Caetano. In the spring of 1974, to the surprise of our government, Caetano was overthrown by another retired general, Antonio Spinosa. Described in some detail by Bill Hyland in his *Mortal Rivals*, the coup was a shock. Spinosa had been an attaché with the Germans at the battle of Stalingrad and, along with a large number of younger officers, bitter toward their government's costly and brutal efforts to put down independence movements in the Portuguese African colonies in Mozambique and Angola. They led a pro-Communist movement that threatened to take over Portugal. By the summer of 1975 the situation was ominous. Finally, with the arrival of Frank Carlucci as the new U.S. ambassador, we were able to rally pro-Western moderates and encourage a counter-coup, which defeated the Communist initiative. Carlucci, another exceptional career Foreign Service officer (and close personal friend), overcame Kissinger's initial reluctance to intervene. Moscow's hopes were dashed. Carlucci went on to become, *seriatim*, deputy CIA director, NSC director, and Secretary of Defense under Reagan, and the mentor of General Colin Powell.

However, the legacy of Portuguese imperial policies in Africa had bred a serious problem in Angola where indigenous Communist forces were winning control

The Portuguese had set November 1975 for the independence of Angola and at that time withdrew their forces from their colony that they had, one might say, misgoverned for two centuries. The Soviets recognized the opportunity for a successful "war of national liberation" and provided increasing support to the Communist movement. Portugal and its colonies had been a distinctly back-burner issue for the United States. In a new and creative move, the Soviets arranged a major transfer of Cuban troops to be sent to support the Communist forces in Angola. U.S. intervention took the form of CIA assistance, which fell short. Administration plans to match the Cuban presence were blocked by a Senate amendment by Senator Dick Clark of Iowa that specifically prohibited any additional CIA funding in Angola. Angola became a Soviet "win," a small but serious reminder that the Cold War was still on. Hyland argued that by passing the Jackson-Vanik amendment we had given up "the carrot" (investment and trade) in our dealings with Moscow; and that with the Clark amendment we had thrown away "the stick." The two were hardly symmetrical, but he had a point.

I had known Dick Clark when he was a staff assistant to Senator John Culver. He had been a college professor of Russian history and visited me at the State Department when I was on the Soviet desk. We had a very friendly relationship. I called on him and Chairman John Sparkman before the Clark amendment on Angola was submitted, and explained that a Communist win (with Soviet and Cuban support) would constitute a serious breach of our containment policy. Clark was troubled by the thought, but adamant against CIA involvement, which he insisted was a "rogue action," not coordinated and approved within the administration. He argued that in the context of Congressional suspicion after Vietnam and Watergate, there would be no stopping his amendment and we would have to "roll with the punch." He did agree to a few minor changes, but nothing to change the prohibition – which, he pointed out, was directed specifically at CIA.

Soviet third-world initiatives, all designed to capitalize on our perceived weakness following Vietnam and Watergate, also were successful in Laos and Cambodia. In Laos,

Communist supporter Prince Suphanawong finally defeated the U.S.-supported Prince Souvanama Phouma after a long ten-year struggle.

In Moscow, the Angola story verified the legitimacy of the commitment to support "wars of national liberation." Longtime Soviet ambassador to the U.S. Anatoliy Dobrynin wrote in his memoir, *In Confidence*, that he had argued in Moscow against such interventions on Angola. He warned that they were deeply offensive to the Ford administration and were only of marginal value. He reported that he was outgunned in the ruling Politburo by chief ideologue Mikhail Suslov, and his colleagues Boris Ponomarev, who was in charge of promoting foreign Communist parties around the world, and military conservatives, Defense Minister Dmitriy Ustinov and Marshall Andrei Grechko. Suslov, Dobrynin explained, considered victories such as Angola verification of his vision that the collapse of colonialism created vacuums that inevitably would be filled by Communist leadership.

We were more successful in dealing with a much more important strategic threat: the vulnerable Panama Canal. For almost a decade perhaps, officials in the Johnson, Nixon, and now Ford administrations were deeply concerned about signs that Communist activists would target the canal. All three, and eventually the Carter administration, supported negotiation with Panama to turn the canal over to the Panamanian government, thereby removing the populist appeal against the U.S. presence.

357

In a nutshell, the arguments that we must maintain our control over the canal and the ten-mile-wide "zone" that split Panama in two for strategic reasons were fraudulent. In fact U.S. citizens living in manicured, U.S.-style villages in the zone were outnumbered by thousands of Panamanians who maintained the villages, and more strategically, did all the manual maintenance of the canal itself. A single disaffected or Communist Panamanian with one hand grenade in his lunch pail or toolbox could put a canal lock out of business.

A second central factor in the debate was the fact that few U.S. commercial ships were still using the canal; its "clientele" was overwhelmingly Japanese vessels transporting Japanese cars and equipment to our gulf ports. In other words, our multi-million-dollar expenses for the canal and the privileged American occupants of the zone were essentially subsidizing Japanese automakers who were, *inter alia*, forcing the closure of U.S. auto plants.

None of these realities had achieved much traction in the U.S. political debate. Ronald Reagan had seized on this as the effective populist message; "we built it, it's ours," was the half-in-jest slogan embraced by a wide range of conservative Republicans and some Democrats. Reagan, at this point, was mounting his first serious race to replace Ford on the Republican ticket, and using the Panama Canal in his campaign.

Ellsworth Bunker, a magnificent, quintessential old-school diplomat, had been appointed the president's man in charge of the Panama Canal negotiations and selling an eventual treaty to Congress. Bunker had a long history of troubleshooting in diplomatic crisis; perhaps his most notable achievement was the successful withdrawal of Dutch colonial rule in Indonesia. He also had been briefly Ambassador in Saigon as the Vietnam War proliferated, and ambassador in India. He was eighty-eight years old at this point. Tough minded, elegant, very Vermont through and through.

I escorted Bunker on several calls on Congress, which were usually discouraging. Inevitably the members would agree about the vulnerability of the canal and were concerned about possible Communist exploitation. One agreed that the canal was "a low-hanging fruit," but added that to support the proposed treaty would be akin to voting to ban guns or end aid to Israel. I was discouraged because we had carefully selected members who I knew to be sophisticated and apartisan about national security issues.

I came up with one winning idea. I phoned my friend Bill Buckley. Bill had earlier served in Mexico for the CIA and, I knew, spoke good Spanish. He was also well-known as a very devout Catholic. One of the most enthusiastic supporters of the treaty that would establish Panama's sovereignty and control over the canal was the Archbishop of Panama, an influential and well-informed leader in Panama. I arranged for Buckley to have a private breakfast with Kissinger, who invited him to visit Panama, and the canal, and meet with the archbishop. He did and returned a committed supporter of the treaty. Buckley's conversion struck a significant body blow to the Reagan forces who insisted we should never give up "our canal."

When the treaty was finally passed in the Carter years, Buckley's contribution had clearly been important. The treaty approval removed a major strategic American vulnerability in the Cold War.

Carter Defeats Ford in 1976

The election outlook between Jimmy Carter and Gerald Ford see-sawed back and forth as November 1976 approached. Within Kissinger's State Department, the mood changed daily. There was agreement that perhaps it would be refreshing to have a change. Carter, an Annapolis graduate, had been a moderate governor in Georgia and shown serious interest in foreign affairs. In the early 1970s, I had held a conference of my USIA Public Affairs officers from Moscow and Eastern Europe in Atlanta, where we received a photo-op with Governor Carter; he kept us for almost two hours in very active discussion about the outlook for essential freedom from Soviet rule for the countries of the Warsaw Pact. We were impressed, as were most people who met him in Atlanta.

However, our loyalty and admiration for Kissinger and genuine respect for Ford, who had moved the country through the crisis of Nixon's resignation, left most of us, at least at the senior level, pulling for Ford (and Kissinger). It was not to be.

After the election, I proposed to Kissinger that he host a farewell reception in the elegant eighth-floor reception room at the department for members of Congress. I was certain, I said, that there would be a good turnout; he had many admirers in Congress, even among adversaries. The eighth-floor reception rooms at the State Department were, and still are, one of Washington's most beautiful sites. Replete with museum-quality American antiques (Thomas Jefferson's desk is on display), the rooms look over the Potomac River and my beloved Lincoln Memorial. Kissinger agreed and kindly invited Lucy and me to join him in the reception line as "co-hosts." We met the secretary and his striking wife Nancy in his office and rode up in the Secretary's elevator together. In a typical Kissinger flourish, he turned to Lucy and said with a big smile, "You know, Lucy, it is always smart to choose career foreign service officers, you are guaranteed at least a modicum of intelligence, they are well-disciplined, and you can always get rid of them!" More than 430 out of 535 members turned out and praised Kissinger with sincerity. A good reflection of his genuine enthusiasm for Congressional relations!

Chapter XII: Carter in for Ford: A Cold War Transition

After "Henry's" triumphant farewell to Congress, the presidential transition began in earnest. Every such transition is historic in its dimensions; this one, after the tumultuous collapse of Nixon's Presidency, and Ford's heroic taking over to lead us out of our dark era, was especially historic.

In Moscow, there was apprehension and fascination at the unique and occasionally bizarre nature of our "transfer of power." There was also an appetite for taking advantage of what seemed to be a period of uncertainty in Washington. Soviet-Cuban forces moved to consolidate their position in Angola. The Soviets stepped up their activities in Central America, which later blossomed into the "Contra affair." And they maintained their nuclear weaponry development. President Carter's selection of Cyrus Vance as Secretary of State was calming, in that he was a known quantity, known to the Soviets and to the U.S. foreign policy establishment, including State Department professionals, for his solid contributions in the extended Vietnam negotiations, and his service in the Johnson Defense Department. Universally regarded as a "real gentleman," he was well respected by both Democratic and Republican members of Congress. Carter's selection for Deputy Secretary of State, Warren Christopher, was not well known and proved to be an enigmatic figure in the Carter administration. Vance and Christopher were both corporate lawyers—dramatically different in approach from historian Kissinger. Carter, however, also turned to a Harvard colleague of Kissinger's, Zbignew Brzezinski, another brilliant historian, to head his National Security Council. The Brzezinski-Vance pairing was reminiscent of the original Kissinger-Rogers pairing. And "Zbig," as he was widely known, wasted no time in establishing his primacy in foreign policy, just as Kissinger had dominated the corporate lawyer, Bill Rogers, in Nixon's administration. For me, it was especially gratifying to have my former professor on the scene.

After the election, in the three-month transition interim, the Kissinger team of Assistant Secretaries dispersed; Larry Eagleburger went off to Yugoslavia as ambassador and my other colleagues also moved on or retired. Undersecretary Phil Habib called me in and proposed that I be nominated to be ambassador to Thailand, where I had served in the early 1950s. Honored and tempted, after discussion with my new wife, Lucy, we decided starting off our new family life 8,000 miles away from our five college-age children was not a good idea. I sought the counsel of my good friends in Congress, Chairman Clem Zablocki of the House Foreign Relations committee, Senator Gale McGhee (both Democrats), and Republican Senator Chuck Percy, and they urged me to stay on at Congressional Relations. Habib warned that the new Carter-Vance team would inevitably want to have their own man; Phil was correct. The Carter White House nominated a former Congressional staffer, Douglas Bennett, to be

Assistant Secretary and I stepped back down to Principal Deputy Assistant Secretary as Bennett's deputy. I remained such for four very active months, but Bennett's philosophy was 180 degrees contrary to my own. My all-career team was soon transformed into a largely former Congressional staff group. At the same time, in the White House itself, President Carter chose a Georgian friend, Frank Moore, as Special Assistant for Congressional affairs, who soon turned out to be singularly inept at playing in the Congressional big leagues. The respected Congressional liaison function that had been led by Bill Timmons and included Tom Korologos in charge of Senate relations became disorganized and ineffective. My tenure in "H" at the Vance State Department was short and frustrating.

Human Rights vs. Containment

Vance's agenda switched the State Department's priority to promoting human rights, first and foremost, around the world. My own approach to this was that "human rights," which Carter, Vance, and Christopher turned into a major policy, was in fact a philosophy, not a policy, and was best promoted by example, not intervention and confrontation.

The new administration was uneasy with Kissinger's cold-blooded dedication to the U.S. national interest, and effective containment of Soviet international imperialism, which subordinated national concerns about the moral values of our allies. True, Kissinger's policies were committed to a Metternichean realism that subordinated traditional

American commitment to democracy, but they reflected the object reality that we faced an aggressive nuclear opponent who exploited every perceived opportunity to project their power into all corners—Angola, Yemen, Laos, Cambodia, Cuba, Bolivia, and Ethiopia.

Human rights as a "policy" first evolved in Congress where an obscure conservative Iowa Republican congressman, H. R. Gross, used his powerful position on the appropriations committee to grill State Department officials testifying on the budget, about the department's "policy on human rights." Gross was soon joined by liberal Democratic congressman Don Frasier of Minnesota and the issue caught on in Congress. I had attempted to harness Gross and Frasier's very sincere interest in the issue by persuading Eagleburger and Kissinger to designate a "human rights officer" in each geographic bureau of the department, who would then report regularly to Chairman Gross and his Democratic colleague Frasier on our efforts to persuade allied governments that reform and increased constituent to democracy were important to the United States. This effort had been successful. When Carter replaced Ford, however, it was not considered adequate by the President and his new administration. Carter, after all, had campaigned on this issue and attacked Ford (and Kissinger) for being cold-blooded and out of step with America's values.

I crossed swords particularly with Deputy Secretary Christopher who was genuinely passionate about human rights as a policy. My argument—that the existing program

365

of designated bureau officers was well received in Congress and no more was necessary—was rejected. Christopher was impatient with any suggestion that Congress was satisfied. He said, "You don't seem to understand, this administration is determined to put human rights upfront, no matter what satisfies Congress." President Carter appointed a full Assistant Secretary for Human Rights and a new bureau was created in the State Department to reflect the new enhanced priority.

Carter's policy also turned out to be a harbinger of the subsequent George W. Bush eight-year commitment to democracy, which he and Condoleezza Rice promoted into a justification for U.S. intervention around the world. At this writing in 2009, under President Obama, it appears that we are returning to a more realistic commitment to the U.S. national interest and concentrating our moral attentions on our own internal short-comings in the human rights field.

Carter's Cold War Achievements

The Carter administration in fact racked up a series of major accomplishments—even "victories"—in the continuing Cold War. In the few months I remained in the State Department Office of Congressional Relations, a number of major initiatives unfolded:

- The successful conclusion of the SALT II arms control treaty with the USSR on May 9, 1979

- The historic Camp David Accords between Israel and Egypt

- Formal establishment of full diplomatic relations with China in 1979

- In Eastern Europe, the return of the crown of St. Stephen to Hungary

- Senator Fulbright's pacifist campaign to shut down Radio Liberty and Radio Free Europe was defeated

President Carter's four-year term was, in fact, a notable success in several critical foreign policy issues. Often underappreciated as a weak period in United States foreign policy terms, President Carter, heavily influenced by the brilliant and hard-charging Brzezinski, continued the fundamental American commitment to containment. Carter's own hands-on involvement, especially in the dangerous, thorny, Middle-East crisis, was and remains unparalleled in history.

Panama Canal Treaty

Rarely seen as a Cold War issue, in fact, the canal posed a serious vulnerability to the United States interests, and by extension, a juicy opportunity for a Soviet inspired "war of national liberation." Presidents Johnson, Nixon, and Ford all committed major efforts to negotiate a resolution of the unsustainable U.S. control and presence in a ten-mile wide strip that divided the sovereign state of Panama in two. The long efforts to overcome the simplistic and nationalistic popular perception that we must hold onto "our Panama Canal" was finally settled by the Carter administration, which won a close Senate victory to ratify the treaty. In the early months of the Carter administration, I continued to lobby the Senate and deflect House initiatives to cripple the treaty through limitations on appropriations.

One of the more amusing incidents occurred when I escorted Ambassador Ellsworth Bunker to meet with the paranoid House Chairman of the maritime committee, Daniel Flood. Flood, a former Shakespearean actor, met us and immediately launched into an uninterrupted tirade of an hour about "America's destiny." After the hour, he looked up and announced that he had to go vote on the floor, thanked Bunker for his briefing, and we left. Bunker was in a state of shock.

We had a somewhat similar experience—though much more positive—when I took Bunker to meet with Senator Joe Biden. Biden was a strong supporter of the Treaty. Long interested in India, Biden talked to former Ambassador to India Bunker about India. He then launched into a statement of his understanding of the Panama Treaty (which was impressively thorough) for twenty minutes. The Senate bells went off and he thanked us and quickly left. Bunker turned to me and said, "Nice to have him with us, but do you realize I never opened my mouth about the canal treaty?" I replied, "Welcome to the Senate!"

When the treaty finally came up for a vote, it produced a solid victory with a major contribution from moderate Republicans, together with most Democrats.

SALT II

SALT I, the first major arms control agreement between the U.S. and the USSR, had managed to cap the headlong production in nuclear weapons, but still allowed unlimited refinement of existing weapons systems on both sides. It is hard to imagine today, but each country had more than 10,000 warheads, each with an explosive power greater than the bomb used at Nagasaki. We were in fact two extremely deadly scorpions in a bottle, threatening annihilation. SALT II negotiations, first carried forward throughout the Nixon and Ford administrations, achieved success in agreeing on goals to reduce those inventories. These negotiations continued under Carter, Vance, and Brzezinski, and agreement was reached in June 1979. However, faced with the unrelenting opposition of Democrat Senator Jackson and an unyielding conservative bloc of Republicans, the treaty faced trouble in the Senate.

Jackson's fundamental opposition to any arms control agreement with the USSR was clearly revealed in his reaction to the successful SALT II negotiations at the Vienna Summit. Jackson denounced the agreement as limiting American freedom to develop nuclear weapons and charged that Carter's trip to the Vienna summit was comparable to Neville Chamberlain's trip to Munich in 1938 to appease Hitler.

In fact SALT II was merely a formal affirmation of the moderately reduced levels agreed to by President Ford in

Vladivostok. It also, for the first time, provided for a viable mutual inspection regime, which in fact was very valuable for the U.S. We toiled away to build a core group of Senate supporters as the negotiations continued between the Soviet and American delegations in Geneva. I recruited individual senators to actually be appointed to the U.S. negotiation team who could then be mobilized in the Senate debate to recount, "I was there," support for the treaty. Senator Biden and Republican Senator John Chaffee became enthusiastic and effective participants in their efforts. Chaffee was uniquely effective because of his heroic war records in World War II and Korea. As a Marine Colonel in Korea, he led a trapped Marine battalion out of the Chosin reservoir to escape. The highly decorated war hero had special respect from his Republican conservative colleagues. For all these efforts, however, the votes for SALT II were not there, especially after the Soviet invasion of Afghanistan. Subsequently observed by both the USSR and U.S. in practice SALT II was never ratified.

Radio Free Europe and Radio Liberty (RFE andRL)

The anti-Vietnam War mood had produced great skepticism about White House and CIA activities. Then a staff member from Senator Case's office, John Marx, apparently acting on his own, "blew the cover" on CIA funding for Radio Free Europe and Radio Liberty to an investigative journalist friend. There was an automatic outcry from Congressional liberals calling for the termination of this secret program. Without exception, scholars and government experts on the Soviet Union and Eastern Europe rallied and insisted that "the radios" were valuable and effective in providing a regular flow of information to the captive populations in the Soviet empire. Efforts to persuade Senator Fulbright and his supporters of this were fruitless. Brzezinski was determined to preserve the function. He accepted the proposal from our "taskforce" to maintain the station's activities under a new, public "Board for International Broadcasting" (BIB) with a small appointed board of governors. This initiative was initially blocked by Fulbright. We needed a champion in the Senate and turned to our old friend Senator Russell Long and his liberal Democratic colleague John Pastore, of Rhode Island. Pastore was reluctant to oppose Fulbright, but signed on when we arranged to have his close friend Tommy Quinn selected for the new board. Brzezinski was particularly influential among the Eastern European diaspora in the U.S. and they made a major effort to coin Congressional support for RFE/RL. With Pastore's leadership we then succeeded in passing legislation and funding for the BIB which still functions in 2009. Distinct from the Voice of America, which presents the official position of the U.S. government and international news, RFE (targeted at Eastern Europe) and RL (targeted at the Soviet Union) presented unfiltered news about internal developments within the captive nations. They still enjoy international acceptance as "semi-official" sources of international news. Brzezinski's sophisticated appreciation of Soviet and East European developments as an academic expert and now as NSC director was critical in saving the stations.

However, my own effectiveness within the Vance-Christopher State Department was declining as the human rights issue loomed larger and larger. I determined, at this point, that the time had come to move on. Lucy and I recognized that after twenty-nine years it was essential to look at a second career to enable me to cope with the costs of five children in college.

CHAPTER XIII. EAST-WEST TRADE; COLD WAR WEAPON

After five fascinating and often bizarre years working with Congress for Kissinger, a change in venue was now obviously desirable. Two options presented themselves: my old friend Frank Carlucci had become deputy director of the CIA. Admiral Stansfield Turner was the director. I had also long known Turner, who had been my sons' Sunday school teacher. Frank proposed that I move to join them to run the CIA's Congressional relations, which had become particularly contentious in the immediate post-Vietnam era. Senator Frank Church, a liberal Democrat, had run a special, very public critical review of the agency's programs, and Congressional budget knives were being sharpened.

A second opportunity arrived at the same time from the Commerce Department. The Bureau of East-West trade was the lead government agency dealing with this contentious sector. Commerce Secretary Juanita Kreps and Frank Weil, who was in charge of the International Trade Administration, offered me the opportunity to become Deputy Assistant Secretary of Commerce and Director of the East-West Trade Bureau. Kreps was a prominent economist from North Carolina but with limited international trade experience. Weil was a successful New York financier, worldwise and a hard-charging executive. They both recognized that trade had become a major factor in the Cold War and a contentious issue within the administration. Trade with the

373

USSR and Eastern Europe was constantly under the spotlight. A means of penetrating the Soviet empire and undermining Moscow's control, trade was also a potentially dangerous source of technology leakage to our adversaries. The challenge was to achieve a balance between effective control of technology transfer and exploiting the needs of the stagnating Soviet and Eastern European economies to our benefit. The battle over the Jackson-Vanik amendment and its adoption by Congress had politicized what had been a technical issue.

You will recall that the Nixon-Kissinger strategy to sustain our security called for offering expanded trade, and investment was progressing to our distinct advantage. However, after Senator Jackson stimulated national support for freedom of emigration from the Soviet Union, the subsequent passage of the Jackson-Vanik amendment effectively eviscerated the "carrot" and turned East-West trade into a highly contentious issue. Most experts on the Soviet Union and Eastern Europe recognized the advantages of a carefully controlled buildup of trade interdependence with Moscow, and especially its appeal to Moscow's restive "allies." On the other hand, hard-line conservatives (mostly Republicans), opposed any trade with the Soviet Union and its so-called allies of the Warsaw Pact on the ground that it strengthened the economies of our adversaries. Senator Jackson and his staff (especially Richard Perle) in fact admitted to me that they favored economic warfare, as opposed to détente.

Both options appealed to me. Both offered to keep me active on Cold War issues. The decisive factor in my choice to accept the East-West trade portfolio was my conviction that a lead position on this scene would eventually prove to be a better platform from which to launch a second career in business. I regretted missing the opportunity to work with my friend Frank Carlucci for whom I had, and retain, great respect and affection. But the direct interaction with leaders in corporate America that the Commerce position offered seemed the most promising avenue.

I arrived at the Department of Commerce with some trepidation. My long experience with my Foreign Service colleagues had given me a sense that Foreign Service officers were the civilian counterparts of the Marine Corps and were unique. To my surprise and delight, when I took over the more than 100 men and women of the Bureau of East-West trade, I found a virtual treasury of talent and competence. There are more PhDs in Commerce than any other department. My two-person Soviet desk had more than twenty years experience, my Romanian director had a law degree from Bucharest, and my Polish director had a PhD in Polish studies. In short, unsung they may have been (several still remain at their posts in 2009) they were in fact dedicated, inspiring, and competent. We also had a full range of similarly qualified experts on selected functional specialties such as energy technology, aircraft, and basic industry in Eastern Europe and the USSR.

Given the centrality and political notoriety that East-West trade had achieved, this superb organization and absolute support of Secretary Juanita Kreps and Undersecretary Frank Weil enabled me to work the trade issues aggressively. And uniquely I also was responsible for coordinating our new, initial trade ties with China. China quickly became the major target of our work.

Eastern Europe- Trade Partner or Soviet Allies?

The Warsaw Pact members of Moscow's alliance had long been recognized as the soft underbelly of the Soviet empire. After the Soviet-led invasion of Czechoslovakia in 1968 to preserve the Brezhnev Doctrine (i.e. Moscow's insistence that once a Communist regime is established, it must never be allowed to depart), frustration and chafing at Moscow's control of their individual national destinies was increasingly evident. You will recall that in 1968, we adopted a policy to expand the presence of the United States in each of the satellite countries to encourage their hopes and instinctive pro-Western sentiments. We did this mindful of the restlessness of Moscow's allies reflected in the periodic outbreak of anti-Moscow demonstrations – 1947, East Berlin; 1953, Budapest; 1968, Dubcek's Prague and riots in Krakow, Poland. By 1978, with my charter to activate trade arrangements throughout the area, I found increasing unrest and even hostility among the "captive nations" toward their Soviet "masters."

I had come to know Romauld Spassowski in my USIA years. Spassowski had since risen to be deputy foreign minister of Poland. As such, he was in charge of President Carter's visit to Warsaw in 1977. Not long after that he returned to Washington as Poland's ambassador, for a second time replacing my good friend Wittold Trampczyns- ki. We quickly renewed our friendship. "Romek" became a rich source of insights into Soviet ambassador Dobrynin's increasingly difficult effort to maintain tight control over his Warsaw Pact colleagues in Washington. Dobrynin was holding weekly meetings with each individual "satellite" ambassador, and a formal monthly working review and dinner with all of them. From Romek (and each of his colleagues) we learned what priorities Moscow was promot- ing and how they attempted to impose discipline over their increasingly uneasy "allies." We also learned from their wives, who were equally resentful of Mrs. Dobrynin's heavy- handed efforts to control them!

About Dobrynin

Anatoly Dobrynin had been Moscow's ambassador in Washington since 1961. He was accredited to our Presidents, from Kennedy through Reagan. He had learned to play the access game and was second to none as a professional representative of his country and its rulers from Khrushchev through Gorbachev. He was fluent, master of the intricacies of our system, and very effective in encouraging confidence in his "understanding" of our policies. He was also extremely facile (surviving numerous purges) and capable of exuding great charm in his efforts to develop "friendships" with important Americans. He worked especially diligently to cultivate "captains of industry" with considerable success. He cherished invitations to attend the Kentucky Derby with prominent American industrialists, who were almost without exception charmed by Dobrynin and his obsequious wife.

Kissinger, with calculation, took full advantage of Dobrynin's eagerness to serve as a "private" channel and plied him with special access (he had his own "pass" to the State Department garage) and private meetings. This added to Dobrynin's sense of self-importance, but also allowed "Henry" to send private, blunt warning signals to Moscow. From my vantage, Kissinger exploited Dobrynin and his access to Moscow's leaders carefully and effectively—he played on Dobrynin's not inconsiderable ego like a fiddle. Nevertheless, most of us were distrustful of Dobrynin—was he an accurate reporter, or did he shape his reports to reflect glory on himself and avoid confronting his Politburo rulers with unpalatable news? While we will probably never know, he does, in his memoirs, *In Confidence,* insist that he regularly warned Brezhnev and Gromyko that Soviet actions like the importation of Cuban mercenaries into Angola and the untimely imposition of an "education tax" on Soviet Jews seeking to emigrate were very badly received in Washington. Whether he, as his claims, also recommended against such actions is open to question.

One thing is clear: charming and friendly as he was to U.S. officials, behind our backs, he warned his Warsaw Pact colleagues to avoid getting "too close" to American officials. According to "Romek" and East European ambassadors, he consistently attacked U.S. officials and our policies in "the most vicious terms." And his wife, Irina, so friendly to Americans, bitterly denounced all things American in her regular meetings with her Warsaw Pact counterparts. The Dobrynins were actively resented by the ambassadors and their wives of Poland, Czechoslovakia, Hungary, Bulgaria, and Romania. They made no attempt to encourage a fraternal atmosphere. Their demeanor was all the more distracting because, according to Spassowski, Dobrynin's KGB station chief, inter alia, ran an aggressive program to control the KGB counterparts in each Warsaw Pact embassy, who actively monitored their own ambassador and staffs on behalf of the KGB and Dobrynin.

When President Carter replaced Ford, Vance did not extend the same special treatment to Dobrynin that Kissinger had. Dobrynin, however, remained preeminent among Communist ambassadors. And, as he explains in *In Confidence*, Dobrynin contended that Vance was often quite candid with him about the problems Vance had with Brzezinski. Knowing Vance, I found it hard to believe that he would complain to Dobrynin about such a thing, but knowing Dobrynin, it is not surprising that he would claim such an intimate relationship.

Poland

As director of the Bureau of East-West trade, I co-chaired the annual U.S.-Polish Council on trade. Soon after assuming my new post, I travelled to Warsaw for the council meeting. Consistent with what Spassowski was reporting, I found palpable unhappiness with Moscow's intrusive presence. My Polish counterpart complained bitterly that his best efforts to win U.S. investment (and other Western investments) were invariably "vetoed" by Moscow. The existence of Moscow's veto power was a constant reminder, he openly said, that Poland was not really a sovereign nation. In fact, the Polish minister of defense, Marshall Rokossovsky, was a Soviet general. This was not a new condition. What was new was the open expression of frustration about it by Polish officials.

Czechoslovakia

A chance to engage with Czechoslovakia presented itself in the form of a dispute over the Czech government's gold reserves, which had been spirited away to the U.S. and England when the Germans invaded in 1938. Instead of returning the gold (worth by then an estimated $600 million) after the war, we held it in reserve, reluctant to return the gold to the new Communist regime. I became a member of the administration's committee to resolve this issue through negotiations with Prague. Return of the gold was inevitable; there was no legal basis for holding it. The Czechs insisted that it be returned, as a sovereign right. The

U.S. was hesitant because of claims by Czech-Americans who had had their property confiscated when the Communists seized control in Prague. Key members of Congress were enlisted by a lawyer—former Senator George Smathers of Florida—to block the return of the gold. Smathers, a high-powered lobbyist, had been a prominent Senate member of the conservative Southern caucus. We overcame Smathers and returned the gold. I travelled to Prague at the invitation of the Czech Minister of Trade and was feted with a ministerial dinner and front-page coverage in *Rude Pravo*, the official government paper. My Czech colleague bragged that he was a hero in Prague because of the gold transfer. He added that the U.S. (and British) action contrasted with Moscow's blatant disdain for Czech sensitivities. Throughout Prague, at this time, we encountered open criticism of Moscow's imperial attitude toward Czechoslovakia.

Bulgaria

I had numerous similar incidents occur when I visited Bulgaria to open the U.S. exhibition at the annual Plovdiv trade fair. Historically the most pro-Russian of Moscow's satellites, even in Bulgaria trade officials carped about Moscow's heavy-handed control of Bulgaria's feeble efforts to invigorate their economy and attract Western investment. A few months later, I accompanied the Bulgarian ambassador in Washington to a major electronics trade show in California. Throughout that trip, the ambassador complained about the limitations on his activities, inspired by Dobrynin!

As we actively interacted with the Warsaw Pact countries on trade issues, it was increasingly clear that Moscow's control was fraying. The Brezhnev Doctrine invasion in 1968 had reinforced the fear of alienating Moscow, but a decade later it was again deteriorating.

Hungary

Hungary, like all of the Eastern European countries, was unique in its own way. The only non-Slavic member of the Warsaw Pact, Hungarians had a long tradition of excellent education and tended to look down on their Slav allies as backward. Hungarian refugee scientists including Edward Teller played lead roles in developing the U.S. nuclear program, and among those who fled Budapest in the 1956 uprising against Moscow were future financiers such as billionaire George Soros. The Department of Commerce, playing to Hungary's appetite for recognition, had concluded a singularly broad and detailed trade agreement designed to promote and protect U.S. investment and joint ventures with Hungarian enterprises. Hungary had an especially advanced chemical industry and was making impressive progress in marketing agro-chemicals on the world market. Soon after my arrival in Commerce, I was visited by a delegation of presidents of American chemical companies to protest Hungarian abuse of their patent rights. Dow, Du-Pont, Cargill, and Monsanto had seen their international market sales of RoundUp and other pesticides and fertilizers suddenly decline, being outsold by Hungarian knockoff products. They insisted that the Hungarian products were clearly based on the theft of their patent rights. In our trade agreements with Hungary, the government of Hungary had agreed to respect U.S. patent rights.

In response, we quickly put together an interagency task force, invited representation of the aggrieved U.S. corporations to join us, and convened a special meeting in Budapest with the Minister of Trade. After three days of contentious meetings—the Hungarians insisting they were within their rights—I asked for a meeting with the Prime Minister and threatened that the U.S. would publicly cancel our trade agreement unless the issue was resolved to the satisfaction of the U.S. corporations. The Hungarian government relented and we moved on to establish a number of effective joint venture agreements between the U.S. corporations and the admittedly advanced Hungarian chemical enterprises.

The net result was a cause for some celebration and resulted in closer, more effective collaboration between Hungary and the United Sates. Hungarian officials were delighted and openly praised "partnership with American corporations" while denouncing to us their forced collaboration with Soviet enterprises, as always producing one-sided benefits for the Soviets.

Poland, Again

At this point in history, Moscow began to panic about increasing restiveness and virtual rebellion against Moscow's puppet regime in Poland. Trade union leaders, including the legendary hero Lech Walensa, began to coalesce into what became *Solidarnost*, a united labor movement committed to reducing and eventually eliminating Soviet exploitation of Poland's failed economy. The Catholic church, the most influential religious institution in Eastern Europe, increased its criticism against the Moscow controlled regime. Highly publicized violent police reactions against individual priests created a series of crises. We, in Washington, received the increasing intelligence flow indicating Soviet troop movements toward Poland's borders. It was clear that Brezhnev, pressured by the cadre of hard-line forces in the Politburo (Suslov, Gromyko, Ustinov, and Marshall Grechko) threatened to intervene unless the beleaguered Polish government cracked down on the growing dissent. Under Soviet direction, Polish General Jaroszelski overthrew the relatively moderate Giereck regime and launched a widespread and often brutal roundup and arrest of suspected dissidents and moderate officials. Jaroszelski did prevent a Soviet invasion and suppressed, for the moment, Poland's move toward greater freedom. He also triggered the final decision by my (by now) close friend, Spassowski, the prominent Polish ambassador to the U.S. to defect.

Spassowski and his devout Catholic wife Wanda had grown steadily more disenchanted with Moscow's domination of Poland. For Romek, it began to grow during his period as deputy foreign minister in Warsaw, after his first tour in Washington as ambassador and subsequent post as ambassador to India. In his senior position at the ministry, and in Communist party councils, he confronted again and again Moscow's intrusions to dictate Poland's ties with the United States. Soviet Prime Minister Kosygin repeatedly "vetoed" Polish agreements with Washington for agricultural loans that would have benefited Poland's desperate agricultural sector. When "Romek" was in charge of the Carter visit to Warsaw, he was summoned to Moscow in advance of the "summit," and was lectured by Soviet deputy foreign minister Georgiy Kornienko, a particularly hard-line deputy to Gromyko about the dangers of collaboration with Washington. Thus, by the time he returned to Washington for his second tour as Poland's ambassador, he was already bitter about Moscow's flagrant intrusions into Poland' activities. And he was increasingly open with me and my State Department colleague Jack Scanlon, Deputy Assistant Secretary for Eastern Europe. (Jack had been in Moscow with me from 1960-1962.)

A key factor in the inevitable defection of Spassowski was the influence of his devoted wife Wanda. Romek had grown up a Marxist. His late father had been a prominent Marxist professor at Warsaw's top university. Caught up in the successive German and Soviet invasions of Poland, he never doubted his commitment to the Communist party of Poland. He became an intelligence officer in the Polish army.

His odyssey is recounted, almost poetically, in his memoir *The Liberation of One* (see Bibliography).

He had progressed rapidly within the post-war Polish Communist government to become ambassador to the U.S., as earlier noted, at the young age of thirty-four. On his first Washington tour, those of us who knew him found him to be tough and a dedicated Communist representative of his government. His sincerity was obvious. He was able to display an occasional glimpse of skepticism and an attractive sense of humor. From the beginning, however, Wanda was friendly, openly devout and critical of her husband's atheistic regime. During his subsequent tour as ambassador to India, he and Wanda experienced a terrible tragedy; their young son, critically depressed, committed suicide. On returning as deputy foreign minister in Warsaw, he threw his efforts into his new position. Wanda, grieving, turned more and more to the church. And she redoubled her campaign to persuade Romek to accept the church as well.

I had introduced Wanda to my mother (who, with my retired father, had returned to live with us and help raise my boys when "C" died in 1970), and to Joan Cormack, the wife of my close friend Tom Cormack, who was by then the executive secretary of CIA (under the infamous Bill Casey). The Cormacks, who had also lost a son in an accident, are devout Catholics. This trio bonded immediately and provided Wanda with a solid support structure.

Thus, Spassowski was well down the road to his conversion, religious and political, when Jaroszelski and his Soviet masters cracked down on Poland's tentative efforts to liberalize its society. Romek met with Scanlon and then me to announce his decision. Scanlon immediately arranged for the FBI to provide protection for the Spassowskis, who were obviously vulnerable to Polish (KGB-controlled) intelligence operatives within the Polish embassy. Efforts by those security officers to apprehend Romek and return him to Warsaw for "consultation" were thereby thwarted. The Spassowski daughter moved in with friends of ours. With Tom Cormack's assistance, Romek and Wanda travelled to Philadelphia where the Catholic Cardinal Kroll accepted Romek into the Church. The dramatic defection by the highest ranking Communist official was over. Poland continued to adjust to the Moscow-sponsored crackdown. Spassowski was condemned, in absentia, to death. To most of us, the handwriting was on the wall for Moscow's control of Poland.

China

While the increasingly active interactions with the Eastern European missions were encouraging in eroding Moscow's totalitarian control of their empire, the opening to China quickly became a dominant factor in U.S. policy. President Nixon and Secretary Kissinger, in a single stroke, had changed the balance of power between Washington and Moscow, when they surprised the world with their sudden visit to Beijing. Nixon and Mao had agreed on a one-China policy to address the Taiwan issue and a broad agreement to move toward full recognition, especially in the trade area. Progress was slow until Mao's death, but then with reformer Deng Xiao Peng in charge, implementation began to unfold. A major formal trade agreement became the keystone. Teams in the State Department, Treasury, Commerce, Justice, Agriculture, and the Defense Department went to work in preparing the United States draft proposal. Many complicated and often contentious issues had to be resolved within our own government, and these internal negotiations were often heated. Particular concern about Chinese exports of textiles, protection of patents, investment guarantees, agricultural sales, and control of strategic items all had to be resolved. The work went on, slowly, but pushed by NSC Adviser Brzezinski.

Meanwhile, an overriding strategic issue had to be resolved: how to reconcile our interest in promoting cooperation with Moscow, especially on controlling the arms race, while taking advantage of the rapprochement with Beijing. This became a major issue between State Secretary Vance and NSC director Brzezinski. Vance favored carefully moving ahead on both fronts – sequentially—one step forward with Beijing and then exploiting Moscow's apprehension about China. This was more or less an extension of Kissinger's successful triangulation policy of encouraging both Moscow and Beijing to exploit their strategic differences. Brzezinski, relishing Moscow's concern, preferred to plunge ahead with Beijing to full recognition, a state visit by Deng Xao Peng to Washington and conclusion of a full trade agreement with "the People's Republic of China." Brzezinski carried the day with President Carter and a China-first policy was adopted. In retrospect, in 2009, that decision seems justified.

Deng Xiao Peng arrived in Washington in 1979 and received an unequaled high-profile reception. The high point was a glamorous evening at the Kennedy Center, hosted by President Carter, where a spectacular program including the Harlem Globetrotters performing on stage around the diminutive Deng (some five feet tall) who professed to love basketball, prominent Chinese-American symphony artists performing, and an emotional closing with a large American children's choir surrounding Deng, who stood at their height, on stage singing "Getting to Know You," from *The King and I.* My Chinese embassy colleagues confirmed to me that Deng was deeply touched by this welcome to the United States. Agreements were concluded across a broad range of subjects, including above all a commitment to conclude the new trade agreement. There was also a major increase in student exchanges, cultural visits, and not publicly, but of critical importance, Chinese agreement to permit CIA/Defense Department operated long-range radar stations on the border of the Soviet Union.

Soon after Deng's visit, the different interagency disputes about our draft trade agreement were driven to conclusion by Brzezinski and his principal Chinese specialist, Professor

389

Michel Oksenberg. The delegation to travel to Beijing to complete negotiation of the agreement was led by Commerce Secretary Kreps and Treasury Secretary Michael Blumenthal. Media interest in the trip was high and a large press corps delegation joined us on Air Force II to fly into Beijing. CBS legendary Asia correspondent Bernie Kalb was the dean of the press delegation which also included the *New York Times*, the *Washington Post*, and the *Wall Street Journal*. It was somewhat amusing to observe the expected jostling between Commerce and Treasury public relations teams to ensure that "their secretary received top billing." I think Kreps was completely at ease in this contest, but Blumenthal seemed somewhat more determined to project his leadership. None of this by-play affected the negotiations, but I found myself, as executive director of the trip, having to intercede from time to time to cool the public relations people.

The formal negotiations opened at the Chinese ministry of foreign affairs with Kreps and Blumenthal in "the chair" for the United States and the Chinese minister of trade for China. It was quite a scene. Juanita, tall and utterly feminine, stood to shake hands with her Chinese counterpart, a diminutive, tough-looking woman in a "Mao jacket," who then turned to greet lanky Mike Blumenthal. Our team included senior representatives of each of our interested departments and our acting Ambassador (chargé d'affairs), Stapleton Roy. "Stape," a career Foreign Service officer, was an invaluable asset. Raised in pre-war China by his missionary parents, Stape was bilingual in Mandarin Chinese and steeped in Chinese history and cultural philosophy. He and Oksenberg provided a steady flow of insights and advice as the complex negotiations unfolded. The Chinese minister with six assistants sat across from us. When Secretary Kreps and Secretary Blumenthal formally presented our several hundred pages' draft proposal, the Chinese minister looked up, smiling, and presented a slender document of fewer than 100 pages. She explained, clearly enjoying the moment, that she was impressed by the volume of the U.S. proposal in contrast to their modest counterproposal. "You see," she said, "we have an advantage here, lawyers were banned from the Chinese Central Kingdom more than 300 years ago!" Laughs were enjoyed by both sides, and individual joint teams appointed to go through the proposals on a sector-by-sector basis.

It is fair to say that we were astounded at how rapidly the negotiations proceeded. Each morning the teams would meet, and then each afternoon, at the Chinese request, our specialists would meet off-the-record to explain to their Chinese counterparts the rationale for the U.S. position on disputed sections. On several occasions our delegates were amazed when their Chinese counterparts would admit that they weren't certain what they should propose and add, "What would you do, if you were my position?" And even more amazingly, often they would accept the U.S. response as their own position. An inspiring reflection of the innate self-confidence of the Chinese who, of course, had centuries of experience behind them. And a revealing difference from invariably defensive and insecure Soviet negotiators. Clearly Deng Xao Peng had ordered that this agreement was to be completed.

The negotiations moved ahead for several days, as the individual task forces one after another reached agreement. Meanwhile, Secretary Blumenthal returned to Washington and Secretary Kreps carried on. We were feted, as though it were in return for Deng's reception in Washington. A major banquet the first night, press included. The next morning, prior to beginning work, we were received personally by Deng Xao Peng, who expressed his determination that our negotiations should succeed. We were driven into the agricultural countryside where Agricultural Undersecretary Ed Schur explained to us the significance of the reform activities we were shown. We hosted a reception at our embassy arranged by chargé Roy and enjoyed an unforgettable feast at Beijing's premiere "duck restaurant." The taskforce ploughed ahead while Secretary Kreps and a few delegates not involved in the technical task force enjoyed a day-long trip down the Kweilin River with its dramatic sandstone towers lining the bank and a fabulous on-boat lunch prepared in huge wok bowls. The Chinese liquor, MaiTai, a throat-burning concoction, was served, but fortunately so was China's outstanding beer Tsingtao.

Finally after six days of task-force work, we had an agreement—with one critical exception: textile trade quotas! In a final plenary meeting in Beijing the Chinese minister and Secretary Kreps squared off. The Chinese held textile sales to the U.S. as the one major area where they could earn hard currency. Secretary Kreps, a North Carolinian with acute appreciation for the concerns of the beleaguered textile industry, resolutely rejected China's request for dramatic increases in the textile quotas that we were proposing— already a significant increase for China. The meeting concluded with Secretary Kreps regretting that agreement was apparently impossible; she announced that therefore we would depart the next day for a one-day stop in Quangzho (Canton) en route to Hong Kong. Added credibility to her resolution was made evident to the Chinese when we publicly briefed the U.S. press delegation about the standoff.

We departed Beijing, as promised, to Quangzhao where we attended a major international trade show and visited another agricultural center. Several of us worked to reinforce Secretary Kreps's unyielding position because we had picked up and sensed that Dang Xao Peng had no intention to allow this historic negotiation to fail. We bet with one another that the Chinese would "cave." Mike Oksenberg and Stapelton Roy, with their long experience in China affairs, were obviously the most qualified to make such a prediction and they did. Lo and behold late in the afternoon, an official from the Minister's office arrived to announce that the Minister was flying down to meet Secretary Kreps with new instructions from Deng. We met with her, signed the historic agreement, and hopped over to Hong Kong.

The then still British-controlled Crown Colony of Hong Kong was one of the world's most vibrant cities. We were bussed into town and arrived at a stately modern hotel, met at the entrance by a bevy of beautiful girls clad in skintight dresses with the sides split up to the waist. Even Juanita had to laugh at our openly animal-like reaction! We had, after all, seen nothing but Mao uniforms for a week.

Secretary Kreps then held a heavily attended press briefing at the U.S.-British Chamber of Commerce in Hong Kong and in understated terms described her historic achievement. I joined her and participated in the discussion of the complex issues we had negotiated. The press delegation was uniformly enthusiastic about the breakthrough and reports about the trip in U.S. media were uniformly positive. Even my friend Bernie Kalb, who had seen decades of U.S. efforts to cope with China, was impressed.

On arrival back in Washington, we found that President Carter and Brzezinski were clearly pleased to see this important step forward with China. A few days later, Ann Wexler, special assistant to President Carter, organized a White House briefing on the trip and the historic new trade agreement. I was asked to join the president in speaking about the agreement. I ventured that U.S.-China trade, which had been running below $1 billion annually, could quickly expand to more than $5 billion annually. The president commented that perhaps I was a bit optimistic. Within two years, we exceeded the $5 billion mark and today in 2009 it runs more than $200 billion.

Earlier Ann Wexler had recruited me periodically to speak at various events around the country. In one unforgettable event, I was sent to Miami to address an audience of 500-plus about the Panama Canal and the potential it presented for Soviet mischief. My speech went off well, but there was a lot of criticism about the decision to "give away our canal." One obviously hostile man stood up and denounced the canal treaty and went on to criticize President Carter for his recent trip to Mexico. In full sincerity, I put him down and characterized Carter's decision to visit Mexico as far-sighted since our relations were extremely important and troubled by trade and immigration issues. As we left the hotel, a man with a strong Southern accent came up to me and said he really appreciated my effective defense of the President. He added, "Jimmy is my neighbor and close friend, and I am going to tell him how well you did." I smiled, and cynically dismissed his comments from my mind. However, when I returned to Washington, Secretary Kreps called me and said, "I don't know what you did in Miami, but the President was really pleased." The next day, Lucy and I were invited to a state dinner at the White House for Japanese Prime Minister Ohira. As we went through the reception line, President Carter took us aside and he thanked me profusely for defending his trip to Mexico. The Southern gentleman really was Carter's neighbor in Plains, Georgia, and he had called the President!

As 1979 wound down, Lucy and I were reinforced in our decision to retire early (at fifty-three) and seek a second career in the private sector to help us escape from our financial bind. Carter had frozen government executive salaries (which for me was $42,000 a year), and inflation was more than ten percent annually. In November a young attorney from Patton, Boggs, and Blow came to seek my views on our Hungarian trade problems. After our meeting, I said to him that I was delighted to assist him, but asked whether he would tell me what his income that year had been as a new young partner at Patton Boggs. He answered $125,000—three times my salary. This revelation closed the decision for us, and I accepted an offer to be corporate vice president with ARMCO, an integrated steel company, for more than three times my government salary—effective January 1, 1980. My new responsibilities covered ARMCO's international investments, including a partnership to build a specialty steel plant in Novolipetsk, Siberia, and Congressional lobbying.

Almost to the day of my resignation on January 1, 1980, Brezhnev, in a last-gasp thrust, launched a massive invasion of Afghanistan. Again, according to Dobrynin's account, this decision was put forth by the collective hard-line leadership group including Suslov, Gromyko, Marshall Grechko, and Defense Minister Ustinov. Dobrynin opines that Brezhnev was in failing health, had shown early signs of dementia and disorientation and was in no condition to stop this latest Soviet aggression. Events in Afghanistan had been deteriorating for several years. In the power vacuum that resulted, the Communist Party of Afghanistan (CPA) seized power with

Moscow's support. Shortly thereafter the CPA split into two warring factions and Communist rule was in jeopardy. Suslov and company viewed this as another Czechoslovakia and acted to apply the "Brezhnev Doctrine" again. This time Moscow sent in more than 200,000 troops and set off a long drawn-out war that eventually sapped Moscow's military and economic viability.

Carter (and Brezhnev) reacted sharply, putting the still-to-be-ratified SALT II treaty on the shelf, placing a complete embargo on trade with the USSR and cancelling U.S. participation in the Olympic Games, scheduled for Moscow.

The immediate hostile reaction of the United States was hardly surprising. We had viewed the overthrow of the friendly, neutral, elected, and admittedly corrupt regime government by the Afghan Communist party as unacceptable. The negative reaction was dramatically reinforced when one of the warring Communist Party factions kidnapped the Ambassador of the United States, Adolph "Spike" Dubs. In a subsequent firefight between the Communist factions, Dubs was assassinated. KGB special advisors were involved in the shootout and there was deep suspicion that they bore responsibility for Dubs's murder. Dubs had been in both Hamburg in 1953 and Moscow in 1961 together with me. I was stunned and applauded President Carter's sharp reaction against Moscow.

More fundamentally the Soviet invasion brought to an end the efforts of those, like Secretary Vance, to balance our rapprochement with Beijing with similar steps with Moscow. It was the end of détente. When Brzezinski directed the ill-fated helicopter intrusion into Iran to rescue the American hostages seized by Khomeini's forces, against Vance's recommendation, it was the final straw. Vance resigned. A turbulent period for Carter who had accomplished a great deal—especially with China. On the other hand, Brezhnev abandoned efforts to ease relations with the U.S., especially bitter about the new Beijing-Washington rapprochement, and weakened by the escalating costs of his Afghan folly.

CHAPTER XIV. EPILOGUE: THE INEVITABLE IMPLOSION OF THE SOVIET UNION

Although the final gasp of the Soviet Union did not occur until 1989, nine years later, the tide of history had clearly turned against Moscow beginning by 1980. Their hold over their restive Eastern European empire was deteriorating, and the accelerating cost and growing public hostility within the USSR toward their "war of choice" in Afghanistan sapped the efficacy of their rule. Brezhnev's dementia had left the arch-reactionary core group of Suslov, Marshall Grechko, KGB chief Yuriy Andropov, and Defense Minister Ustinov in charge of the war in Afghanistan and the failing efforts to suppress growing Eastern European restiveness. And Suslov et. al. were completely out of touch with evolving Russian attitudes.

Brezhnev, who finally died in 1983, was followed by KGB leader Yuri Andropov. My Soviet acquaintances cheered his assumption of power because they believed he was far more sophisticated and possessed demonstrated executive capabilities, in contrast to Brezhnev who had become disoriented and permitted growing corruption and incompetence. However, Andropov was quickly disabled by a kidney infection and forced to operate while depending on dialysis to survive. In less than two years, in 1984, he in turn died and was replaced by Brezhnev's protégé, the pedestrian, corrupt Konstantin Chernenko. (Chernenko also quickly became ill and died in 1985.) The dramatic sudden series of leadership changes added to the strong sense within the Warsaw Pact that power at the center of the "empire" was collapsing.

The always dangerous, delicate balance between American and Soviet nuclear-tipped missile inventories remained dangerous. While SALT I had established some mutual restraints on numbers, they still remained at more than 10,000 war-heads on each side. The SALT II treaty concluded in 1979 included modest reductions in these totals, but President Carter had decided not to press for Senate confirmation of SALT II when the Soviets invaded Afghanistan. Nonetheless the new limitations were observed by both sides. What remained was an uneasy stand-off, dependent on a determination by both sides not to "launch" by mistake.

On July 27, 1982 (after my retirement), I led a joint Soviet-American Trade Council dinner on the cruise boat *Enticer*, which circled Manhattan while we ate dinner and listened to speeches by both sides. I had a long, private conversation with Evgeniy Shershnev, Soviet ambassador Dobrynin's deputy, who was presumed to be the top KGB official in the United States. After several vodkas, Shershnev became candid about Brezhnev's decline and hopeful about Andropov's takeover. Shershnev was deeply impressed by the beauty and power of New York, particularly as we passed under the incredible Brooklyn Bridge. He rhapsodized over its engineering and explained that he had been trained as an engineer. After passing the bridge, he, in an anxious tone, launched into a distressed discussion of our nuclear standoff and concern that President Reagan was increasing the danger of war. He admitted that the Soviet Union could not try to match the U.S. "build-up" but would increase their preparedness by adopting a lower threshold to "Launch-on-warning." A stark reminder of how close we remained to a nuclear holocaust. I quickly shared this conversation with my friend Frank Carlucci, Deputy Secretary of Defense.

In 1985, Mikhail Gorbachev replaced Chenenko. Young, with a record of successful management during his rapid ascent within the Communist Party, Gorbachev re-staffed the government with better educated and vigorous young colleagues. He retired Brezhnev's old Politburo cronies and launched fundamental changes to modernize the Party and its programs. Gorbachev introduced two radical changes, *perestroika* (restructuring the economy and reducing the huge military machine) and *glasnost* (opening up the previously closed society, dependent on a paranoid dedication to secrecy). He replaced the hard-line Gromyko with Eduard Shevardnadze, former KGB chief in Georgia who launched a sweeping change in Soviet foreign policy. Gorbachev accepted an invitation from President Reagan to visit the United States and had a highly successful tour, mingling with crowds on the street in Washington and winning considerable popularity in American media coverage. All of these actions were a welcome turn away from the unyielding hostile Soviet position that had heretofore only gradually shifted away from the darkest days of Stalin's brutal rule.

However, these same actions, relaxing the totalitarian nature of the Soviet government, also stoked the growing resistance of the East European Warsaw Pact members to Moscow's control. By 1987 the complete collapse of the Soviet empire was evident. East Germans, sensing the growing weakness of Moscow's control, started fleeing, first within the permitted vacation areas in Hungary. Budapest, in turn, began to allow East Germans to leave Hungary to flee to West Germany. *The wall had been breached.* In my mind, Hungary's decision to open the gates validated our long policy to encourage the Hungarian appetite for freedom from Moscow's total control.

In Poland, the labor movement *Solidarnost* established virtually a parallel government. And Gorbachev acquiesced in this development. The Berlin wall was dismantled. The stampede was on. Soviet foreign minister Shevardnadze accepted an invitation from Reagan's then Secretary of State, James Baker, to spend several days at Baker's ranch in Wyoming. In a historic exchange Baker persuaded Shevard-nadze to agree that Moscow should allow the Warsaw Pact nations to go free. What we had always assumed would be a bloodbath when the Soviet empire collapsed, happened practically without a shot being fired, a monument to Baker's diplomatic skills.

Change in Washington

Back in 1980, meanwhile, President Jimmy Carter had finished his promising reign with a series of failures. The fall of the Shah of Iran and subsequent seizure of our embassy staff by Iranian revolutionaries posed a dramatic challenge to President Carter. And yet, there was virtually nothing that the United States could do. The world's great nuclear power appeared impotent and Carter's image as a "weak" President became ingrained. The desperate helicopter raid to free the hostages collapsed when two of our helicopters crashed into each other, adding to that image. My colleague and close friend Bruce Laingen was the senior hostage. His heroic and dignified performance under the 400-plus day internment reflected great credit on the U.S. after the Iranians released the hostages as President Reagan replaced Carter.

Carter was also plagued by the economic recession that had begun under President Ford and had resisted all of Ford's and Carter's actions to "restart the economy." Reagan, seizing on these problems, easily defeated Carter's reelection effort. Reagan's campaign charged Carter with "losing Afghanistan, Yemen, Angola, and Nicaragua," ignoring of course, his historic achievements with China, unrelenting containment of the USSR, the conclusion of SALT II, and ratification of the Panama Canal Treaty.

Reagan came to power and promptly reinvigorated the fundamental internal division that had bedeviled Nixon, Ford, and Carter over how to maintain "containment" and, by this time, finish off the Soviet Union. In this instance the internal struggle was between Secretary of State Haig and

George Schultz, promoting engagement and containment, and hard-line Secretary of Defense Caspar Weinberger and CIA director Bill Casey (reinforced by my ubiquitous friend Richard Perle who became Assistant Secretary of Defense), a trio who promoted confrontation, all-out economic war, and continued buildup of our massive nuclear arsenal. Reagan, in the final analysis, wisely relied primarily on the sage advice of Schultz, who achieved primacy in dealing principally with Moscow.

In 1989, with its external empire in the Warsaw Pact lost, the Soviet Union itself fell apart. First Gorbachev and then, Boris Yeltsin, who overthrew Gorbachev, presided over the largely peaceful breaking away of the Baltic states: Ukraine, Kazakhstan, Kyrgyzstan, Uzbekistan, Belarus, Turkmenistan, and Tajikistan, which joined loosely in a former Soviet states group, which in turn quickly became nominal only.

The Cold War was over.

Cold War Myths

1. Both sides share blame for the Cold War.

Some revisionist historians, seeking, as is their wont, a new interpretation of this post-war period, have built a case that the collapse of the war-time alliance with the USSR was not inevitable. They contend that Western and especially American hostility to Soviet hegemony over Eastern Europe confronted Moscow with an impossible challenge that could have been avoided. The reality is the opposite. It takes a historic leap of faith to ignore Moscow's immediate violation of its commitments in the Yalta and Potsdam agreements, which could have produced a peaceful reconstruction of the USSR itself and Europe. Stalin's post-war brutality and relentless push to expand Soviet control of liberated Europe, and the subsequent campaigns of Khrushchev and Brezhnev to consolidate their hold of East Germany and rush into power vacuums that developed as European colonial control of Africa and Southeast Asia created Cold War confrontations around the globe.

The iron curtain was a reality!

2. "Reagan won the Cold War."

I hope it is clear from this account that all U.S. presidents, from Harry Truman through Ronald Reagan, contributed to this historic "victory" over Soviet imperialism. Reagan, in fact, deserves great credit for his effective personal engagement with Gorbachev, and sustaining our military superiority and political containment of Moscow's expansion efforts. Reagan, as established by James Mann in *The Rebellion of Ronald Reagan* (see Bibliography), was also dedicated to reducing and even ending the existence of our terrifying nuclear inventories of the two super-powers. In fact, in the Reykjavik summit meeting with Gorbachev he had to be restrained by his advisers from both State and Defense from agreeing to a proposal by Gorbachev to destroy all nuclear weapons on both sides. Their argument that this would leave Moscow's still massive conventional forces in a

405

dominant position in Europe was undoubtedly correct at the time. Today, in 2009, that conventional force has withered to a shadow of itself, and a goal of a nuclear weapons-free world which President Obama has expounded is compelling.

However, credit for the Cold War outcome must embrace first and foremost the creators of "containment," President Truman and George Kennan, the career Soviet specialist diplomat, who in his historic dispatch of 1945 ("the long telegram") laid out the arguments for a long-term commitment to prevent Soviet expansion. Truman personally deserves the greatest recognition. He recognized the dangers the vacuum created by the disarmament of the victorious Western government after World War II. And against a major tide of popular opinion that was determined to consume the fruits of our victory; committed the United States to force Soviet troops out of Northern Iran; intervened against the Communist takeover of Greece; moved to block Communist takeover efforts in Western Europe (which were very real in 1946-1948) with the Marshall Plan and then NATO; and intervention in Korea. There are many heroes in the Truman period, including General Marshall, Dean Acheson, Republican Senator Arthur Vandenberg, and James Forrestal.

Each presidential administration continued the policy of containment, without exception: Eisenhower's prudent disengagement in Korea and commitment to NATO; Kennedy's firm stand on Berlin and dramatic rebuff of Khrushchev's Cuban missile initiative; Nixon's opening to

China and arms control negotiations (SALT) with the Soviets; Carter's continuation of the SALT process, extricating us from the Panama Canal and his little recognized support for new weapons systems such as the MX missile, nuclear submarine forces and the cruise missile program; and finally Reagan.

All in all a remarkable national commitment to the forty-year policy of containment. It worked!

3.   Roosevelt sold out Eastern Europe at Yalta.

As described in chapter two, the Yalta Agreement did not yield control over Eastern Europe to the Soviet Union. In fact, had Stalin fulfilled his obligations under Yalta, the countries of Eastern Europe would have held free elections and established sovereign governments. The cold hard fact of the presence of massive Soviet troops in occupation of the "liberated states" of Eastern Europe is what determined Communist control over those states.

4. Soviet occupation of East Germany and Berlin's vulnerable location within the Soviet zone of Germany was a product of weak Western diplomacy by Truman at Potsdam.

In fact, once again, the fate of East Germany was a reflection of the reality of the presence of more than a half million Soviet troops in East Germany after the war ended. President Eisenhower correctly recognized this reality in agreeing to the occupation zones in Germany. He also participated in the decision to eschew a race to capture Berlin, allowing the surging Red Army to do this. In so deciding, he saved thousands of inevitable U.S. and British casualties, and recognized that the Soviets—who had lost eleven million men and women in their battle against the Nazi invasion— deserved "the honor" of capturing Berlin.

The Incredible Tapestry That Is America

A unique advantage and complication for the United States in facing Soviet power throughout the forty-year Cold War is found in the very "tapestry" President Obama describes. The Soviet Union faced unrelenting pressure, reflecting its imposed domination of its Warsaw Pact allies, and eventually from the multiplicity of peoples that made up the Soviet Union. Their control of their Pact allies depended on the massive presence of Soviet occupation troops in the Eastern Europe nations that never abandoned their appetite for independence.

In contrast, the United States population has included millions of immigrants, rich in the culture and language of the world, who chose and often battled to become Americans. It is difficult to imagine our success in eroding and finally defeating Soviet control over Eastern Europe without the invaluable contributions of our immigrant population.

VOA, Radio Liberty, and Radio Free Europe were of critical importance in our campaign to maintain American influence in the Soviet empire; they were dependent on hundreds of post-war immigrants who wrote the daily scripts and broadcast the reports back into their native lands. I first became aware of this resource in my first assignment as we processed tens of thousands of Ukrainians, Balts, Czechs, Hungarians, Bulgarians, Romanians, and thousands of refugees fleeing Soviet control from the Caucasus-Central Asian areas that had been subjugated by Czarist Russia and the Soviet Union.

I personally benefited from the wise advice of former Soviet General Alexander Barmine (who had defected early in the 1950s), and Ukrainian-American diaspora leader Lev Dobriansky as I worked to hone the cultural and VOA messages into the Soviet Union and Eastern Europe during my five years at USIA.

At the same time this "incredible tapestry" created serious complications for U.S. policymakers in the Cold War, and since. The Greek-American community effectively organized in a diaspora group, AHEPA, and raised an impressive war-chest which it used to influence congressmen and senators on behalf of Greece. Initially this support buttressed President Truman's brave decision to intervene against the Soviet-sponsored drive by the Greek Communists, which seemed on the brink of success in 1947. Subsequently however, and continuing even today in 2009, AHEPA's influence has been dedicated to limiting U.S. assistance to Greece's historic enemy, Turkey. As Turkey became the largest contributor of troops to NATO and provided a significant combat force to UN forces battling North Korea in the early 1950s, AHEPA-inspired congressional limitations on military assistance to Turkey clearly cut across our Cold War policies.

A second, little discussed diaspora influence directed largely against Turkey came from the small, tightly knit, very wealthy Armenian-American community. Again, this influence persists today. Armenian anti-Turkish sentiments center on the history of the slaughter of millions of Armenians by Turkish Ottoman forces during the collapse of the Ottoman Empire at the end of World War I. Even though this gruesome event occurred almost a century ago, the international Armenian diaspora continues to demand recognition that the fate of Turkey's Armenians be acknowledged as "genocide."

Another, this time much-discussed example, was the effective Jewish-American campaign against trade and arms-control agreements with the USSR. This effort, led by the heavily financed committee AIPAC, succeeded in creating and passing the Jackson-Vanik amendment, which tied the hands of the United States as it tried to actively engage with Moscow and create an interdependence which could have hastened the end of Soviet expansionism. Supporters of this policy, like my old friend the late former congressman Charlie Vanik, insisted that passage of the law bearing his name led to the end of Soviet limitations on Jewish emigration from the USSR. Critics of Jackson-Vanik point out that emigration from the USSR was increasing (30,000 were allowed in 1973) as Nixon's engagement with Moscow progressed; after Jackson-Vanik passed, emigration virtually ceased for several years. Jackson-Vanik was a reflection of deeply-held concerns in the United States, and undoubtedly contributed to today's reality that freedom of emigration from the former Soviet Union is firmly established.

Similar ethnic based organizations of Ukrainian-American, Polish-American, Hungarian-American, etc., exercise strong and sometimes disproportionate influence over American foreign policy.

Aaron David Miller, in *The Much Too Promised Land*, discussing the contentious issue of AIPAC influence over U.S. Middle East policy, captured the critical need for balance: "In Kissinger's, Carter's, and Baker's diplomacy, the pursuit of the national interest trumped the political interest. And, this is as it should be. When Presidents lead on foreign policy, domestic constituencies and lobbies usually follow, albeit sometimes uneasily."

We are indeed empowered by the rich tapestry of our population, but it takes a strong, sensitive President to harness these resources effectively.

ANNOTATED BIBLIOGRAPHY

Ausland, John. *Kennedy, Khrushchev: The Berlin Crisis 1961-64*. Scandinavian University Press,1996. Ausland was a key member of the Berlin task force in the State Department and early made the direct connection between Khrushchev's Cuban caper and the fundamental confrontation in Berlin.

Bacevich, Andrew J. *The Limits of Power: The End of American Exceptionalism*. Metropolitan Books, 2008. This slim (180 pages) volume is an exquisite analysis of the folly of imperialism, cast today in the Bush doctrine of preemptive warfare. Bacevich, a decorated combat veteran, lost his son, 1ˢᵗ Lieutenant Bacevich, in the current Iraq War.

Bailey, Anthony. *Along the Edge of the Forest: An Iron Curtain Journey*. Random House,1983. A fascinating account of a journalist's trip along the Soviet barrier dividing Germany.

Baker, John A. *Italian Communism: The Road to Legitimacy and Autonomy*. National Defense University Press, 1989. Baker, a brilliant career Foreign Service officer with Moscow experience, produced an insightful study of the Italian C.P., which played a major role in post-war Italy and came close to taking power in Italy.

Behrman, Greg. *The Most Noble Adventure: The Marshall Plan and the Time When America Helped Save Europe*. Free Press, 2007. A superb, highly acclaimed history of the Marshall Plan and the outstanding men who mobilized

U.S. financial assistance to avert the collapse of the European economic structure in the years immediately following the War.

Beisner, Robert. *Dean Acheson: A Life in the Cold War.* Oxford University, 2006. An overly long but rich account of Acheson's key role in developing U.S. post-war policy and drawing the line on the sand as the Cold War unfolded.

Blake, George. *No Other Choice: An Autobiography.* Simon & Schuster,1990. Blake, discussed in my chapter on Berlin, was in British MI5 as a "captain" in uniform. His book is an attempt at justifying his perfidy and reveals the clever psychological techniques used by the KGB. Other instances of KGB psychological success included the renowned Swedish Colonel Stig Wennerston and Aldrich Ames of CIA.

Blasier, Cole. *The Giant's Rival: The USSR and Latin America.* Pittsburgh Press, 1987. Professor Blasier, perhaps the preeminent scholar on Soviet activities in Latin America, tells a little-known story of the extensive Soviet efforts to build on their success with Castro to create a hemisphere network of Soviet influence.

Daniloff, Nicholas. *Of Spies and Spokesmen: My Life As a Cold War Correspondent.* University of Missouri Press, 2008. Daniloff served in Moscow for four years in the UPI bureau and two more years as *U.S. News* bureau chief. In between, he covered the State Department and White House for UPI in Washington. A fascinating journalist's eye view. A descendant of a famous Decembrist revolutionary in Czarist Russia, Nick attracted a lot of KGB attention in the USSR.

Dobbs, Michael. *One Minute to Midnight: Kennedy, Khrushchev, and Castro on the Brink of Nuclear War.* Knopf, 2008. Dobbs was the *Washington Post* correspondent in Moscow for four years. His account of the Cuban Missile Crisis is based extensively on Soviet documents now available and his personal trips to Cuba. Dobbs makes it apparent that we were much, much closer to a nuclear conflict than anyone appreciated, except President Kennedy and his small "ex-Comm" cabinet-level team.

Doboynin, Anatoly. *In Confidence: Moscow's Ambassador to America's Six Cold War Presidents.* Time Books, 1995. A well-written but self-serving account of the Soviet Ambassador's long tour in Washington. His experience is unique, but his autobiography reflects the selective view we all suspected he reflected back to Moscow. He strove to seem friendly and wise, courting CEOs and willingly serving Kissinger as a key messenger.

Doder, Dusko. *Shadows and Whispers.* Random House, 1986. A fascinating and insightful account of the turbulent period after Brezhnev's death when Andropov, Chernyenko, and Gorbachev followed in rapid succession. Doder's instincts were unmatched.

Fursenko, Anatoly and Timothy Naftali. *Khrushchev's Cold War: The Inside Story of an American Adversary.* Norton, 2006. Relying on new Soviet documents, this account reveals the disputes within the Politburo and pressures on Khrushchev as Khrushchev "rolled the dice" again and again in his campaign to force the West out of Berlin.

Gaddis, John Lewis. *We Now Know: Rethinking Cold War History*. Oxford University Press, 1998. Gaddis, an academic, has written three books analyzing the origins and actions of the Cold War. They all suffer from his lack of personal participation, but this most recent volume includes interesting recently opened Soviet material.

Hamilton, Ian. *Agent of Choice*. Penguin Books, 1962 (out of print). Swedish defense attaché Stig Wennerstron was one of Moscow's most valuable espionage catches. His story illustrates the sophistication of KGB recruiting techniques.

Hyland, William G. *Mortal Rivals: Superpower Relations from Nixon to Reagan*. Random House, 1987. Hyland, a career CIA analyst of Soviet affairs, became Kissinger's top advisor on the USSR. Candid, clearly written, Hyland's book is a very interesting "insider" account.

Judt, Tony. *Postwar: A History of Europe Since 1945*. Penguin Books, 2005. A superb, balanced, well-written survey of the Cold War years as Europe recovered from the devastation of two World Wars.

Kalb, Marvin and Bernard Kalb. *Kissinger*. Little, Brown, & Co., 1974. A firsthand account that reveals Kissinger's superb efforts to harness media interest at a time of unequaled vulnerability of the U.S because of Watergate and Vietnam.

Karnow, Stanley. *Vietnam: A History*. Viking,1983. Karnow, the dean of journalist-historians of Asia (see also his *Mao and China*) produced a sweeping review of Indochina during World War II and through the Cold War. Fascinating insights into the evolution of Communist Vietnamese leaders and the doomed French effort to reclaim Indochina after Word War II.

Kissinger, Henry. *White House Years*. Little, Brown & Co.,1979. Written as only Henry Kissinger can write, these rich perspectives on his tenure at the NSC and State Department are a must-read source.

Kissinger, Henry. *Years of Renewal*. Simon & Schuster, 1999.

Kissinger, Henry. *Years of Upheaval*. Little Brown, & Co., 1992.

Mann, James. *The Rebellion of Ronald Reagan: A History of the End of the Cold War*. Viking, 2009. Mann provides an excellent, readable account of Reagan's consistent commitment to end the Cold War and banish nuclear weapons. Particularly interesting account of the battle between Defense Secretary Weinburger and Secretary of State Shultz and James Baker as to whether to confront and isolate or engage and negotiate with Moscow. Reagan eventually came down on the side of Shultz and Baker.

Matlock, Jack. *Autopsy on an Empire*. Random House, 1995. A sweeping insight into the final collapse of the Soviet empire by our outstanding Ambassador to Moscow. Matlock, over three assignments to Moscow, went from an astute observer in 1960-62 (when we served together) to an active participant in Soviet policy-making, as Gorbachev strove to cope with the collapse of Soviet power.

Miller, Aaron David. *The Much Too Promised Land*. Bantam Books, 2008. Miller, a key U.S. negotiator in the Arab-Israeli dispute, served under three presidents with distinction. His book is a superb, balanced account of the Byzantine ongoing effort to resolve this cardinal issue.

Murphy, David, Sergei Kondrashev, and George Bailey. *Battleground Berlin: CIA vs. KGB in the Cold War*. Yale University Press, 1997. A fascinating collaborative effort by top CIA and KGB operatives in Berlin.

Oberdorfer, Don. *The Turn: From the Cold War to the New Era*. Poseidon Press, 1991. Veteran *Washington Post* reporter Oberdorfer presents an engrossing blow-by-blow account of the final years of the Soviet regime. He accompanied Secretary Schulz and President Reagan to their historic summits. His insights into the fierce ideological struggle between Schulz and Defense Secretary Weinburger are particularly fascinating.

Schechter, Jerrold and Peter Deriabin. *The Spy Who Saved the World: How a Soviet Colonel Changed the Course of the Cold War*. Scribner's, 1992. Schechter, a Time-Life correspondent in Moscow and NSC official, joins with

Deriabin, a top KGB official, to document the dramatic thirty-year espionage career.

Schaffer, Howard B. *Ellsworth Bunker: Global Troubleshooter, Vietnam Hawk.* Univeristy of North Carolina Press, 2003. A warm and definitive treatment of one of our most accomplished statesmen. His leadership in the drawn-out but successful negotiation of the Panama Canal Treaty is particularly valuable. His tour in Saigon, it appears, was largely a frustration.

Slusser, Robert. *The Berlin Crisis of 1961: Soviet-American Relations and the Struggle for Power in the Kremlin, June-November, 1961.* Johns Hopkins University Press, 1973. An excellent detailed recounting of the day-to-day confrontation.

Sorensen, Ted. *Counselor.* HarperCollins, 2008. A remarkably open, personal account of the Kennedy presidency. Predictably very generous to JFK, but especially enlightening about Kennedy's perception of Khrushchev.

Spassowski, Romuld. *The Liberation of One.* Harcourt, Brace, Jovanovich. 1981. Ambassador Spassowski's memoir is a brilliant account of his evolution from a dedicated Marxist into a devout Catholic. He was the highest ranking defector in the Cold War.

Taubman, William. *Khrushchev: The Man and His Era.* Norton, 2003. The definitive biography of Khrushchev. Fascinating insight into one of the most important players in the devastating history of the Soviet Union and the Cold War.

Weinstein, Alan. *Perjury: The Hiss-Chambers Case.* Random House, 1997. The most definitive account of the bizarre affair of Alger Hiss. His career dominated the scene in Washington politics and provided the keystone in the anti-Communism campaign that led to the election of Richard Nixon and jeopardized President Truman's efforts to rebuild American military strength to counter Soviet imperialism. While Weinstein's excellent book leaves little doubt that Hiss was a Soviet agent, there is still a great sense of mystery about what motivated Hiss and whether his actions had any serious consequences. What is not in question is that those who seized on the case—Senators McCarthy, Wherry, and Taft, to create an atmosphere of fear and insecurity in the U.S.—did complicate our national resolve as we worked to contain Soviet imperialism around the world, a classic case of keeping our eye on the wrong ball.

Whitney, Craig. *Spy Trader: Germany's Devil's Advocate & the Darkest Secrets of the Cold War.* Turner Books, 1996. A fascinating account of the play between the Soviet zone of Germany, the so-called German Democratic Republic, and the U.S. and West German officials and the exchange of captured spies.

APPENDIX A

Title IV, Section 402 of the Trade Bill of 1974, "The Jackson-Vanik Amendment"

TITLE IV—TRADE RELATIONS WITH COUNTRIES NOT CURRENTLY RECEIVING NONDISCRIMINATORY TREATMENT

Sec. 401. Exception of the Products of Certain Countries or Areas.

Except as otherwise provided in this title, the President shall continue to deny nondiscriminatory treatment to the products of any country, the products of which were not eligible for the rates set forth in rate column numbered 1 of the Tariff Schedules of the United States on the date of the enactment of this Act.

Sec. 402. Freedom of Emigration in East-West Trade.

(a) To assure the continued dedication of the United States to fundamental human rights, and notwithstanding any other provision of law, on or after the date of the enactment of this Act products from any nonmarket economy country shall not be eligible to receive non-discriminatory treatment (most-favored-nation treatment), such country shall not participate in any program of the Government of the United States which extends credits or credit guarantees or investment guarantees, directly or indirectly, and the President of the United States shall pot conclude any commercial agreement with any such country, during the period beginning with the date on which the President determines that such country—

(1) denies its citizens the right or opportunity to emigrate;

(2) imposes more than a nominal tax on emigration or on the visas or other documents required for emigration, for any purpose or cause whatsoever; or

(3) imposes more than a nominal tax, levy, fine, fee, or other charge on any citizen as a consequence of the desire of such citizen to emigrate to the country of his choice,

and ending on the date on which the President determines that such country is no longer in violation of paragraph (1), (2), or (3).

(b) After the date of the enactment of this Act, (A) products of a nonmarket economy country may be eligible to receive nondiscriminatory treatment (most-favored-nation treatment), (B) such country may participate in any program of the Government of the

United States which extends credits or credit guarantees or investment guarantees, and (C) the President may conclude a commercial agreement

with such country, only after the President has submitted to the Congress a report indicating that such country is not in violation of paragraph (1), (2), or (3) of subsection (a). Such report with respect to such country shall include information as to the nature and implementation of emigration laws and policies and restrictions or discrimination applied to or against persons wishing to emigrate. The report required by this subsection shall be submitted initially as provided herein and, with current information, on or before each June 30 and December 31 thereafter so long as such treatment is received, such credits or guarantees are extended, or such agreement is in effect.

(c) (1) During the 18-month period beginning on the date of the enactment of this Act, the President is authorized to waive by Executive order the application of subsection (a) arid (b) with respect to any country, if he reports to the Congress that—

(A) he has determined that such waiver will substantially promote the objectives of this section; and

(B) he has received assurances that the emigration practice!, of that country will henceforth lead substantially to the achievement of the objectives of this section.

(2) During any period subsequent to the 18-month period referred to in paragraph (1), the President is authorized to waive by Executive order the application of subsections (a) and (b) with respect to any country, if the waiver authority granted by this subsection continues to apply to such country pursuant to subsection (d), and if he reports to the Congress that—

(A) he has determined that such waiver will substantially promote the objectives of this section; and

(R) lie has received assurances that the emigration practices of that country will henceforth lead substantially to the achievement of the objectives of this section.

(3) A waiver with respect to any country shall terminate on the day after the waiver authority granted by this subsection ceases to be effective with respect to such country pursuant to subsection (d). The President may, at, any

time, terminate by Executive order any waiver granted under this subsection.

(d)(1) If the President determines that the extension of the waiver authority granted by subsection (c) (1) will substantially promote the objectives of this section, he may recommend to the Congress that such authority be extended for a period of 12 months. Any such recommendation shall—

(A) be made not later than 30 days before the expiration of such authority;

(R) be made in a document transmitted to the House of Representatives and the Senate setting forth his reasons for recommending the extension of such authority; and

(C) include, for each country with respect to which a waiver granted under subsection (c)(1) is in effect, a determination that continuation of the waiver applicable to that country will substantially promote the objectives of this section, and a statement setting forth his reasons for such determination.

(2) If the President recommends under paragraph (1) the extension of the waiver authority granted by subsection (c) (1), such authority shall continue in effect with respect to any country for a period of 12 months following the end of the 18-month period, referred to in subsection (c) (1), if, before the end of such 18-month period, the House of Representatives and the Senate adopt, by an affirmative vote of a majority of the Members present and voting in each House and under the procedures set forth in section 153, a concurrent resolution approving the extension of such authority, and such resolution does not name such country as being excluded from such authority. Such authority shall cease to be effective with respect to any country named in such concurrent resolution on the date of the adoption of such concurrent resolution. If before the end of such 18-month period, a concurrent resolution approving the extension of such authority is not adopted by the House and the Senate, but both the House and Senate vote on the question of final passage of such a concurrent resolution and—

(A) both the House and the Senate fail to pass such a concurrent resolution, the authority granted by subsection (c) (1) shall cease to be effective with respect to all countries at the end of such 18-month period;

(B) both the House and the Senate pass such a concurrent resolution which names such country as being excluded from such authority, such authority shall cease to

422

be effective with respect to such country at the end of such 18-month period; or

(C) one House fails to pass such a concurrent resolution and the other House passes such a concurrent resolution which names such country as being excluded from such authority, such authority shall cease to be effective with respect to such country at the end of such 18-month period.

(3) If the President recommends under paragraph (1) the extension of the waiver authority granted by subsection (c)(1), and at the end of the 18-month period referred to in subsection (c)(1) the House of Representatives and the Senate have not adopted a concurrent resolution approving the extension of such authority and subparagraph (A) of paragraph (2) does not apply, such authority shall continue in effect for a period of 60 days following the end of such 18-month period with respect to any country (except for any country with respect to which such authority was not extended by reason of the application of subparagraph (B) or (C) of paragraph (2)), and shall continue in effect for a period of 12 months following the end of such 18-month period with respect to any such country if, before the end of such 60-day period, the House of Representatives and the Senate adopt, by an affirmative vote of a majority of the Members present and voting in each House and under the procedures set forth m section 153, a concurrent resolution approving the extension of such authority, and such resolution does not name such country as being excluded from such authority. Such authority shall cease to be effective with respect to any country named in such concurrent resolution on the date of the adoption of such concurrent resolution. If before the end of such 60-day period, a concurrent resolution approving the extension of such authority is not adopted by the House and Senate, but both the House and Senate vote on the question of final passage of such a concurrent resolution and—

(A) both the House and the Senate fail to pass such a concurrent resolution, the authority granted by subsection (c)(1) shall cease to be effective with respect to all countries on the date of the vote on the question of final passage by the House which votes last;

(B) both the House and the Senate Dass such a concurrent resolution which names such country as being excluded from such authority, such authority shall cease to be effective with respect to such country at the end of such 60-day period; or

(C)   one House fails to pass such a concurrent resolution and the other House passes such a concurrent resolution which names such country as being excluded from such authority, such authority shall cease to be effective with respect to such country at the end of such 60-day period.

(4) If the President recommends under paragraph (1) the extension of the waiver authority granted by subsection (c) (1), and at the end of the 60-day period referred to in paragraph (3) the House of Representatives and the Senate have not adopted a concurrent resolution approving the extension of such authority and subparagraph (A) of paragraph (3) does not apply, such authority shall continue in effect until the end of the 12-month period following the end of the 18-month period referred to in subsection (c) (1) with respect to any country (except for any country with respect to which such authority was not extended by reason of the application of subparagraph (B) or (C) of paragraph (2) or subparagraph (B) or (C) of paragraph (3)), unless before the end of the 45-day period following such 60-day period either the House of Representatives or the Senate adopts, by an affirmative vote of a majority of the Members present and voting in that House and under the procedures set forth in section 153, a resolution disapproving the extension of such authority generally or with respect to such country specifically. Such authority shall cease to be effective with respect to all countries on the date of the adoption by either House before the end of such 45-day period of a resolution disapproving the extension of such authority, and shall cease to be effective with respect to any country on the date of the adoption by either House before the end of such 45-day period of a resolution disapproving the extension of such authority with respect to such country.

(5) If the waiver authority granted by subsection (c) has been extended under paragraph (3) or (4) for any country for the 12-month period referred to in such paragraphs, and the President determines that the further extension of such authority will substantially promote the objectives of this section, he may recommend further extensions of such authority for successive 12-month periods. *Any* such recommendations shall—

(A)   be made not later than 30 days before the expiration of such authority:

(B) be made in a document transmitted to the House of Representatives and the Senate setting forth his reasons for recommending the extension of such authority; and

(C) include, for each country with respect to which a waiver granted under subsection (c) is in effect, a determination that continuation of the waiver applicable to that country will substantially promote the objectives of this section, and a statement setting forth his reasons for such determination.

If the President recommends the further extension of such authority, such authority shall continue in effect until the end of the 12-month period following the end of the previous 12-month extension with respect to any country (except for any country with respect to which such authority has not been extended under this subsection), unless before the end of the 60-day period following such previous 12-month extension, either the House of Representatives or the Senate adopts, by an affirmative vote of a majority of the Members present and voting in that House and under the procedures set forth in section 153, a resolution disapproving the extension of such authority generally or with respect to such country specifically. Such authority shall cease to be effective with respect to all countries on the date of the adoption by either House before the end of such 60-day period of a resolution disapproving the extension of such authority, and shall cease to be effective with respect to any country on the date of the adoption by either House before the end of such 60-day period of a resolution disapproving the extension of such authority with respect to such country.

(e) This section shall not apply to any country the products of which are eligible for the rates set forth in rate column numbered 1 of the Tariff Schedules of the United States on the date of the enactment of this Act.

NIMBLE BOOKS LLC